Changing the Industrial Geography in Asia

Changing the Industrial Geography in Asia

The Impact of China and India

Shahid Yusuf

Kaoru Nabeshima

THE WORLD BANK
Washington, D.C.

ISBN: 978-0-8213-8240-0
eISBN: 978-0-8213-8438-1
DOI: 10.1596/978-0-8213-8240-0

Library of Congress Cataloging-in-Publication Data
Yusuf, Shahid, 1949–
   Changing the industrial geography in Asia : the impact of China and India / by Shahid Yusuf and Kaoru Nabeshima.
      p. cm.
   Includes bibliographical references and index.
   ISBN 978-0-8213-8240-0 — ISBN 978-0-8213-8438-1 (electronic)
   1. Industrialization—China. 2. Industrialization—India. 3. Industrialization—Asia. 4. China—Economic policy—2000- 5. India—Economic policy—1991- 6. China—Foreign economic relations. 7. India—Foreign economic relations. I. Nabeshima, Kaoru. II. Title.

HC427.95.Y867 2010
338.095—dc22

                                                                                      2010022089

Cover design: Edelman Design Communications

Contents

Tables

Acknowledgments

This is the final volume of a series of publications emerging from a project on East Asia's Prospects, cosponsored by the government of Japan. It was written in close collaboration with the East Asia and Pacific Regional Office in the World Bank. We gratefully acknowledge the financial backing of the government of Japan through its Policy and Human Resources Development Fund, which supported both the research we conducted in preparing this volume and its publication.

We began working on this book when we were both part of the Development Economics Research Group (DECRG) of the World Bank. However, much of the writing was done at the World Bank Institute (WBI), to which we moved in early 2009. While in DECRG, we benefited from the support given by Martin Ravallion, and in WBI we were fortunate in receiving equally strong backing from Roumeen Islam and Raj Nallari. Once Shahid Yusuf retired from the Bank, Shahidur Khandker kindly agreed to take over the East Asia Project until the book was finalized, and we owe him and William Martin, his manager, our thanks for their generous assistance at a very critical stage in the completion of the volume.

The book began to take shape following the publication of a volume on China and India called *Dancing with Giants,* to which both of us contributed. The others who participated in that project stimulated and sharpened our own thinking on the topic, especially Alan Winters, and as the writing on the current volume progressed, we benefited from conversations with colleagues who had an interest in the topic. The final manuscript was enriched and improved by comments from Ardo Hansson, Vikram Nehru, and Arvind Virmani; our thanks to them all for sharing their ideas, insights, and views. We are also grateful to Lopamudra Chakraborti and Rory Birmingham, who provided peerless research assistance throughout the course of the study.

Our debts to Patricia Katayama, Cindy Fisher, and Denise Bergeron at the World Bank Office of the Publisher are little short of mountainous. Once again they have expertly shepherded the volume from manuscript stage to final form, cheerfully accommodated changes in the schedule, and helped us surmount some bumps along the way. We cannot thank them enough. Last but not least, the editors at Publication Services have our appreciation for their dedicated effort at polishing the manuscript.

About the Authors

Shahid Yusuf holds a PhD in economics from Harvard University and a BA in economics from Cambridge University. He joined the World Bank in 1974 as a Young Professional and while at the Bank spent more than 35 years tackling issues confronting developing countries. During his tenure at the World Bank, Dr. Yusuf was the team leader for the World Bank–Japan project on East Asia's Future Economy from 2000 to 2009. He was the director of the *World Development Report 1999/2000, Entering the 21st Century*. Prior to that, he was economic adviser to the senior vice president and chief economist (1997–98), lead economist for the East Africa Department (1995–97), and lead economist for the China and Mongolia Department (1989–93).

Dr. Yusuf has written extensively on development issues, with a special focus on East Asia, and has also published widely in various academic journals. He has authored or edited 23 books on industrial and urban development, innovation systems, and tertiary education. His three most recent books are *Development Economics through the Decades* (2009); *Tiger Economies under Threat* (coauthored with Kaoru Nabeshima, 2009); and *Two Dragonheads: Contrasting Development Paths for Beijing and Shanghai* (also coauthored with Kaoru Nabeshima, 2010). Dr. Yusuf currently consults with the World Bank and other organizations.

Kaoru Nabeshima holds a PhD in economics from the University of California, Davis, and received his BA in economics from Ohio Wesleyan University. During his tenure at the World Bank, he served as an economist in the Bank's Development Research Group and, subsequently, as a consultant for the World Bank Institute. He is currently a senior researcher at the Institute of Developing Economies–Japan External Trade Organization (IDE-JETRO).

Dr. Nabeshima's recent publications include *Postindustrial East Asian Cities* (coauthored with Shahid Yusuf, 2006); *How Universities Promote Economic Growth* (coedited with Shahid Yusuf, 2007); *Growing Industrial Clusters in Asia* (coedited with Shahid Yusuf and Shoichi Yamashita, 2008); *Accelerating Catch-Up: Tertiary Education and Growth in Africa* (coauthored with Shahid Yusuf and William Saint, 2008); *Tiger Economies under Threat* (coauthored with Shahid Yusuf, 2009); and *Two Dragon Heads: Contrasting Development Paths for Beijing and Shanghai* (coauthored with Shahid Yusuf, 2010).

Abbreviations

ASEAN	Association of Southeast Asian Nations
BOP	balance of payments
BPO	business process outsourcing
COE	collectively owned enterprise
DRC	dynamic revealed competitiveness
DRCP	dynamic revealed competitiveness position
EU	European Union
EU15	Austria, Belgium, Denmark, Finland, France, Germany, Greece, Ireland, Italy, Luxembourg, the Netherlands, Portugal, Spain, Sweden, and the United Kingdom
FDI	foreign direct investment
FTA	free trade agreement
GDP	gross domestic product
GHG	greenhouse gas
GLI	Grubel-Lloyd Index
ICT	information and communication technology
IP	intellectual property
IT	information technology
ITES	information technology–enabled services
MNC	multinational corporation
OECD	Organisation for Economic Co-operation and Development
PPP	purchasing power parity
PRD	Pearl River Delta
R&D	research and development
RCA	revealed comparative advantage
S&T	science and technology
SEZ	special economic zone
SMEs	small and medium enterprises
SOE	state-owned enterprise
TVE	township and village enterprise
USPTO	U.S. Patent and Trademark Office
WTO	World Trade Organization

1

Introduction

During a 13-year period extending from roughly 1995 to 2008, the world economy experienced an upheaval resulting from a great burst of globalization that brought the 20th century to a close. The new century is being ushered in by a second upheaval following a severe financial crisis that plunged the global economy into recession in 2008–09. Through an analysis of industrial trends, patterns, and national manufacturing capabilities that emerged after 1985, this volume examines the consequences of the first upheaval for Asia's industrial geography and explores the likely outcomes of the second upheaval for industrial development and trade across the Asia region.

The first upheaval witnessed a massive migration of manufacturing industries and certain business services from advanced countries to developing economies. This migration transformed East and parts of South Asia into the industrial heartland of the world. The second upheaval, which could continue for a decade or more, will most likely consolidate Asia's industrial preeminence; in addition, it could result in the redistribution and concentration of industrial activities in the two most populous and fastest-growing economies in Asia—China and India. The growth of Asia's share of global manufacturing activities and major business services is already tilting the balance of economic power in Asia's favor (Grether and Mathys 2006). In 1973, one-quarter of purchasing power parity (PPP) adjusted world gross domestic product (GDP) came from Asia while 51 percent came from the West. By comparison, as of 2003, Asia's share had risen to 43 percent, surpassing the West's 40 percent share (see table 1.1).[1]

---

[1]Using nominal exchange rates, East Asia's share of global GDP in 2006 was 20 percent compared to 31 percent for Europe and 32 percent for North America. This provides another perspective on the relative weights of the different regions (Cohen-Setton and Pisani-Ferry 2008).

Table 1.1 Shares of World GDP, 1820–2030

	1820	1950	1973	2003	2030
Western Europe	23.0	26.2	25.6	19.2	13.0
United States	1.8	27.3	22.1	20.7	17.3
Other Western offshoots[a]	0.1	3.4	3.3	3.1	2.5
West	**25.0**	**56.8**	**50.9**	**40.4**	**32.8**
China	32.9	4.6	4.6	16.8	23.8
India	16.0	4.2	3.1	6.1	10.4
Japan	3.0	3.0	7.8	6.1	3.6
Other Asia[b]	7.4	6.8	8.7	13.6	15.4
Latin America	2.1	7.8	8.7	7.7	6.3
Eastern Europe and former USSR	9.0	13.1	13.8	6.1	4.7
Africa	4.5	3.8	3.4	3.2	3.0
Rest	**75.0**	**43.2**	**49.1**	**59.6**	**67.2**
Asia as % of world	**59.3**	**14.9**	**24.2**	**42.6**	**53.3**

Source: Maddison 2008.
a. Australia, Canada, and New Zealand.
b. Includes Bangladesh and Pakistan from 1950.

A continuing increase in Asia's share will have major implications for the rest of the world, especially if China and India are the principal gainers. This increase is therefore one of the issues that we explore in this book. The second issue concerns the shape of Asian industrial geography in the coming decade. If the two Asian giants become the industrial equals of the United States, Germany, and Japan, such parity will have ramifications for trade and growth worldwide, for the future of development in China and India, and for industrialization elsewhere in East and South Asia.

The focus of this volume is on China and India. We see them as the principal beneficiaries of the first upheaval, roughly bookended by the crises of 1997–98 and of 2008–09, and as being among the prime movers whose economic footprints will expand most rapidly in the coming decades. If these two countries do come close to realizing their considerable ambitions, their neighbors in Asia and their trading partners throughout the world must be ready for major adjustments. The changes in industrial geography and in the pattern of trade since the mid-1990s have already been far-reaching. Nothing on a comparable scale occurred during the preceding two decades of the 20th century. These developments offer instructive clues concerning the possible direction of changes in the future. However, in the interest of manageability, our analysis is centered on the dynamics of industrialization, as these have a large bearing on the course of development. Within this context, reference is made to trade, foreign direct investment, and the building of technological capabilities, which together constitute a major subset of the factors responsible for the shape not only of the industrial geography of the past but also of the industrial geography yet to come.

The striking feature of development in South and East Asia in the second half of the 20th century is the degree to which Japan dominated the industrial landscape and how the Japanese model[2] triggered the first wave of industrialization in four East Asian economies[3]—the Republic of Korea; Taiwan, China; Hong Kong, China; and Singapore. These four so-called tiger economies were the early starters, and each has become a mature industrial economy. Indeed, Hong Kong, having transferred almost all of its manufacturing activities to the Pearl River Delta,[4] has morphed into a postindustrial economy.

China Awakens

A first wave of industrialization in East Asia commenced with the revival of Japan's industry, beginning in the mid-1950s, and the rapid technological progression of Japanese firms in the two subsequent decades. Ten years later, Japan was joined by the economies of Hong Kong, China; the Republic of Korea; Singapore; and Taiwan, China. From the 1970s onward, industrial change stirred and quickly gathered momentum in Malaysia and Thailand, and to a lesser degree in Indonesia and the Philippines. These four countries constituted the second wave of "fast followers"[5] in Asia, their industrialization guided and partially financed by foreign direct investment (FDI) that resulted in a base of exporters oriented mainly toward markets in the United States and Japan. China entered the fray in the 1980s following a landmark decision by the government in 1978[6] to rapidly modernize

---

[2]The course and pace of industrialization in Korea and Taiwan, China, was influenced by development during the period when both economies were Japanese colonies.

[3]The so-called flying geese model, first described by Akamatsu (1962), has been elaborated and formalized by numerous commentators (see Kasahara 2004; Kojima 2000; and Kojima and Ozawa 1985). According to Ozawa (2003), the performance of the East Asian economies depended upon the global environment created and maintained by the United States for trade, investment, and structural upgrading. Japan both benefited from the Pax Americana and went on to complement the pull exerted by the U.S. economy by serving as an "industrial upgrading intermediary for the East Asian regions and an augmentor of industrial capacity through its FDI and technology transfer to neighboring countries" (p. 705).

[4]Hong Kong, China, is now the services-providing hub of the Shenzhen–Hong Kong urban region, with only 4 percent of its GDP sourced from manufacturing. On Hong Kong, China's transformation, see Berger and Lester (1997); Enright, Scott, and Dodwell (1997); and Tao and Wong (2002).

[5]See Mathews and Cho (2000).

[6]At the now almost legendary Third Plenum of the Eleventh Central Committee held in December 1978. This was followed by gradual reform of state-owned enterprises (SOEs). For details on SOE reform, see Yusuf, Nabeshima, and Perkins (2005).

the economy, but it was not until the mid-1990s that China emerged as a significant exporter and recipient of FDI (see figure 1.5 on page 11 and figure 1.8 on page 18). The remarkable aspect of China's industrial development and prowess as a trading nation is the sheer speed with which it came out of a state of economic backwardness, social turmoil associated with the aftermath of the Cultural Revolution, and political disarray following the death of Mao Zedong and the arrest of the Gang of Four[7] in 1976. Once the government committed itself to reform and catching up with its neighbors, the country's latent entrepreneurial talent and neglected potential for industrialization were mobilized at incredible speed. This was achieved with the help of organizational resources, the calibrated application of market-based incentives,[8] the opening of the economy to FDI and to trade via the special economic zones (SEZs) and the Foreign Trade Corporations, and most important, heavy and sustained investment in both production facilities and the infrastructures undergirding industrial development. A little more than a decade after China began adopting market institutions and incentives and promoting exports, it was hard on the heels of Asia's front-running tiger economies.

India Gathers Speed

After a long spell of sluggish growth at a rate of just 3 percent per year, the pace of India's growth quickened in the early 1980s (to 5.5 percent between 1980 and 1991) in response to a dribble of reforms emanating from the Congress-led government under Indira Gandhi (Panagariya 2008a; Virmani 2004). These reforms intensified following the balance of payment (BOP) crisis of 1991.[9] But it was not until almost the end of the 1990s that India's strengthening economic performance came to international notice, and that because of a fortunate conjuncture of circumstances: India's slowly accumulating capabilities in the information and communication

---

[7]The so-called Gang of Four was a group of individuals who were most closely associated with Mao in the last few years of his life and were responsible for interpreting and implementing his instructions. They were Jiang Qing, Zhang Chunqiao, Yao Wenyuan, and Wang Hongwen. The Gang was arrested in October 1976, less than a month after Mao's death on September 9th, 1976.

[8]A relaxation of controls over the production and pricing of some commodities and the instituting of a dual pricing system were among the earlier reforms. The growth impetus provided by economic opening and institutional reforms is analyzed by Ding and Knight (2008).

[9]Commentators differ in the significance they assign to the limited reforms introduced in the early 1980s and the modest growth acceleration that resulted. Liberalizing policies and devaluation following the crisis of 1991 also raised growth to only about 6 percent. After 2003, growth surged to 9 percent (Rodrik and Subramanian 2004; Bhalla 2004; Panagariya 2008b).

Table 1.2 GDP Growth
annual %

Country	1997	1998	1999	2000	2001	2002	2003	2004	2005	2006	2007	2008
China	9.3	7.8	7.6	8.4	8.3	9.1	10.0	10.1	10.4	11.6	13.0	9.6
India	4.1	6.2	7.4	4.0	5.2	3.8	8.4	8.3	9.4	9.7	9.1	7.1

Source: World Development Indicators Database.

technology (ICT) sector[10] and in information technology–enabled services (ITES) were suddenly in great demand because of the assumed threat to computer systems posed by the start of the year 2000 (Y2K) and by the adoption of the Euro as the common European currency. Both generated an urgent need for software writing and debugging—skills that India had been nurturing domestically and via its diaspora of professionals. This demand was reinforced by the advent of business services outsourcing models embraced by U.S. corporations, which are always eager to pare their costs and capitalize on the opportunities presented by ICT for off-shoring back-office functions. The off-shoring of these functions was followed by that of others, such as code writing, personnel management, and research.[11] India's location in an advantageous time zone, offering the capability of handing off tasks at the end of the working day in the United States, compounded the attraction of lower costs. Catalyzed by these developments in ITES and business process outsourcing (BPO) services, India's growth accelerated to more than 7 percent per year between 1997 and 2007 (see table 1.2). Even though India's manufacturing sector accounted for just 15 percent of GDP in 2000, and its exports mainly comprised resource-based products and light manufactures, the spillover effects from the IT sector embellished its reputation as an exporting economy with substantial human capital resources, and India was quickly inducted into the ranks of late industrializers. If China constituted the third wave of industrializing Asian economies, the entry of India can be considered the fourth wave, which also included another rapidly growing late starter, Vietnam.

First China, then India, generated ripples and radically altered the parameters governing the pace and composition of development in all other countries. By

---

[10]These grew out of the excellence of India's Institutes of Technology (the first was established in 1950), the expanding diaspora of highly skilled professionals, a few strategic investments by multinational corporations (MNCs) that mapped out the possibilities starting in the mid-1980s, the light regulation of the ICT sector, and the fortuitous creation of information technology (IT) infrastructure and institutions in a small number of cities containing entrepreneurial firms and skilled workers.

[11]IT expanded the spectrum of tradable services and enlarged the export options available to developing countries. Offshored services now include legal, architectural, and medical services and the number of tradable services continues to expand.

2008 China had achieved a GDP ranking surpassed only by the United States and Japan. In exports, it overtook first the United States and then Germany to become the world's leading exporter in 2009; and in 2010, it edged out Japan to become the world's second largest economy. All of this was achieved by an economy with an 11th-place GDP ranking in 1990, based on nominal exchange rates. India had a 12th-place GDP ranking in 1990 based on nominal exchange rates, and it maintained this position in 2008. Measured by purchasing power, however, China's GDP ranks second and India's moves up to fourth.[12] Moreover, China and India are on track to widen their lead over other economies because they have proven unusually resilient in the face of the global recession. Whereas most other economies contracted during 2009, or at best barely grew, the large domestic market and the stimulus measures introduced by China and India[13] enabled these two countries to expand by over 9 percent and over 6 percent, respectively. And even if the growth of world trade during the medium term remains sluggish, the two are better positioned than the majority of their competitors to maintain relatively high rates of GDP growth on the strength of domestic demand, and to continue enlarging their shares of global trade.

The Puzzle of Growth Miracles

Economists have been struggling to come to terms with the phenomena presented by the performance of the two countries. Backward-looking cross-country analysis suggests that growth accelerations[14] tend to be self-limiting, with countries regressing to a global norm (Easterly and others 1993). The correlation of growth rates between successive decades is weak (Durlauf, Kourtellos, and Tan 2008). Only a very few economies have avoided this tendency to oscillate around a global mean. Almost all are in East Asia,[15] and several have approached but not equaled the rates China has been able to sustain over a quarter of a century. India is not in the same league yet, but its GDP growth since 1980 handily exceeds the global average for developing countries, and during 2003–08 its performance almost equaled China's.

Recent economic history recognizes a small number of "growth miracles," including Germany in the 1960s through the 1970s, Japan from the 1950s through

---

[12]See Maddison (2009).

[13]The magnitude of the stimulus ranged from 5.9 percent of GDP in China, to 4.2 percent of GDP in the Russian Federation, 3.5 percent of GDP in Korea and 2.0 percent of GDP in the U.S. (see Pisani-Ferry 2010).

[14]Growth accelerations have proven difficult to predict. A handful of sustained efforts at reform have led to long-term acceleration, but most such episodes soon peter out (Hausmann, Pritchett, and Rodrik 2004).

[15]Botswana is the lone exception.

the 1970s, and Korea from the mid-1960s through the 1980s. By juxtaposing the performance of China and India with that of Germany, Japan, and Korea,[16] we can gain a sense of how the two ongoing Asian economic miracles compare with earlier episodes and also find evidence to support the thesis of our study, which is that economic performance on this grand scale reconfigures industrial geography even as it transforms the pattern of trade.

Before the East Asian tiger economies burst upon the world stage, it was the performance of Germany and Japan that was the stuff of economic legend. These were the economies with the highest growth rates in the latter half of the 1950s and 1960s, and it was their nonpareil performance that underpinned the growth model of the immediate postwar era. Both Germany and Japan were reconstructing at great speed in the 1950s, restoring infrastructure and productive capacity destroyed during the Second World War by drawing upon the institutions and, more important, the human resources[17] that had survived the savage conflict.[18] During 1948–55, Germany benefited from the resources and industrial technology transferred via the Marshall Plan and through the provision of Mutual Security Assistance (Giersch, Pague, and Schmieding 1993; DeLong and Eichengreen 1993; and Comin and Hobijn 2010). This, in conjunction with reforms and the absorption of almost 10 million refugees, helped to sustain GDP per capita growth rates at an average of 6.5 percent during 1955–59 at a time when global GDP per capita growth averaged 2.5 percent.[19] Until the eve of the first oil crisis in 1973, Germany's per capita growth was robust, averaging 3.7 percent from 1960 through 1973. In only two years—1963 and 1967—did it slow significantly (see figure 1.1). Growth was propelled by a healthy level of investment, ranging between 26 and 30 percent from 1965 to 1972 (figure 1.3), supported by domestic savings that were approximately equivalent (see figure 1.4). Exports, mainly of manufactures as Germany regained its industrial vigor, provided additional demand push and rose steadily to reach almost 25 percent of GDP by 1975 (figure 1.5). Domestic-resource mobilization thus made a vital contribution at a time when international capital transfers were seriously hamstrung by the global scarcity of capital and regulatory constraints on its mobility.

---

[16]On this comparison, see also Winters and Yusuf (2007).

[17]Maddison (2006) remarks that when he visited Japan in 1961, GDP was rising by 1 percent every month.

[18]See Soete (1985). As David Weinstein (1995) has established in the case of Japan, the postwar distribution of industry mimicked the prewar industrial geography, reflecting the persistence of institutions and the rootedness of skills and infrastructures. Germany's metallurgical and engineering industries were gravely damaged. Other industries were less affected, as was the overall level of the capital stock. Overall, the war destroyed about a quarter of Germany and Japan's capital stock (Wolf 1993).

[19]Both Japan and Germany benefited from the virtual elimination of military spending that had annexed almost a quarter of GDP.

Figure 1.1 **Per Capita GDP Growth of Germany and Japan (Deviation from World per Capita GDP Growth)**

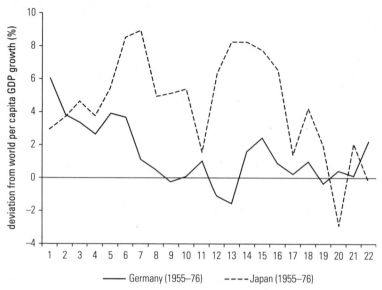

Source: Maddison 2009.

By the mid-1970s Germany had rejoined the ranks of the advanced industrial nations by effectively leveraging and augmenting its stock of human capital and technological capabilities—an amazing achievement, given the scale of destruction during wartime and the economic dislocation associated with the division of the country into two parts.

Japan's revival was assisted by the demand for resource-based industrial products such as petrochemicals, steel, and non-ferrous metals and for a variety of manufactures generated by the Korean War of 1951–53, but that is only part of the story. In spite of severe losses—human and structural—Japan also emerged from the Second World War with its base of skills and knowledge substantially undiminished.[20] It also embraced reconstruction and reindustrialization with equal fervor, raising the ratio of investment to GDP from negligible levels in the late 1940s to an average of 36 percent between 1960 and 1973 (see figure 1.3). This was well above the rate achieved by Germany and was reflected in Japan's growth in per capita GDP, which averaged 8.7 percent—5 percentage points higher than for Germany (see figure 1.1).

---

[20]In the immediate postwar years, Japan also had to absorb nearly 6 million of its nationals who were repatriated from China, Korea, and Taiwan, China.

Figure 1.2   Per Capita GDP Growth of China, India, and the Republic of Korea (Deviation from World per Capita GDP Growth)

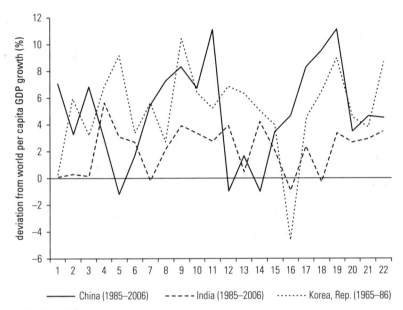

China (1985–2006)   India (1985–2006)   Korea, Rep. (1965–86)

Source: Maddison 2009.

Japan's savings, much like Germany's, were on par with investment. The country's development was mostly financed from domestic sources except during the very early stages. To earn the needed foreign exchange, Japan depended upon exports of manufactures, starting with light consumer items and, in the 1960s, diversifying rapidly into consumer electronics, transport equipment, capital goods, and industrial raw materials. As Japan narrowed technology gaps and the quality of its products (such as cameras and radios) improved and acquired brand recognition, the leading Japanese firms and trading companies that spearheaded the export drive deepened their penetration of markets in developing and developed countries. Japan's ratio of exports climbed steadily to about 10 percent of GDP in 1960 and kept pace with the growth of the economy thereafter (figure 1.5).

Enter Korea

Korea joined the list in the mid-1960s, about a decade after the emergence of Germany and Japan. Korea also had been ravaged by the war of 1951–53, and the wounds ran deep. Unlike the other two countries, Korea was not well endowed with human capital, technological capacity, or an established business infrastructure,

Figure 1.3 Gross Capital Formation

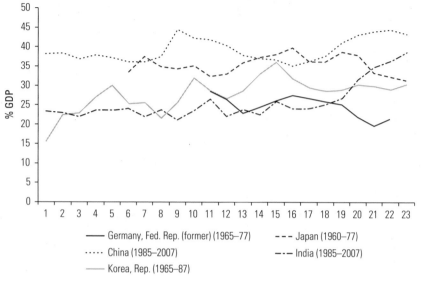

Source: Maddison 2009.

Figure 1.4 Gross Domestic Savings

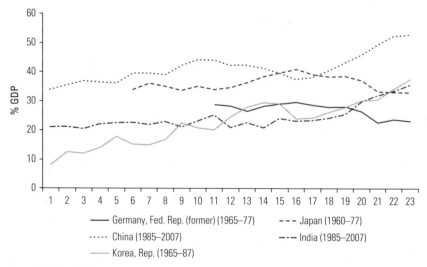

Source: Maddison 2009.

Figure 1.5 Exports of Goods and Services

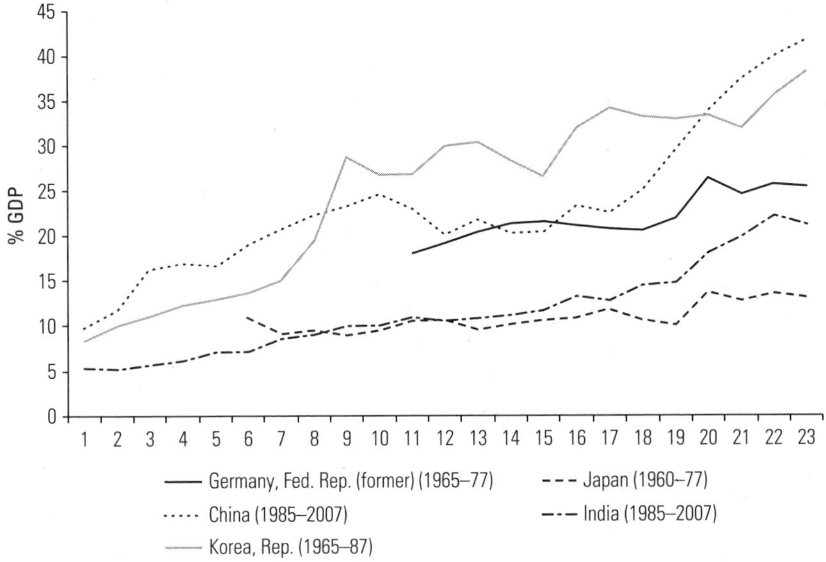
45
40
35
30
25
20
15
10
5
0
% GDP
1 2 3 4 5 6 7 8 9 10 11 12 13 14 15 16 17 18 19 20 21 22 23
Germany, Fed. Rep. (former) (1965–77)
Japan (1960–77)
China (1985–2007)
India (1985–2007)
Korea, Rep. (1965–87)

Source: Maddison 2009.

but the nucleus of business organizations created in the 1920s and 1930s under Japanese occupation survived. Koreans were quick to learn; and the government, firmly committed to industrialization, mobilized the country's material and entrepreneurial resources through a combination of leadership, exhortation, directed credit and other incentives, the setting and close monitoring of production and exports targets,[21] and frequent reminders of the external threat. Spurred by exports and capital formation, growth reached an average per capita rate of 7.8 percent during 1965–75 and 6 percent during 1976–85 (see figure 1.2). Exports, a mere 8 percent of GDP in 1965, averaged 32.7 percent of GDP during 1984–85 (see figure 1.5). Domestic savings also rose in Korea, but not as steeply as in Japan; the country relied to a greater degree on foreign assistance than did either Japan or Germany, and on overseas borrowing to bridge the gap between investment and domestic savings (see figure 1.3 and figure 1.4). However, by the 1990s, domestic savings and investment were in balance.

This brief overview of the fast-paced development of Germany, Japan, and Korea over a period of two decades underscores the contribution of investment

[21] President Park Chung-hee actively supervised the enforcement of the export targets through monthly meetings with industrial leaders.

financed by domestic savings. In Korea's case, this was supplemented by foreign borrowing. In all three countries, growth was led by the manufacturing sector and resulted from the pyramiding of manufacturing capabilities. Export demand helped the country to realize scale economies, induced technological change, and increased productivity. Both Germany and Japan were soon able to move beyond the assimilation of technology to introduce their own innovations—a few of which proved to be highly disruptive to the status quo.[22] What has not yet been emphasized is the role of the government in guiding, coordinating, and financing the activities of the key players, public and private; in supplying the needed infrastructure services; in building a system for producing skills of the appropriate type and quality; in promoting technology acquisition so as to narrow gaps in quality and productivity; and in stimulating innovation through increased research. Governments worked closely with the business community and, in the case of Germany and Japan, with the labor unions to help them strengthen their competitiveness vis-à-vis other firms in international markets. Large firms, mostly conglomerates, were the driving forces in the three economies and key to the creation of brand image and export success. In Germany and Japan, midsize companies (called the *Mittelstand* in Germany) also contributed significantly.[23] They acquired considerable political muscle in both countries; in Germany they had government backing—and were the beneficiaries of support from specialized banking institutions. Small and medium-sized firms had a lower industrial profile in Korea, despite government efforts to encourage the entry of firms into the small and medium enterprise (SME) sector through targeted financing, industrial extension and vocational training schemes.

China Sets a New Benchmark

These three countries constituted the economic outliers until China began casting off the shackles of a planned autarchic system to draw abreast with its East Asian neighbors. China has now dramatically raised the bar. Between 1985 and 2006, China's per capita GDP rose at an average rate of 7 percent per year, and its share of global GDP (at nominal exchange rates) increased from 2.5 percent in 1985 to 6 percent in 2007, equal to that of Germany (see figure 1.7). By 2008 it had climbed to 8 percent, exceeding the share of Japan. The PPP-adjusted share of global GDP presents an even more striking picture. China started out in

---

[22]The transistor radio, the pocket calculator, the Walkman, and subcompact cars being among the best known.

[23]From European experience and other research on exporting firms, it appears that the top 10 percent of exporting firms account for between 70 percent and 96 percent of exports. On balance, these are medium or large firms that are more productive than the average firm, and they tend to export a number of products each to several locations (Mayer 2007).

1985 with a larger share of GDP compared with the other countries—about 7 percent. This increased steadily to 17 percent in 2006, whereas Japan's share after 20 years of rapid growth was 7.5 percent in 1976. Germany's share, after first rising, had gradually dipped below 6 percent by 1976, and Korea's share had risen to just over 1 percent of global GDP in 1986 following two decades of development (see figure 1.6). Whether nominal GDP or PPP-adjusted GDP is used as the yardstick, China's economic performance is unprecedented. This is mirrored in trade statistics (see table 1.3). Among large countries (and even including not-so-large ones), China has a share of trade (exports plus imports) relative to GDP that is the highest, at 74 percent in 2007. Japan's share was 27 percent in 2005; Korea's was higher—90 percent in 2007—but it is a smaller economy. In 1985 the ratio of exports and imports to China's GDP was 24 percent—an increase in openness that was nothing short of spectacular for an economy that, less than a decade earlier, had been one of the world's most isolated. Although China started out in the early 1980s as an exporter of raw materials, foodstuffs, energy, and processed materials, its export composition changed radically, and over 93 percent of its exports are now manufactures. More than the three other countries, China has depended on manufacturing to achieve growth. Value added by manufacturing (in total GDP) was a little less than 35 percent in 1985 and almost 33 percent in 2005. It was 22 percent in Japan and 28 percent in Korea (table 1.4).

Figure 1.6   Share of World GDP

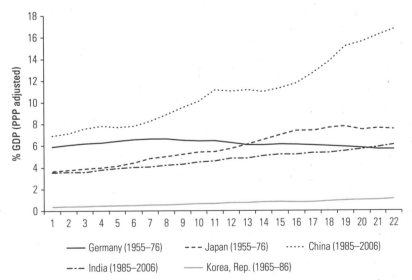

% GDP (PPP adjusted)

——— Germany (1955–76)   - - - Japan (1955–76)   ····· China (1985–2006)

—-– India (1985–2006)   ——— Korea, Rep. (1965–86)

Source: Maddison 2009.

Figure 1.7   Global Share of Nominal GDP

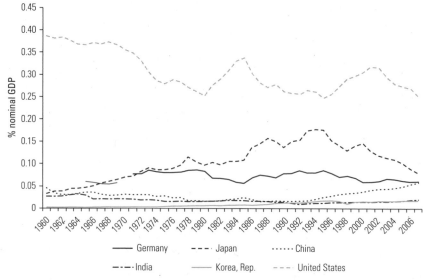

Source: World Development Indicators Database.

Table 1.3   Trade
        % GDP

Country/economy	1980	1985	1990	1995	2000	2005	2007
Singapore	—	—	—	—	—	448.3	433.0
Malaysia	111.0	103.2	147.0	192.1	220.4	212.1	200.1
Taiwan, China	104.1	93.0	86.5	92.8	105.3	124.2	139.8
Thailand	54.5	49.2	75.8	90.4	124.9	148.2	139.0
Korea, Rep.	72.0	63.4	57.0	58.8	78.5	82.2	90.4
Philippines	52.0	45.9	60.8	80.5	108.9	99.3	84.8
China	21.7	24.0	34.6	43.9	44.2	69.3	74.2
Sri Lanka	87.0	64.0	68.2	81.6	88.6	73.6	68.8
Indonesia	54.4	42.7	49.1	54.0	71.4	64.0	54.7
Bangladesh	23.4	18.8	19.7	28.2	33.2	39.6	46.5
India	15.6	13.1	15.7	23.1	27.4	42.5	45.7
Pakistan	36.6	33.2	38.9	36.1	28.1	35.3	35.3
Japan	28.4	25.3	20.0	16.9	20.5	27.3	33.6

Source: World Development Indicators Database.
Note: — = not available.

Table 1.4   Manufacturing Value Added
% GDP

Country/economy	1980	1990	2000	2005	2007
Thailand	21.5	27.2	33.6	34.7	34.8
China	40.2	32.7	32.1	32.8	34.0
Malaysia	21.6	24.2	30.9	29.6	28.0
Korea, Rep.	24.5	27.3	29.4	28.4	27.9
Indonesia	13.0	20.7	27.8	27.4	27.0
Singapore	28.9	27.3	27.7	27.1	25.5
Taiwan, China	35.3	31.2	23.8	23.2	24.1
Philippines	25.7	24.8	22.2	23.2	22.0
Japan	—	—	22.2	21.6	21.2
Pakistan	15.9	17.4	14.7	18.6	19.0
Sri Lanka	17.8	14.8	16.8	19.5	18.5
Bangladesh	13.8	13.1	15.2	16.5	17.8
India	16.7	16.7	15.6	15.8	16.3

Source: World Development Indicators Database.
Note: — = not available.

India in the Global Scales

Compared to China and the three other countries, India is still in a catch-up phase. Its share of global GDP at nominal exchange rates was 1.85 percent in 1985 and 2.16 percent in 2007 (see figure 1.7). The PPP-adjusted share of global GDP was 3.5 percent in 1985 and 6.1 percent in 2006, or about one-third of China's share (figure 1.6). Perhaps the feature that most differentiates India from China and the three other economies is the low ratio of manufacturing value added in GDP—just 16.3 percent, a value that remained unchanged between 1985 and 2007 (see table 1.4). This is one of the reasons that India's exports rose from 0.5 percent in 1985 to only 1.4 percent of global trade in 2007 (table 1.5), although the ratio of trade to GDP increased sharply—from 13 percent in 1985 to 46 percent in 2007 (see table 1.3).

Savings, Investment, Technology, and Growth: A Comparison

The data on trade and manufacturing reveal the unusual nature of China's performance and the lesser, but still impressive, scale of India's growth. Additional insight comes from the time series on investment and savings. China has been a champion investor since 1985. The ratio of investment to GDP was 38 percent in the mid-1980s—greater than in Germany, Japan, and Korea at any time during

Table 1.5   Global Share of Exports of Goods and Services
  percent

Country/economy	1980	1990	2000	2005	2007
China	0.9	1.6	3.5	6.4	7.7
Japan	6.2	7.3	6.4	5.0	4.7
Korea, Rep.	0.9	1.7	2.6	2.6	2.5
Singapore	—	—	—	2.2	2.1
Taiwan, China	0.9	1.7	2.2	1.8	1.6
India	0.5	0.5	0.8	1.2	1.4
Malaysia	0.6	0.8	1.4	1.2	1.2
Thailand	0.3	0.7	1.0	1.0	1.0
Indonesia	1.1	0.7	0.8	0.7	0.7
Philippines	0.3	0.3	0.5	0.4	0.4
Bangladesh	0.0	0.0	0.1	0.1	0.1
Pakistan	0.1	0.1	0.1	0.1	0.1
Sri Lanka	0.1	0.1	0.1	0.1	0.1

Source: World Development Indicators Database.
Note: — = not available.

their high-growth years—and 43 percent in 2007 (see figure 1.3). Amazingly, savings have handily outperformed investment, rising from 34 percent in 1985 to 52 percent in 2007 and 2008 (see figure 1.4). Research has struggled to explain this unmatched savings performance of households and the business sector alike. The rate of household saving (almost 28 percent) in 2008 is linked to the increase in disposable incomes; to the limited availability of financing for consumer durables; to precautionary motives sharpened by concerns over the adequacy of social security and medical insurance; to the need to make provisions for education and marriage; and, for some households, to the pressure exerted by low interest rates on savings deposits (Prasad 2009).

Domestic investments have been supplemented by FDI; this has provided capital for certain segments of industry with limited access to financing (Huang 2005), facilitated technology transfer,[24] and helped connect Chinese firms to international production networks. As a share of GDP, FDI in China was 0.54 percent in 1985 and oscillated between 3 percent and over 4 percent between 2000 and 2007. This is far

---

[24]There is a sizable literature on the spillovers from FDI, which broadly makes the case for technology transfer more in the vertical dimension than the horizontal. The contribution of FDI to the growth of China's industrial regions and productivity are empirically examined by Tuan and Ng (2007) and Tuan, Ng, and Zhao (2009). Mutually advantageous spillover between foreign and local firms are highlighted by Wei, Yingqi, Liu, and Wang (2008).

above the levels attained by Germany, Japan, Korea, and India. It is only in the past few years that the ratio of FDI to GDP in India has begun approaching that of China. In 2007 India was in second place, with an FDI-to-GDP ratio of almost 2 percent (figure 1.8).

India's accelerating rate of growth is also closely linked to buoyant investment. The rate of investment to GDP was 23 percent in 1985 and 39 percent in 2007 (figure 1.3). Since 1998 it has been on an upward trend, buttressed by sharply rising domestic savings (figure 1.4). Depending upon how the domestic and global macroeconomic and climate environments evolve over the next decade, the demand for infrastructure and from the manufacturing sector can sustain high rates of growth fueled by surging investment.

It is notable that over a long period of time—extending from 1860 to the present—leading economies such as the United States and the United Kingdom have deviated relatively little from their trend growth rates of per capita GDP, averaging 1.9 percent annually for the United States and 1.4 percent for the United Kingdom (see figure 1.9). Germany, Japan, and Korea stand out because their growth rose above long-term trends for significant stretches of time, beginning in the 1960s (see Figure 1.9). The long-run growth rates for Germany, Japan, and Korea are 1.8 percent, 3.4 percent, and 6.3 percent, respectively. In Korea, growth dipped below the trend rate during an economically and politically stressful period starting in 1979[25] and extending into the early 1980s, after which the economy quickly regained its stride. However, both Japan and Korea have been in a below-trend mode and may be facing an enduring trend deceleration.[26] China, with a long-term growth rate of 5 percent, is consistently surpassing its growth trend, which began in the late 1990s (see figure 1.7). Whether India can match China's performance (or possibly raise the bar yet again) remains to be seen. Currently, India's long-run trend rate of per capita income growth is 2.6 percent. Per capita income growth edged above the trend line in the late 1990s and has remained above it ever since. Whether India can equal or improve on China's record will depend upon how its economy fares in the aftermath of the 2008–09 crisis and the period of slower growth of the global economy that is forecast; we will discuss this issue later in this volume.

Thus far, we have concentrated on a handful of the determinants and handmaidens of growth: investment, trade, the manufacturing sector, and domestic savings. But growth in the leading economies is also tied to gains in productivity arising from technological progress and innovation.[27] Because increased human

---

[25]President Park was assassinated in October 1979.

[26]Both countries are attempting to reverse deceleration by trusting in research and development (R&D) to deliver the kind of innovation that will sustain a high rate of productivity growth.

[27]Comin and Hobijn (2010) underscore the role of total factor productivity (TFP) in explaining the differences in the levels of GDP among countries. They also draw attention to the technical assistance provided by the U.S. to Germany and Japan after the second World War that assisted these countries to catch up.

Figure 1.8   Share of FDI in GDP

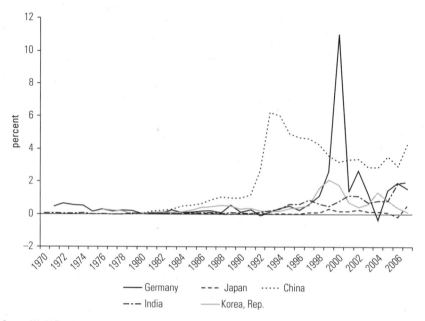

Source: World Development Indicators Database.

capital contributes to technological advance, and patents are a frequently cited indicator of innovation, we have inserted measures of tertiary-level education and of patents granted to residents of Germany, Japan, and Korea into our charts tracking long-run GDP growth to see if there is an apparent correlation. As can be seen from the figures, the spread of tertiary education appears to be unrelated to the acceleration of growth in Germany, Japan, and Korea (see figure 1.9). Patenting began increasing in the 1960s in Japan and, to a lesser extent, in Germany once their national innovation systems were restored after the disruption caused by the war. In Korea, patenting gained momentum after 2000, 35 years into an era of rapid growth (see figure 1.10). The implication is that the long spell of "miraculously" high growth was mainly a function of capital investment in productive assets and infrastructure; technological catch-up with the frontrunner (the United States) through absorption of both embodied and disembodied technologies; and, in the earlier years of productivity, gains arising from the transfer of resources from the rural sector to the urban economy. The deepening of human capital certainly contributed to the closing of the technology gap. Whether tertiary education and innovation supported growth during the past decade in Germany and Japan is less clear; however, it is likely that they are enabling these two countries and Korea to sustain the competitiveness of their vital export-oriented manufacturing industries. Recent estimates of the sources of growth by Jorgenson and Vu

Figure 1.9   Per Capita GDP Growth and Labor Force with Tertiary Education

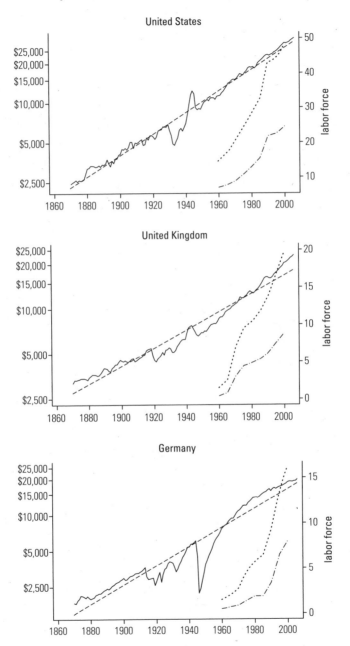

(*continued on next page*)

Figure 1.9   *(continued)*

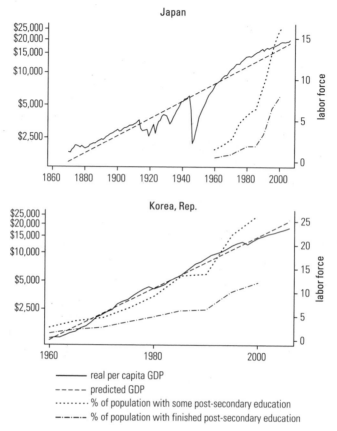

Source: Barro and Lee 2000; Maddison 2006.

(2009) reaffirm the leading role of capital for 14 major economies from 1989 to 2006. Between 1989 and 1995, capital was the source of 54 percent of the growth in these economies. Total factor productivity (TFP) or the aggregated gains in productivity from all sources including capital and labor, provided less than one-fifth. Between 2000 and 2006, the contribution of capital had declined to 41 percent; however, it was larger than the 36 percent contributed by TFP.

For China (figure 1.11), the quickening in tertiary education and patenting are fairly recent phenomena, becoming noticeable in the last decade—that is, since the end of the 1990s, with patenting taking off after 2001. The growing supply of skills in China has contributed to the assimilation of technology in manufacturing and in key services. The available supplies during 1985–2000 were adequate to

Figure 1.10   Per Capita GDP Growth with Patents

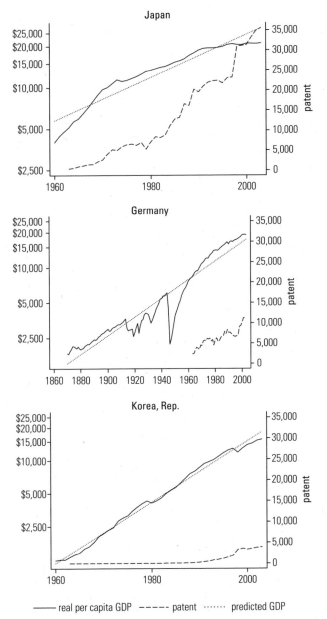

Source: Barro and Lee 2000; Maddison 2006.

Figure 1.11 Per Capita GDP Growth and Labor Force with Tertiary Education: China

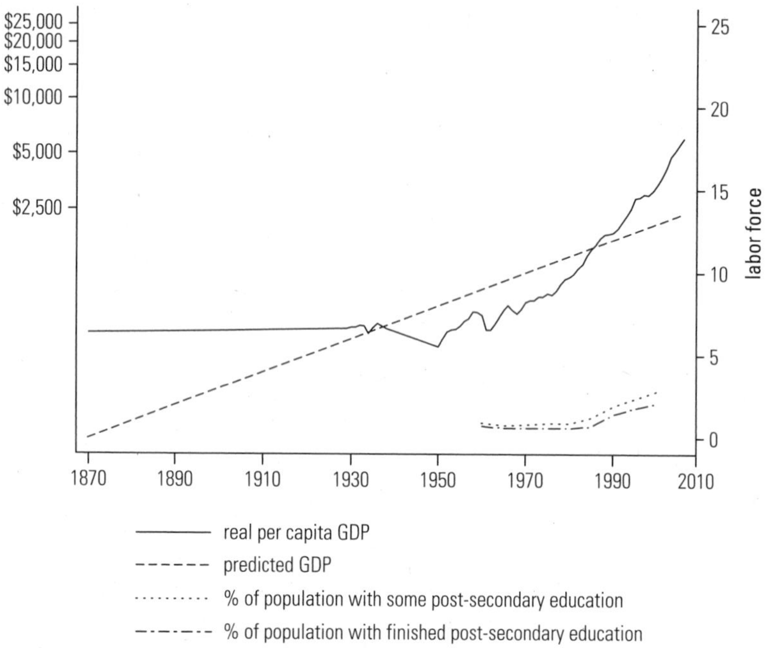

─────── real per capita GDP

------ predicted GDP

·········· % of population with some post-secondary education

─·─·─·─ % of population with finished post-secondary education

Source: Barro and Lee 2000; Maddison 2006.

accommodate the codified technologies being imported. As for the future, tertiary-level skills, continuing technological assimilation, and innovation seem poised to increase their contribution to productivity.

India's overall growth of per capita GDP has no relation to changes in the supply of tertiary-level skills and the flow of patenting (figure 1.12), both of which are only now beginning to pick up. However, it is clear that the quality of India's slender stock of high-level manpower (Altbach 2006) is behind the success of its IT industry and its islands of advanced manufacturing capabilities, which together have catalyzed India's export gains and rapid growth.

In a Class of Its Own

The Chinese economy is in a class by itself. To a lesser degree, India is also, although it trails China by a wide margin. Neither Germany, Japan, nor Korea turned in an economic performance comparable to what China has done for more than 30 years. Only Japan's GDP achieved a scale equivalent to that of

Figure 1.12   Per Capita GDP Growth and Labor Force with Tertiary Education: India

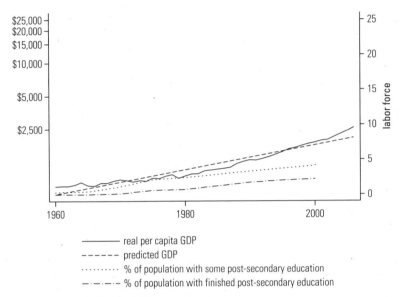

———— real per capita GDP
– – – – – predicted GDP
· · · · · · · · · % of population with some post-secondary education
– · – · — · – % of population with finished post-secondary education

Source: Barro and Lee 2000; Maddison 2006.

China. Tables 1.6 and 1.7 show the income levels of all five countries in 1950 and how much these levels had risen by 1999. Korea leads by a wide margin, with a 39-fold increase, followed by China. In this company, Germany's less than sixfold increase seems minuscule, and India also has a long way to go. Although both Germany and Japan were major trading nations in the mid-1970s, their impact on the industrial geography of the surrounding countries was relatively modest. It should be remembered that in the 1960s and 1970s there were many barriers to trade and labor mobility, countries were partially insulated from competition, and capital flows were severely circumscribed by controls. By the time the Chinese economy began its remarkable ascent, globalization[28] was tearing down barriers to trade and the international circulation of capital. China was quick to profit from such openness and, through a series of measures packed into less than

---

[28]The dismantling of barriers to trade began in earnest with the Kennedy Round of trade negotiations completed in 1964 and continued with the Tokyo and Uruguay Rounds, the last finalized in 1994. The United States and European countries began to gradually lift capital controls in the 1980s, and industrializing began joining in during the 1990s.

Table 1.6   Per Capita Income in 1950
international dollars of 1990

Country	Per capita income
Germany	3,881
Japan	1,926
Korea, Rep.	770
India	619
China	439

Source: Fogel 2009.

Table 1.7   Expansion Multiples of GDP, 1950–99
ratio of GDP in 1999 to GDP in 1950

Country	Ratio
Korea, Rep.	38.93
China	25.59
Japan	16.09
India	8.11
Germany	5.50

Source: Fogel 2009.

15 years, has become more open to trade than Japan or the United States.[29] China's readiness to exploit the opportunities presented by the global integration of trade, the integration of financial markets, and the huge increase in FDI has accelerated the pace of export-oriented industrialization.[30] The off-shoring of production by firms in the advanced countries along with China's own capacity to reinvent itself as an open, quasi-capitalist economy in a matter of years have greatly magnified its impact on the global economy in general—and Asian countries in particular. China has emerged as a formidable competitor for other industrializing Asian nations across a wide range of manufactured products, straddling the full span of technologies and labor intensities. China's cost-effective mastery of assembly line–type operations and its growing readiness to invest overseas also make it an expanding market for the products and resources of other countries, as well as a source of FDI in extractive industries and in light manufacturing. As China's economic size has expanded, so too has its influence on the industrial

[29]The ratio of trade to GDP in China on the eve of reform was a little over 10 percent (Ding and Knight 2008).

[30]China's exports surged noticeably once it became a member of the WTO in 2001.

geography of the Asian region. Unless the process of trade and capital integration slows drastically[31] or is reversed, China's influence relative to that of Japan and the United States will continue to grow. It will be especially prominent with respect to the industrialization of Asian countries.

India, a smaller and less industrialized economy with a modest volume of manufactured exports, has thus far had a negligible influence on the industrial contours of other Asian nations. It was slower to embrace globalization and to tear down the high tariff walls. India's tense relations with its immediate neighbors have hampered the economic integration of the South Asia region, with implications for intra-industry trade and the scale and composition of industry both in India and in the rest of South Asia. Relative to the manufacturing sectors of other fast-growing economies, India's is small, and much of it serves the domestic market. This has prevented India from emulating East Asian rates of growth. The experience of other high-achieving economies suggests that the manufacturing sector in India might have to almost double its share of GDP, or at the very least exceed 25 percent of GDP, for growth rates in the high single digits to be sustained. The domestic market could absorb the bulk of the increased production; however, exports also would need to play a vital role. This would be predicated on the expansion of the global market and, most important, the Asian regional trading regime. Side by side with China's growth, a double-digit growth in India's manufacturing (were it to materialize) would have far-reaching implications for the industrial prospects of India's trading partners. The gains for other countries will be a function of India's openness, the flowering of intra-industry trade, effective behind-the-border trade facilitation, and a dismantling of regulations that currently limit access by foreign producers to Indian markets. As with Japan, if effective openness materializes slowly, the opportunities for other countries to benefit from India's industrialization will be constrained.

These factors (and others, to be examined in later chapters) will compose the forces shaping Asia's industrial geography. The remainder of the book is divided into five chapters. Chapter 2 encapsulates the story of China's industrialization. It delineates the key features of China's industrial sector and trends in subsectoral growth. It shows how the composition of the sector of value added is changing and examines how industrialization is reflected in the mix and growth of exports. The latter part of Chapter 2 covers the same ground for India.

Chapter 3 examines how the comparative advantages of China and India are evolving and identifies factors that will affect competitiveness and openness to imports.

Chapter 4 discusses how China and India have affected industrialization in other Asian countries over the past decade and examines how the industrial structures,

---

[31]Integration is being promoted through numerous regional trading arrangements, which reached a total of 166 in mid-2009, with many more in the pipeline. See "The Noodle Bowl" (2009) and Desker (2004).

exports, and comparative advantages of other Asian countries are developing. We also discuss possible directions of diversification. We build upon this analysis to look toward the future to suggest how the dynamics of industrialization and trade in Asia could determine the industrial geography of the region under plausible assumptions.

Chapter 5 examines five factors that are likely to influence the industrial geography in Asia, and the final chapter concludes with the industrial strategies needed in Asian countries to sustain and improve their prosperity.

References

Akamatsu, Kaname. 1962. "A Historical Pattern of Economic Growth in Developing Countries." *Journal of Developing Economies* 1(1): 3–25.

Altbach, Philip G. 2006. "Tiny at the Top." *Wilson Quarterly* (Autumn): 49–51.

Barro, Robert J., and Jong-Wee Lee. 2000. *International Data on Educational Attainment: Updates and Implications.* CID Working Paper 042, Center for International Development, Harvard University, Cambridge, MA.

Berger, Suzanne, and Richard Lester. 1997. *Made by Hong Kong.* New York: Oxford University Press.

Bhalla, G. S. 2004. "Agricultural Development in India and China: Comparative Experience and Future Collaboration." *Panchsheel and Beyond Cooperation in Development.* New Delhi: Centre for Developing Societies.

Cohen-Setton, Jeremie and Jean Pisani-Ferry. 2008. "Asia-Europe: The Third Link." Bruegel Working Paper 2008/04, Bruegel, Brussels.

Comin, Diego, and Bart Hobijn. 2010. "Technology Diffusion and Postwar Growth." In *NBER Macroeconomics Annual 2010.* Cambridge, MA: National Bureau of Economic Research.

DeLong, J. Bradford, and Barry Eichengreen. 1993. "The Marshall Plan: History's Most Successful Structural Adjustment Programme." In *Postwar Economic Reconstruction and Lessons for the East Today,* ed. Rüdiger Dombusch, Wilhelm Nolling, and Richard Layard, 189–230. Cambridge, MA: MIT Press.

Desker, Barry. 2004. "In Defence of FTAs: From Purity to Pragmatism in East Asia." *Pacific Review* 17(1): 3–26.

Ding, Sai and John Knight. 2008. "Why Has China Grown So Fast? The Role of Structural Change." Economic Series Working Paper 415, University of Oxford, Department of Economics, Oxford, UK.

Durlauf, Steven N., Andros Kourtellos, and Chih Ming Tan. 2008. "Are Any Growth Theories Robust?" *Economic Journal* 118(527): 329–46.

Easterly, William, Michael Kremer, Lant Pritchett, and Lawrence H. Summers. 1993. "Good Policy or Good Luck? Country Growth Performance and Temporary Shocks." *Journal of Monetary Economics* 32(3): 459–83.

Enright, Michael J., Edith E. Scott, and David Dodwell. 1997. *The Hong Kong Advantage.* Hong Kong: Oxford University Press.

Fogel, Robert W. 2009. "The Impact of the Asian Miracle on the Theory of Economic Growth." NBER Working Paper 14967, National Bureau of Economic Research, Cambridge, MA.

Giersch, Herbert, Karl-Heinz Pague, and Holger Schmieding. 1993. "Openness, Wage Restraint, and Macroeconomic Stability: West Germany's Road to Prosperity 1948–1959." In *Postwar Economic Reconstruction and Lessons for the East Today*, ed. Dornbusch, Rudiger, Wilhelm Nolling, and Richard Layard. Cambridge, MA: MIT Press.

Grether, Jean-Marie, and Nicole A. Mathys. 2006. "Is the World's Economic Center of Gravity Already in Asia?" http://www.etsg.org/ETSG2007papers/grether.pdf.

Hausmann, Ricardo, Lant Pritchett, and Dani Rodrik. 2004. "Growth Accelerations." NBER Working Paper 10566, National Bureau of Economic Research, Cambridge, MA.

Huang, Yasheng. 2005. *Selling China: Foreign Direct Investment during the Reform Era*. New York: Cambridge University Press.

Jorgenson, Dale W., and Khuong M. Vu. 2009. "Growth Accounting within the International Comparison Program." *ICP Bulletin* 6(1): 3–28.

Kasahara, Shigehisa. 2004. *The Flying Geese Paradigm: A Critical Study of Its Application to East Asian Regional Development*. United Nations Conference on Trade and Development.

Kojima, Kiyoshi. 2000. "The 'Flying Geese' Model of Asian Economic Development: Origin, Theoretical Extensions, and Regional Policy Implications." *Journal of Asian Economics* 11: 375–401.

Kojima, Kiyoshi, and Terutomo Ozawa. 1985. "Towards a Theory of Industrial Restructuring and Dynamic Comparative Advantage." *Hitotsubashi Journal of Economics* 26(2): 135–45.

Maddison, Angus. 2006. "World Population, GDP and Per Capita GDP," 1-2003 AD. http://www.ggdc.net/maddison/Historical_Statistics/horizontal-file_03-2006.xls.

———. 2008. "The West and the Rest in the World Economy 1000–2030." *World Economics* 9(4): 75–99.

———. 2009. "World Population, GDP and Per Capita GDP," 1-2006 AD. www.ggdc.net/ maddison/Historical_Statistics/horizontal-file_03-2009.xls

Mathews, John, and Dong Sung Cho. 2000. *Tiger Technology: The Creation of a Semiconductor Industry in East Asia*. Cambridge Asia-Pacific Studies. Cambridge, New York, and Melbourne: Cambridge University Press.

Mayer, Thierry. 2007. "The Internationalization of European Firms: New Facts Based on Firm-Level Evidence." EFIM Report European Firms & International Markets.

"The Noodle Bowl." 2009. *Economist*, September 3, 2009.

Ozawa, Terutomo. 2003. "Pax Americana–Led Macro-Clustering and Flying-Geese-Style Catch-up in East Asia: Mechanisms of Regionalized Endogenous Growth." *Journal of Asian Economics* 13: 699–713.

Panagariya, Arvind. 2008a. "Transforming India." In *Sustaining India's Growth Miracle*, ed. Jagdish N. Bhagwati and Charles W. Calomiris. New York: Columbia Business School Publishing.

Panagariya, Arvind. 2008b. *India: The Emerging Giant*. New York: Oxford University Press.

Pisani-Ferry, Jean. 2010. "China and the World Economy: A European Perspective." Bruegel Policy Contribution 2010/03, Bruegel, Brussels.

Prasad, Eswar. 2009. "Rebalancing Growth in Asia." NBER Working Paper Series 15169, National Bureau of Economic Research, Cambridge, MA.

Rodrik, Dani, and Arvind Subramanian. 2004. "From 'Hindu Growth' To Productivity Surge: The Mystery of the Indian Growth Transition." NBER Working Paper 10376, National Bureau of Economic Research, Cambridge, MA.

Soete, Luc. 1985. "International Diffusion of Technology, Industrial Development and Technological Leapfrogging." *World Development* 13(3): 409–22.

Tao, Zhigang, and Yue-Chim Richard Wong. 2002. "Hong Kong: From an Industrial City to a Centre of Manufacturing-Related Services." *Urban Studies* 39(12): 2345–58.

Tuan, Chyau, and Linda Fung-Yee Ng. 2007. "The Place of FDI in China's Regional Economic Development: Emergence of the Globalized Delta Economies." *Journal of Asian Economics* 18(2): 348–364.

Tuan, Chyau, Linda Fung-Yee Ng, and Bo Zhao. 2009. "China's Post-Economic Reform Growth: The Role of FDI and Productivity Progress." *Journal of Asian Economics* 20(3): 280–93.

Virmani, Arvind. 2004. "India's Economic Growth." ICRIER Working Paper 122, New Delhi.

Wei, Yingqi, Xiaming Liu, and Chengang Wang. 2008. "Mutual Productivity Spillovers between Foreign and Local Firms in China." *Cambridge Journal of Economics* 32(4): 609–31.

Weinstein, David E. 1995. "Evaluating Administrative Guidance and Cartels in Japan (1957–88)." *Journal of the Japanese and International Economies* 9: 200–23.

Winters, L. Alan, and Shahid Yusuf. 2007. *Dancing with Giants: China, India, and the Global Economy.* Washington, DC: World Bank.

Wolf, Holger C. 1993. "The Lucky Miracle: Germany 1945–1951." In *Postwar Economic Reconstruction and Lessons for the East Today,* ed. Rudiger Dornbusch, Wilhelm Nolling, and Richard Layard. Cambridge, MA: MIT Press.

Yusuf, Shahid, Kaoru Nabeshima, and Dwight H. Perkins. 2005. *Under New Ownership: Privatizing China's State-Owned Enterprises.* Stanford, CA: Stanford University Press.

2

Development Experience
of China and India

Two stylized facts of significance emerge from the experience of fast-growing Asian economies and of other developing economies. First, rapid growth of GDP is correlated with the expansion of manufacturing industry. Figure 2.1 shows the relationship between average real growth in manufacturing value added and real growth in GDP for developing countries between 1995 and 2005. The data come from World Development Indicators, maintained by the World Bank. The trend line represents a simple bivariate regression.[1] From the figure, it is apparent that the slope is positive. While causality is hard to establish, the result suggests that one percentage point increase in manufacturing value added growth is associated with 0.33 percentage point increase in GDP growth.

Second, each of the high-achieving Asian economies relied on exports of manufactures generated by the development of competitive industries—which were quick to exploit international market opportunities. Manufactured goods composed as much as 90 percent of the exports of the Philippines during 1996–2006 and about 50 percent of the exports of Indonesia and Vietnam. The other countries ranged in between, with the East Asian economies clustered near the upper end (Asian Development Bank 2009). Net exports contributed between 10 percent and almost 50 percent of the growth of the East Asian economies. Korea, Indonesia, Malaysia, the Philippines, and Thailand derived more impetus from net exports during 1995–2000. Hong Kong, China; Taiwan, China; Singapore; and Japan drew more of their growth from exports during 2000–06 (See figure 2.2, Haltmaier and others 2007, and Prasad 2009). However,

---

[1]The regression result is $y = 0.029556 + 0.3259912x$. Adjusted R-square was 0.2987. The t-value associated with the coefficient estimate was 7.39.

Figure 2.1 Relationship between GDP Growth and Growth in Manufacturing Value Added

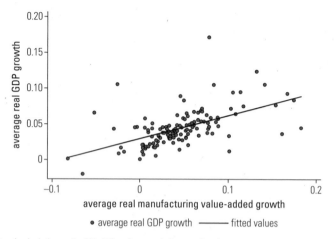

Source: Authors' calculations using World Development Indicators Database.

Figure 2.2 Percentage Point Contribution of Real Net Exports to GDP Growth in Asia

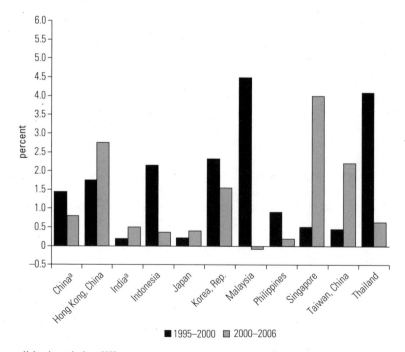

Source: Haltmaier and others 2007.
a. China and India data are through 2005.

irrespective of contribution of net exports, export growth in the aggregate and tradable sectors was the principal source of technological and entrepreneurial dynamism in these economies.[2]

China's Industrial Development

China is a manufacturing economy par excellence, and the genesis of this sectoral dominance can be traced to the consistent preference for manufacturing as a growth driver. This began in the 1950s; in the earlier decades, the government pursued an autarchic development strategy on ideological grounds, and this strategy targeted heavy industries such as ferrous metals and machinery. Consumer goods had a relatively small share of the total. The U.S. embargo on trade with China and the virtual cessation of trading links with the former Soviet Union provided added inducement for China to build a broad domestic industrial base using whatever technologies were within its reach. By the 1960s, more than a third of China's GDP originated in the industrial sector. This rose to 45 percent by the end of the 1970s.[3] The reforms that blended elements of the market economy into Chinese socialism did nothing to dilute the significance assigned to manufacturing; however, the government began altering the composition of the manufacturing sector. This process continues as China's policy makers revise their objectives and raise their sights every few years.

The opening of China's economy stimulated the development of manufacturing activities with export potential and increased the salience of light manufactures—including consumer electronics, textiles, apparel, toys, footwear, furniture, and leather goods—in which China enjoyed a comparative advantage, given the abundance of labor relative to capital.[4] The transfer of facilities for producing such goods from Hong Kong to special economic zones (SEZs) and cities in the Pearl River Delta contributed to this compositional shift.

By adopting a more decentralized approach to development, reinforced by fiscal and other incentives encouraging localized entrepreneurship (both private and quasi-public), the central government further encouraged the diversification of industry. The early 1980s saw the start of a boom in township and village enterprises (TVEs) producing a wide range of consumer goods, agricultural implements and machinery, pulp and paper, chemicals, metal products, and other

[2] Imports have been no less important in transferring technology and as a source of competition. As Ding and Knight (2008) show, the contribution of imports to China's growth rivals that of exports.

[3] A deliberate relocation of industry and skilled workers from coastal cities to inland areas starting in the mid-1960s and extending through the mid 1970s misallocated resources and caused hardship. However, it did transfer technology to the interior of China.

[4] On the aligning of production with comparative advantage, see Lin (2009).

goods.[5] The TVEs were mostly small enterprises serving local markets as these took root, but by the latter part of the 1980s TVEs had become a major source of light manufactures for export. In fact, 21 percent of China's total exports in 1991 were by TVEs (Perotti, Sun, and Zou 1999). Thus, policies promoting manufacturing for export—fueled by foreign direct investment (FDI) and reforms that permitted TVEs to flourish—began widening the domestic market for a variety of manufactured goods.

Starting in the mid-1990s, China began diversifying into the assembly of higher-tech electronic products, machinery, and office equipment. This was paralleled by the targeting of the auto and other heavy industries as pillars of China's economy, an action that also galvanized the petrochemical sector. Over the last decade, these three subsectors have become the foremost drivers of industry.

Strengthening industrial capabilities and increasing evidence of competitiveness encouraged policy makers to begin building China's national innovation system to induce the design, development, and production of more sophisticated products. The objective is to move the economy decisively beyond assembly to activities with higher added value and potentially greater profitability. This process, which began gathering momentum in the late 1990s, is continuing, with Chinese firms and universities sinking more money into R&D to stimulate product and process innovation.

Tracking the sectoral and subsectoral developments in industrial production over almost three decades reveals both the speed of industrial growth and the compositional changes that have contributed to it. Figure 2.3 indicates that as of 1980, a little less than half of China's GDP originated in the industrial sector, while 30 percent was from agriculture. By the mid-1980s, agriculture was losing ground, being displaced by services; the two curves form a virtual mirror image, with agriculture's share shrinking as the share of services shoots upward. Industry, however, has more or less maintained its position, ending in 2006 close to where it started (table 2.1). By 2008, agriculture's share dropped below 10 percent, industry's share stood at 48 percent, and that of services was at about 42 percent.

When the output of manufacturing as a whole is broken down into its constituent parts, another kind of transition is apparent. In 1980, about 40 percent of production was composed of light manufactures, with food products and textiles being the two largest (see figure 2.4). The balance of industrial output originated in subsectors producing intermediate products and machinery and equipment. Ten years later, the share of textiles, apparel, and food products was

---

[5]TVEs had their roots in the rural industrialization efforts that commenced in the early 1970s. See Womack and Jones (1994). There is a sizable literature on the genesis of TVEs, the ownership structure of these entities, and the role of local governments. See, for example, Findlay, Watson, and Wu (1994); Pei (1996); Chen (1998); Chen and Rozelle (1999); Oi (1999); and Khanna (2007), who uses the example of the company TCL to illustrate how TVEs provided a springboard for the growth of larger firms.

Figure 2.3   Composition of GDP (Supply Side), China

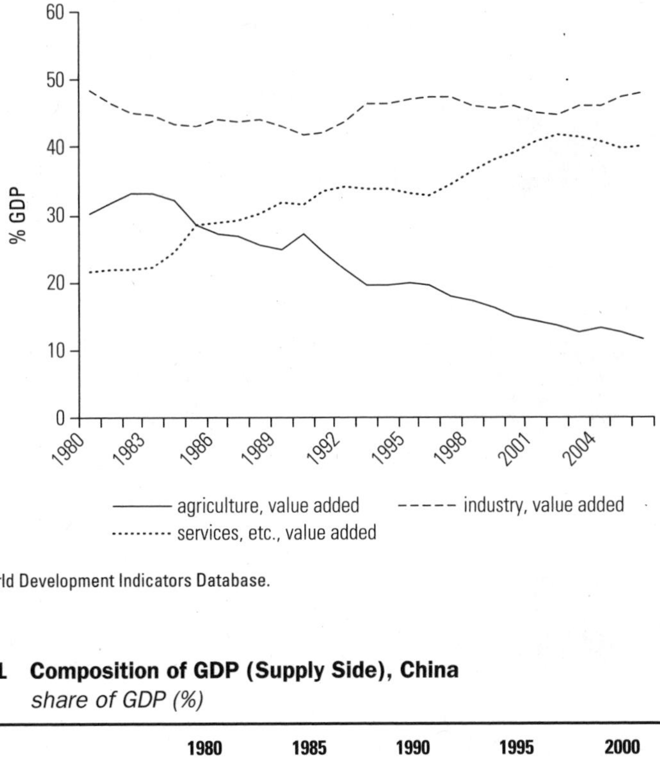

Source: World Development Indicators Database.

Table 2.1   Composition of GDP (Supply Side), China
share of GDP (%)

Series	1980	1985	1990	1995	2000	2006
Industry, value added	48.5	43.1	41.6	47.2	45.9	48.1
Services, etc., value added	21.4	28.5	31.3	33.1	39.3	40.2
Agriculture, value added	30.1	28.4	27.0	19.8	14.8	11.7

Source: World Development Indicators Database.

in decline, whereas that of industrial intermediates such as chemicals, glass, and rubber products was expanding. This tendency had become more pronounced by 2003, by which time textiles, apparel, foodstuffs, and leather products accounted for just one-fifth of output. The biggest gainer over this entire period was electronics (including electrical machinery), followed by transport equipment. Four years later, the scale of the electronics sector, broadly defined, is even more prominent—as is that of transport equipment and allied industries such as ferrous metals, petroleum, coking, and chemicals. Together these four subsectors were responsible for 22.2 percent of the value of manufacturing output in 2007. If we add to these the production of machinery and other metal products, the total swells to 43.2 percent of aggregate manufacturing output (see table 2.2).

Figure 2.4   Industrial Composition by Type of Manufactures of China, 1981, 1990, and 2003

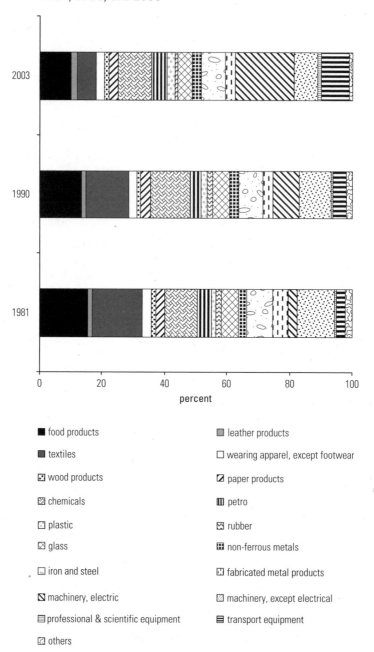

■ food products

■ textiles

▣ wood products

▨ chemicals

▢ plastic

▨ glass

▢ iron and steel

◩ machinery, electric

▤ professional & scientific equipment

▨ others

■ leather products

□ wearing apparel, except footwear

▨ paper products

▥ petro

▨ rubber

▦ non-ferrous metals

▣ fabricated metal products

▨ machinery, except electrical

▦ transport equipment

Source: UNIDO INDSTAT3.

Table 2.2   Industrial Composition of China, 2007

Sector	Gross industrial output Value (100 million yuan)	Composition (%)
National total	352,950.1	
Processing of food from agricultural products	17,496.1	5.0
Manufacture of foods	6,071.0	1.7
Manufacture of beverages	5,082.3	1.4
Manufacture of tobacco	3,776.2	1.1
Manufacture of textiles	18,733.3	5.3
Manufacture of textile apparel, footwear, and caps	7,600.4	2.2
Manufacture of leather, fur, feather, and related products	5,153.5	1.5
Processing of timber; manufacture of wood, bamboo, rattan, palm, and straw products	3,520.5	1.0
Manufacture of furniture	2,424.9	0.7
Manufacture of paper and paper products	6,325.5	1.8
Printing, reproduction of recording media	2,117.6	0.6
Manufacture of articles for culture, education, and sports activities	2,098.8	0.6
Processing of petroleum, coking, processing of nuclear fuel, and manufacture of raw chemical materials and products	44,649.7	12.7
Manufacture of medicines	6,361.9	1.8
Manufacture of chemical fibers	4,120.8	1.2
Manufacture of rubber	,462.4	1.0
Manufacture of plastics	8,120.4	2.3
Manufacture of nonmetallic mineral products and metal products; and smelting and pressing of non-ferrous metals	45,038.4	12.8
Smelting and pressing of ferrous metals	33,703.0	9.5
Manufacture of general and special-purpose machinery	29,007.5	8.2
Manufacture of transport equipment	27,147.4	7.7
Manufacture of electrical machinery and equipment	67,550.8	19.1
Manufacture of artwork and other manufacturing	3,387.7	1.0

Source: National Statistical Bureau of China 2008.
Note: Mining; recycling of disposal waste and production; and supply of power, gas, and water are excluded from the national total. The composition is thus focused solely on manufactures.

Over the 26-year period from 1980 to 2006, industry was consistently the principal source of growth, followed by services, with agriculture falling behind as its growth slowed and its share diminished (see table 2.3). Meanwhile, services have pulled abreast of industry; their contribution is on the rise across the spectrum. This trend is likely to persist, with services pulling ahead, as in other middle- and

Table 2.3 Average Shares of Contribution to Growth, China
percent

	Consumption	Government spending	Investment	Net exports
1970s	39.0	16.7	50.7	−6.5
1980s	50.3	14.6	32.8	2.4
1990s	34.3	17.3	34.3	14.0
2000s	31.2	13.8	47.6	7.4

Source: World Development Indicators Database.

high-income economies (McKinsey Global Institute 2010). This might happen soon, if international trade grows more slowly.

A partitioning of the sources of growth in China indicates how sectoral change came about. Bosworth and Collins (2007) estimate that physical capital and total factor productivity contributed 3.2 percent and 3.8 percent, respectively, to China's GDP growth between 1978 and 2004.[6] During 1993–2004, their contributions were 4.2 percent and 4.0 percent, respectively (see table 2.4). Within this context, the role of industry overshadows the other sectors. As table 2.5 shows, capital and TFP respectively contributed 2.2 percent and 4.4 percent of growth during 1978–2004, and 3.2 percent and 6.2 percent from 1993–2004.[7] Although industry-specific data are lacking, empirical evidence from other countries suggests that TFP has risen much faster in the electrical and nonelectrical machinery subsectors (Jorgenson, Ho, and Stiroh 2007). This has added to the prominence of these industries and raised the average increase of TFP for manufacturing as a whole.

Over the same two periods, services derived 2.7 percent of its growth from capital and 1.9 percent from TFP (1978–2004). The contribution of TFP to services fell to just 0.9 percent per year between 1993 and 2004. Clearly, industry has lived up to its international reputation for productivity growth, and its future role could well influence how rapidly China's GDP continues expanding.

---

[6]This estimate can be compared with others by He and Kuijs (2007). The sources of growth in China are estimated by, among others, Wang and Yao (2003); Badunenko, Henderson, and Zelenyuk (2008); and Urel and Zebregs (2009). All of them find that capital played the leading role. According to some estimates, China's TFP growth during 1990–2008 was even higher—almost 4 percent—reflecting not just the effects of labor transfer to the urban industrial sector but also China's extraordinary success at absorbing technology and catching up ("Secret Sauce" 2009). On the research dealing with productivity see Syverson (2010).

[7]A more recent estimate by Kuijs (2010) pegs the contribution of TFP during 1995–2009 at 2.7 percent and the contribution of capital at 5.5 percent.

Table 2.4   Sources of Growth: China, India, and East Asia, 1978–2004
annual rate of change (%)

Period		Output	Employment	Output per worker	Physical capital	Land	Education	Factor productivity
					Contribution of			
Total economy								
1978–2004	China	9.3	2.0	7.3	3.2	0.0	0.2	3.8
	India	5.4	2.0	3.3	1.3	0.0	0.4	1.6
1993–2004	China	9.7	1.2	8.5	4.2	0.0	0.2	4.0
	India	6.5	1.9	4.6	1.8	0.0	0.4	2.3
East Asia excluding China								
1960–80		7.0	3.0	4.0	2.2	—	0.5	1.2
1980–2003		6.1	2.4	3.7	2.2	—	0.5	0.9
1980–93		7.3	2.7	4.6	2.6	—	0.6	1.4
1993–2003		4.5	2.0	2.5	1.8	—	0.5	0.3

Source: Bosworth and Collins 2007.
Note: — = not available.

Table 2.5   Sources of Growth by Major Sector, 1978–2004
annual rate of change (%)

Period		Output	Employment	Output per worker	Physical capital	Land	Education	Factor productivity
					Contribution of			
Industry								
1978–2004	China	10.0	3.1	7.0	2.2	—	0.2	4.4
	India	5.9	3.4	2.5	1.5	—	0.3	0.6
1993–2004	China	11.0	1.2	9.8	3.2	—	0.2	6.2
	India	6.7	3.6	3.1	1.7	—	0.3	1.1
Services								
1978–2004	China	10.7	5.8	4.9	2.7	—	0.2	1.9
	India	7.2	3.8	3.5	0.6	—	0.4	2.4
1993–2004	China	9.8	4.7	5.1	3.9	—	0.2	0.9
	India	9.1	3.7	5.4	1.1	—	0.4	3.9

Source: Bosworth and Collins 2007.
Note: — = not available.

The productivity advantage of the industrial sector in China is underscored by the trend increase in the value of output per worker. Figure 2.5 indicates that output per worker in industry equaled that in services through 1984, then briefly dropped below services, and then began decisively pulling ahead after 1994. Value added per worker has consistently been higher in industry as a share of total value

Figure 2.5 Output per Worker by Sector, China, 1978–2004

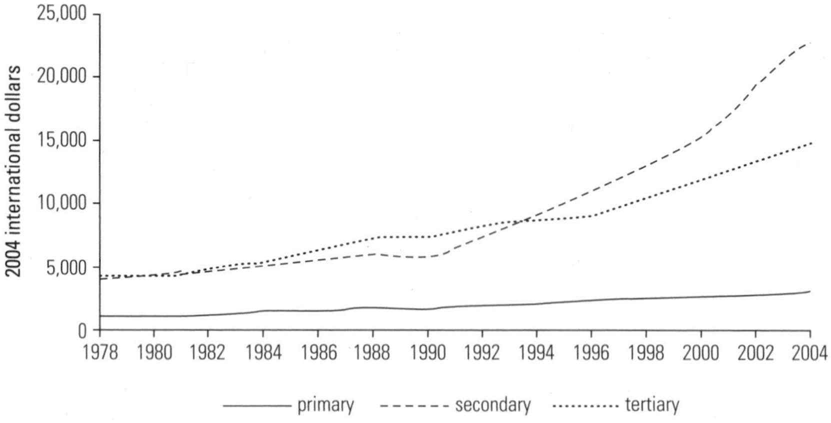

Source: Bosworth and Collins 2007.

added (see table 2.6). In 1978, value added by services was about half that of industry. By 1993 the gap had narrowed, with services accounting for a third of industry's share. As of 2004, the share of services was unchanged; but that of industry had risen to 58 percent. Moreover, the growth of output per worker in industry doubled between 1978–93 and 1993–2004 from 2.4 percent to 5.0 percent per year. The tertiary sector's share also increased, but only from 1.1 percent to 1.7 percent (table 2.7).

The flip side of these gains in industrial productivity is declining employment. This is a worldwide and disquieting trend in manufacturing—no growth or even negative growth in jobs. China's vast manufacturing sector employed 98 million in 1995. By 2002 the number had fallen to 83 million,[8] after a decade of double-digit growth.

Three decades after the start of reform, China's share of global output and value added have swelled enormously. By 2009 China was the world's leading manufacturer of iron, steel, cement, aluminum, and glass. In Asia, China is the largest or the second largest producer (after Japan) in virtually every major product group; it overtook Korea in transport equipment in 2008, and by the end of 2009 the order volume in China's shipyards exceeded that of Korea in terms of compensated gross tonnage (54.96 million compensated gross tonnage). In textiles, garments, furniture, toys, and leather products it towers over other countries and, along with Japan, claims a large share of the market for

---

[8]This number is from the *China Labour Statistical Yearbook 2007.*

Table 2.6   Value Added and Employment by Industry as Share of Total
percent

		Primary	Secondary	Tertiary	Total
Value added					
1978	China	28	48	24	100
	India	44	24	32	100
1993	China	17	51	33	100
	India	33	28	39	100
2004	China	9	58	33	100
	India	22	28	50	100
Employment					
1978	China	71	17	12	100
	India	71	13	16	100
1993	China	56	22	21	100
	India	64	15	21	100
2004	China	47	23	31	100
	India	57	18	25	100

Source: Bosworth and Collins 2007

Table 2.7   Sectoral Growth in Output per Worker, 1978–2004
contribution to growth (%)

		Total	Primary	Secondary	Tertiary	Reallocation
1978–93	China	6.4	1.2	2.4	1.1	1.7
	India	2.4	0.6	0.5	0.7	0.6
	Difference	4.0	0.6	1.9	0.5	1.0
1993–2004	China	8.5	0.7	5.0	1.7	1.2
	India	4.6	0.5	0.9	2.1	1.2
	Difference	3.9	0.2	4.1	−0.4	0.0

Source: Bosworth and Collins 2007.

electronics. The contrast between China's share in the early 1980s and 20 years later is striking; it testifies to China's remarkable capability to industrialize, not just in a few areas, but across the entire range of subsectors (see figures 2.6, 2.7, 2.8, and 2.9 for shares in 1981 and 2002).

China's early commitment to industrialization—and, since 1978, its investment in and steady upgrading of its manufacturing and technological capabilities—is yielding extraordinary dividends in terms of productivity, industrial diversification,

Figure 2.6 Share in Global Output, Textiles, 1981 and 2002
percent

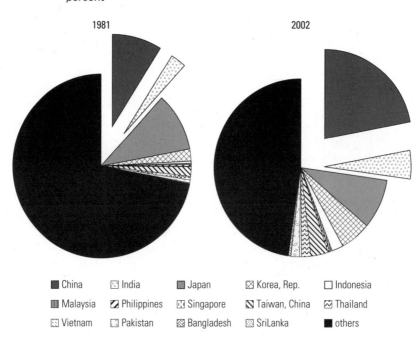

Source: UNIDO INDSTAT3.
Note: Data for Bangladesh are from 1981, 1990 and 1998; for Pakistan, 1981, 1990 and 1996; for the Philippines, 1981, 1990, and 1997; for Sri Lanka, 1981, 1990, and 2001; for Taiwan, China, 1981, 1990, and 1996; and for Vietnam, 2000 and 2002.

and growth.[9] Three factors have helped to ensure the success of industrialization in generating rapid growth: exports, urban development, and efforts at rapidly augmenting technological capabilities, in chronological order.

Export Composition and Growth

As noted in chapter 1, China is an unusually open economy for its size, with a high ratio of trade to GDP. It is also the most successful exporting nation on record. Aided by globalization and the international redistribution of manufacturing capacity, China's exports have risen faster than those of its closest competitors—Germany, Japan, and Korea (see table 2.8). The composition of its exports also has changed significantly. In 1985, over 60 percent of China's

---

[9]However, provincial resistance to the exit of marginal and inefficient producers has slowed the gains in productivity, especially in the materials processing and transport industries. It has also resulted in the accumulation of excess capacity.

Figure 2.7   Share in Global Output, Wearing Apparel (except Footwear), 1981 and 2002
percent

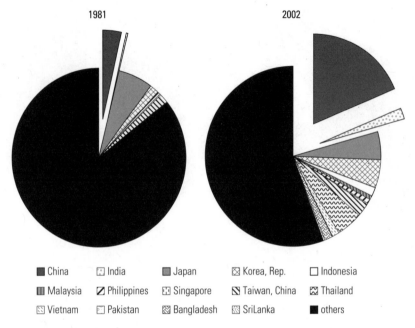

Source: UNIDO INDSTAT3.
Note: Data for Bangladesh are from 1981, 1990 and 1998; for Pakistan, 1981, 1990 and 1996; for the Philippines, 1981, 1990, and 1997; for Sri Lanka, 1981, 1990, and 2001; for Taiwan, China, 1981, 1990, and 1996; and for Vietnam, 2000 and 2002.

exports were resource- and agriculture-based products and primary products. Electronics and other high-technology products accounted for a little more than 5 percent of the total. Five years later, the share of the former product group had been cut almost by half; by 2006, it was down to 12 percent. The big gainers were exports of electronics, telecommunications products, and office equipment, the shares of which grew from 5.4 percent in 1985 to more than one-third in 2006. Underlying this remarkable performance was a technological revolution that produced a flow of new products feeding a seemingly insatiable demand worldwide. The other export categories that raised their shares were engineering products, processed exports, and automotive products.[10] Collectively, their

[10]Exports of electrical machinery and transport equipment accounted for 36 percent of Asia's exports in 1992. By 2006 their share had risen to 56 percent on average and to 70–80 percent for Malaysia, Singapore, and the Philippines (Asian Development Bank 2009).

Figure 2.8 Share in Global Output, Leather Products, 1981 and 2002
percent

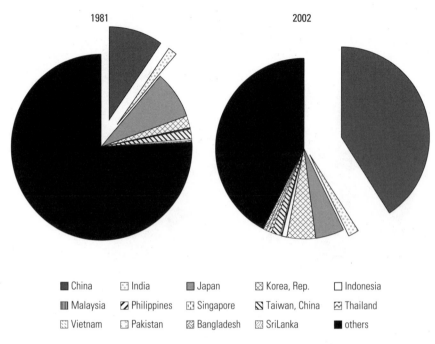

1981   2002

■ China   ⊡ India   ■ Japan   ⊠ Korea, Rep.   □ Indonesia

▥ Malaysia   ▧ Philippines   ⊡ Singapore   ◩ Taiwan, China   ⊠ Thailand

▧ Vietnam   ▢ Pakistan   ▨ Bangladesh   ▨ SriLanka   ■ others

Source: UNIDO INDSTAT3.
Note: Data for Bangladesh are from 1981, 1990 and 1998; for Pakistan, 1981, 1990 and 1996; for the Philippines, 1981, 1990, and 1997; for Sri Lanka, 1981, 1990, and 2001; for Taiwan, China, 1981, 1990, and 1996; and for Vietnam, 2000 and 2002.

share rose from under 13 percent in 1985 to 22 percent in 2006. In the intervening years, the share of textiles, garments, footwear, and other light manufactures peaked at 47 percent in 1995 before settling to 32 percent in 2006 (see figure 2.10 and table 2.9).

Starting out as an exporter of primary and resource-based products in the first half of the 1980s, China recast itself as the premier producer of textiles and light manufactures from 1985 to 1995. This is a typical pattern for a late industrializer emerging from a state of industrial backwardness—but one that was developed in an amazingly short period of time. Ten years later, while maintaining its strong presence in light manufactures, China elbowed out competitors around the world to emerge as the leading exporter of electronics and high-tech products—many assembled—and among the top 10 exporters in other major product categories

Figure 2.9   Share in Global Output, Electric Machinery, 1981 and 2002
percent

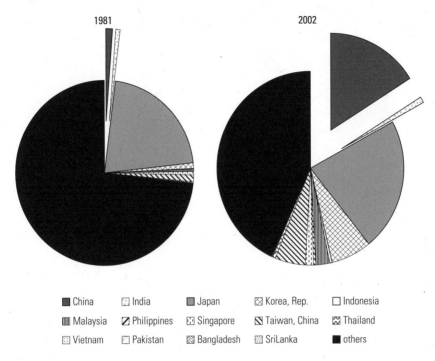

1981   2002

■ China   ⊡ India   ■ Japan   ⊠ Korea, Rep.   □ Indonesia

▥ Malaysia   ▨ Philippines ⊞ Singapore   ◱ Taiwan, China   ⊠ Thailand

⊠ Vietnam   ⊡ Pakistan   ⊠ Bangladesh   ▨ SriLanka   ■ others

Source: UNIDO INDSTAT3.
Note: Data for Bangladesh are from 1981, 1990 and 1998; for Pakistan, 1981, 1990 and 1996; for the Philippines,
1981, 1990, and 1997; for Sri Lanka, 1981, 1990, and 2001; for Taiwan, China, 1981, 1990, and 1996; and for Vietnam,
2000 and 2002.

Table 2.8   Exports of Goods and Services
current US$ billions

Country	1980	1985	1990	1995	2000	2005	2007
China	20.2	30.5	68.0	168.0	279.6	836.9	1342.2
Japan	144.7	193.6	316.8	480.9	512.7	652.5	771.0
Korea, Rep.	20.5	30.9	73.7	149.1	208.9	334.5	442.2
Germany	186	176.6	425.2	604.3	634.2	1141.6	1549.4

Source: World Development Indicators Database.

Figure 2.10 Export Composition of China by Technology Class

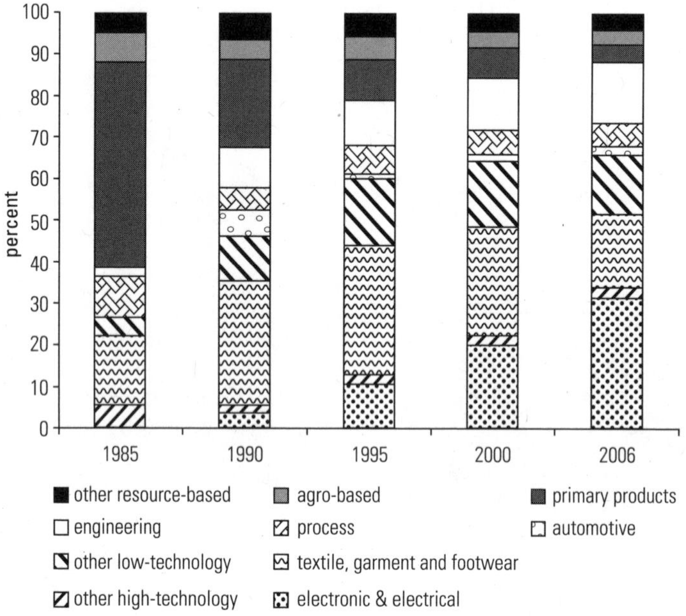

Legend:
- ■ other resource-based
- □ engineering
- ◣ other low-technology
- ▨ other high-technology
- ■ agro-based
- ▨ process
- ⊠ textile, garment and footwear
- ⊡ electronic & electrical
- ■ primary products
- □ automotive

Source: Authors' calculations using UN Comtrade data.

(see table 2.10). The items in which China's presence is insignificant are automotive and processed primary commodities (table 2.11), although, as discussed below, China's profile in automotive products is likely to rise.[11] Such a drastic transformation of export composition is unusual, even among East Asian economies. In the early days, Japan's exports were also dominated by low-tech products, mainly garments and textiles (see figure 2.11), but the shift toward medium- and high-tech products there was slower. In comparison, Korea completed the transition much more quickly, first through a rapid increase of

---

[11]China became the largest single market for automobiles in 2009, with sales of 13.6 million units, compared to 10.4 million in the United States, long the world leader (*China Daily* 2010). However, China's domestic manufacturers have thus far managed to sell practically no cars overseas, aside from a trickle in Russia, Ukraine, Eastern Europe, and Latin America. How quickly this might change and whether China is able to enter the market for battery-powered or hybrid vehicles could significantly affect the course of future industrialization and the growth of exports to Asia and other countries. Haddock and Jullens (2009) foresee a bright future for the global auto industry as demand from the BRICs (Brazil, the Russian Federation, India, and China) rises and technology evolves.

Table 2.9 China Export Composition by Technology Class

percent

Country	Year	Electronic and electrical	Other high technology	Textile, garment, and footwear	Other low technology	Automotive	Process	Engineering	Primary products	Agro-based	Other resource-based
China	1985	0.7	4.7	17.0	4.0	0.5	10.0	1.9	49.5	7.2	4.6
	1990	3.7	1.7	30.1	11.0	6.1	5.4	9.8	21.0	4.8	6.5
	1995	10.9	2.3	31.1	15.8	1.0	7.3	10.7	10.0	5.3	5.6
	2000	20.2	2.5	25.9	16.0	1.5	5.8	12.5	7.4	3.9	4.4
	2006	31.4	2.6	17.6	14.2	2.1	5.7	14.7	4.3	3.3	4.1

Source: Author's calculations using UN Comtrade data.

Table 2.10 Export Composition by Technology Class, 2006
percent

Country	Electronic and electrical	Other high technology	Textile, garment, and footwear	Other low technology	Automotive	Process	Engineering	Primary products	Agro-based	Other resource-based
China	31.4	2.6	17.6	14.2	2.1	5.7	14.7	4.3	3.3	4.1
India	2.9	4.3	17.6	12.8	3.1	9.2	7.6	15.3	3.3	23.9
Japan	19.4	4.7	0.9	7.8	22.8	8.8	26.5	1.9	2.2	5.0
Korea, Rep.	31.1	5.7	3.7	7.8	13.9	10.1	18.6	2.8	2.2	4.1

Source: Author's calculations using UN Comtrade Data.

Table 2.11   Global Rank and Share of Exports by China and India, 2006

Technology class	China Rank	China Share (%)	India Rank	India Share (%)
HT1	1	16.84	35	0.18
HT2	8	3.66	24	0.58
LT1	1	26.71	6	3.17
LT2	1	12.40	21	1.32
MT1	12	2.05	29	0.36
MT2	3	6.38	21	1.12
MT3	4	8.50	30	0.45
PP	16	2.16	33	0.87
RB1	5	4.86	38	0.51
RB2	8	3.92	9	3.62

Source: Authors' calculations based on UN Comtrade data.
Note: HT1 = electronic and electrical products; HT2 = other high-technology products; LT1 = textiles, garments, and footwear; LT2 = other low-technology products; MT1 = automotive products; MT2 = process industry; MT3 = engineering products; PP = primary products; RB1 = agriculture-based products; RB2 = other resource-based products. Technology classification is based on Lall (2000).

Figure 2.11   Export Composition of Japan by Technology Class

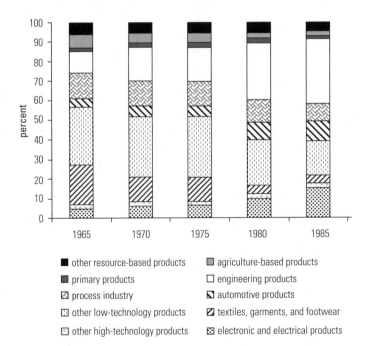

- ■ other resource-based products
- ■ primary products
- ⊠ process industry
- ⊡ other low-technology products
- ⊡ other high-technology products
- ▨ agriculture-based products
- □ engineering products
- ◨ automotive products
- ◪ textiles, garments, and footwear
- ⊠ electronic and electrical products

Source: Authors' calculations using UN Comtrade data.

medium-tech exports in the 1980s and later by rising exports of high-tech products in the 1990s (see figure 2.12).

India's presence in the global manufactured exports market is limited mainly to low-tech (textiles, garments, and footwear) and resource-based products.

China's compelling production and export statistics are only one strand in the story of China's industrialization. Industrial capacity requires investment, and China has led the field in this regard. Furthermore, several complementary developments have made it possible to translate raw industrial capacity into the capability that has catapulted China into the front ranks of industrial economies. These developments include urbanization and the organizational skills forged by the Communist Party.

The Urban Focus of Industry

Industrial development is primarily an urban phenomenon. China's rural industry supported industrial change during the 1980s and early 1990s, but much of the action was in China's cities. On the eve of China's big industrial push in 1980, the

Figure 2.12 Export Composition of the Republic of Korea by Technology Class

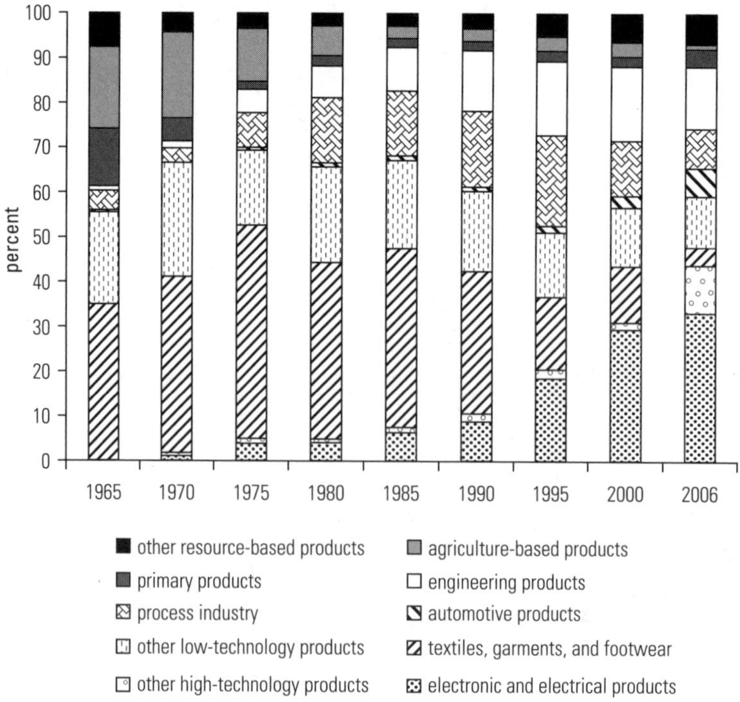

- ■ other resource-based products
- ■ primary products
- ⊠ process industry
- ▥ other low-technology products
- ▤ other high-technology products
- ▥ agriculture-based products
- ☐ engineering products
- ◩ automotive products
- ▨ textiles, garments, and footwear
- ⊠ electronic and electrical products

Source: Authors' calculations using UN Comtrade data.

Table 2.12 **Industry's Contribution to GDP Growth in Four Chinese Cities**
percent

		Contribution to GDP Growth			
	Share of industry in GDP	Primary	Secondary	of which industry	Tertiary
Chongqing	38.1	8.0	51.1	43.0	41.0
Guangzhou	39.5	1.8	39.2	—	59.0
Shanghai	43.5	0.3	46.9	44.9	52.7
Tianjin	52.7	1.0	61.7	57.3	37.2

Source: National Statistical Bureau of China 2008.
Note: — = not available.

rate of urbanization was a mere 29 percent.[12] The Bureau of Statistics counted 189 cities in 1978. Urbanization began accelerating in the mid-1980s, pushing the urban share of the population to 42 percent; as of 2007, China counted 651 cities.[13] The notable feature of the vast majority of China's cities, with the exception of Beijing and a few others, is that they are primarily industrial cities. Manufacturing is prominent in each one, accounting for between one-third and one-half of GDP. Even in megacities such as Shanghai, Tianjin, Guangzhou, and Chongqing, manufacturing is the engine of growth. Tianjin derives more than half of its growth from industry (see table 2.12). Other, smaller cities also depend upon industry for much of their growth.

Cities have contributed to growth through scale and urbanization economies. Urban industrial development has mediated the transfer of workers from low-value-added jobs in rural areas to higher-value-added jobs in urban manufacturing activities. By consciously tying their own growth and prosperity to manufacturing, Chinese cities made it possible for the country to build a vast industrial base in a matter of years and to realize large gains in productivity. In most developing countries, the absence of such a focus has meant that industrialization has flagged, technological spillovers have been meager, fewer productive jobs have been created, the export potential has not been fully tapped, and income growth has fallen far short of objectives.

Cities in China have promoted industrialization by encouraging investment and entrepreneurship, but it is not the urban business environment in China that has been responsible for the pace of industrialization. According to the World Bank's *Doing Business Surveys*, China ranked 89th in 2009, far behind Malaysia and Korea, with the obstacles to starting a business and the difficulties in obtaining

---

[12]For economic and ideological reasons, the Chinese authorities tightly controlled urbanization prior to the 1980s. See Yusuf and Wu (1997, pp. 38-42).

[13]See Yusuf (2009). If the migrant population is included in the total, the urbanization rate in 2008 was approximately 50 percent, or 650 million people in all.

necessary construction permits and licenses identified as the principal weaknesses. China has promoted industrial change through a multitude of fiscal and price incentives, combined with heavy investment in urban infrastructure financed through the leasing of land, and by borrowing from banks.[14] By providing serviced land (industrial and technology parks are a favored vehicle for attracting industry) and sinking resources into energy, transport, water, and housing, as well as into other urban amenities and services, urban centers in China created the conditions in which industry could flourish. The availability of a literate, trainable workforce has also proven to be a considerable asset. Furthermore, a generation of public officials who firmly believe in the desirability of industrializing (and whose careers depend primarily upon economic outcomes) have spared no effort in trying to make China's cities industrial success stories.[15] The leadership and drive of municipal officials and their focus on a few economic objectives has been vital in translating policies into actions.

With encouragement from the government, state-owned banks have channeled China's abundant savings (not all of it, of course, but a substantial part) into developing cities and augmenting manufacturing capacity. The efforts aimed at neutralizing the effects of the 2008–09 global crisis vastly increased the scale of bank lending for these purposes. Thus, industrialization in China has been synonymous with urbanization; together these forces have stimulated a growth spiral and are responsible for many of the gains in productivity referred to previously.

The urban axes of China's industrialization have been given insufficient attention; these were and are the foci of an industrial system and the determinants of its dynamism. Urban centers of all sizes have been at the forefront of the efforts to forge a labor force suited to the needs of industry. China's investment in basic education provided the foundations for an industrial workforce. The ongoing highly ambitious efforts to upgrade the quality of human capital are being spearheaded by urban investment in secondary and tertiary education, vocational training,[16] and R&D. The great surge in the flow of human capital that began in the 1980s—first at the level of secondary education, then a decade later in tertiary education (see table 2.13)—was concentrated in the cities and paced by the rapid expansion in manufacturing activities. These activities generated revenues for public services, created jobs, and gave rise to the demand for an upgrading of skills.

In chapter 4 we will have more to say about R&D and tertiary education; here, it suffices to note that Chinese cities were quick to respond to government signals

---

[14]This is viewed as the fiscal Achilles heel of many municipalities, and fiscal sustainability will be a challenge for many in the years ahead.

[15]At times, this has come at the cost of environmental objectives.

[16]Inland cities are giving greater emphasis to vocational training in an effort to attract more industry from coastal areas where cost pressures are rising.

Table 2.13 Gross School Enrollment, China
percent

Share of total population	1985	1990	1995	2001	2007
Primary	120.4	127.5	116.9	117.4	112.3
Secondary	31.3	37.7	50.9	65.0	77.3
Tertiary	—	—	—	9.9	22.9

Source: World Development Indicators Database.
Note: — = not available.

to ramp up their education systems so that industry would not be constrained by a lack of skills. Moreover, the vital tertiary-level skills, which are buttressing China's transition to more sophisticated manufactures and services, are the result of efforts by municipalities to build local innovation systems adequate for the challenges posed by a 21st-century global environment.

Organizational Capacity

China's urban environment was especially conducive to industrialization for one additional reason: the presence of organizational skills. Although China's original industrial template was borrowed from the Soviet Union, over time it was significantly modified. With the adoption of the Third Front program, a highly dispersed yet centrally directed approach to development, industrialization was fostered throughout the country (Naughton 1988). What was earlier described as a "cellular" economic model embedded industrial (and technological) capabilities in many parts of China, some of which had been unsuited for the development of industry (Donnithorne 1967). The upshot of this approach, reinforced by the scale and organizational efficacy of the Communist Party, was threefold. First, a large number of production units were created, many of them vertically integrated out of necessity because suppliers were unreliable, the transport system was backward, and the logistics capacity was primitive. Second, industrial breadth was cultivated within provinces (and often within municipalities), a strategy that endowed virtually every part of the country with an industrial base—one, in many respects, quite uniform in composition. This is apparent from tables 2.14 and 2.15, comparing three advanced coastal provinces with three of the least developed interior provinces in terms of industrial composition. Larger industrial enterprises tended to be highly self-contained, catering to most of their essential requirements, because internal trade was hindered by local mercantilism and a multiplicity of barriers to trade, and the services sector was severely underdeveloped. Vestiges of this are still apparent in the numerous auto assembly plants, steel and cement mills, engineering firms, and producers of chemicals and fertilizers of suboptimal size scattered throughout China. Many of the state enterprises and collectives continue to provide employees with a multiplicity of services, although these are being cut back.

Table 2.14   Gross Regional Product by Three Strata of Industry, China, 2008
percent

Region	Composition (GRP = 100)				
	Primary industry	**Secondary industry**	**Industry**	**Construction**	**Tertiary industry**
Interior provinces					
Henan	14.4	56.9	51.8	5.6	28.6
Hunan	18.0	44.2	38.3	6.7	37.8
Sichuan	18.9	46.3	39.4	8.2	34.8
Coastal provinces					
Jiangsu	6.9	55.0	49.7	5.8	38.1
Zhejiang	5.1	53.9	48.2	6.4	41.0

Source: National Statistical Bureau of China 2009.

Table 2.15   Share of Total Industrial Output Value by Type of Enterprise, China, 2008
percent

Region	Enterprises of light industry	Enterprises of heavy industry
Interior provinces		
Henan	31	69
Hunan	28	72
Sichuan	32	68
Coastal provinces		
Guangdong	38	62
Jiangsu	27	73
Zhejiang	41	59

Source: National Statistical Bureau of China 2009.

The third outcome of dispersed cellular development orchestrated by the Communist Party was the necessary inculcating of organizational capabilities for managing production, adapting technologies, creating a provincial (or national) supply chain and distribution system (however rudimentary), and improvising solutions as the need arose.[17] This organizational capital—formal and informal via connections—and the induced entrepreneurship has, in hindsight, proven a

---

[17]Bloom and Van Reenen (2010) point out that the role of management in raising productivity and managerial and organizational skills—plus investment in information and communication tehnology (ICT)—also seem to explain the productivity advantage of the United States over Europe (Gordon 2003). Although much doubt has been cast on the quality of management in Chinese state-owned enterprises (SOEs) and collectively owned enterprises (COEs) their achievement to date in absorbing technology and raising productivity suggests that factory management skills might not be meager after all.

considerable asset. Localized autonomy seemingly coexisted with a disciplined responsiveness to directions from the leadership in Beijing.

China had access to resources few developing countries could muster as a result of the scale, geographical distribution, and scope of production capabilities (however primitive); the accumulated local organizational skills; and the relays built into the command system. The party organization and its penetration made it possible to mobilize resources on a scale unimaginable in other countries. Once the leadership committed to a strategy, it was possible, with the help of incentives and sanctions stiffened by party discipline, to pursue countrywide development programs and achieve certain narrow objectives in short order. In other words, the organization building and state-directed industrialization that preceded the reform era made it possible for the central authorities to launch, finance, and largely implement an industrial Big Push involving thousands of counties and municipalities.

Other countries have created organizations with comparable heft, but none has succeeded in imbuing them with an enduring discipline and the flexibility to form a vast, decentralized industrial program. This is not to imply that the organization was without flaws, or that China has not had to wrestle with slippages and problems of accountability, corruption,[18] and other ill effects arising from the undue exploitation of discretionary power. There have been these problems and others. The organizational relays are not flawless, and signal distortion and misinterpretation have been recurring (albeit still manageable) phenomena. The unerring ability to meet targets determined by the government has frequently led to questions over the accuracy of statistics used to establish programs. However, the broad and very tangible achievements are reliable testimonials. In the late 1970s China was in dire economic straits. After a decade of political strife and social upheaval, it lagged far behind Japan and Korea. In economic terms it was tiny, with just 1.8 percent of global GDP (at nominal exchange rates), and devoid of internationally competitive industrial assets. But unlike the Soviet Union, the untidy socioeconomic structures that had congealed over almost three difficult—and occasionally strife-torn—decades had huge latent potential, which reform was able to release. By steadily increasing doses of market incentives, the government channeled the entrepreneurial energies released into public sector–led development using organizational skills, leavened by ideology that was periodically reoriented as circumstances and objectives changed. Table 2.16 shows that China's real industrial output has grown at a consistently high rate since 1978, with a peak average annual growth rate of 15 percent during 1993–97. The other determinants of industrialization described in this chapter all played their part; however, the piecemeal adoption of market institutions alone could not have

---

[18]On China's struggle to cope with corruption, see Pei (2008) and Manion (2004); and with regard to organizational crime, see "China's Other Face" (2009).

Table 2.16 Industrial Output Growth: China, 1978–2008

Period	Average real increase in added value of industrial output (%)
1978–82	9.1
1983–87	13.1
1988–92	11.9
1993–97	15.4
1998–2002	9.2
2003–08	13.1

Source: Chinability.com 2009; World Bank 2009.

produced such dramatic industrial outcomes. In the 1980s and the 1990s, economic science offered no clear recipes for transitioning economies or for how transition might be combined with growth. Transitioning countries had to learn by doing. In hindsight, China—which eschewed a Big Bang deconstruction of the socialist system—emerges as the most adept learner. The Chinese state and its organizational apparatus directed, coordinated, organized, and incentivized. It also selectively harnessed market forces, pragmatically adjusting its ideological bearings to meet economic objectives. Now, as China's industrial development enters a new phase in a global environment that could be on the cusp of major changes, the virtues of this approach will be severely tested.

India's Development Experience

India's growth gained speed in the early 1980s, after a dribble of reforms had dismantled some of the regulations that had shackled the economy since the period soon after independence; but the economy did not begin a virtuous spiral led by industry (and supported in due course by exports), as happened in China. The Indian economy muddled along without the benefit of a well-articulated development strategy that was consistently and forcefully pursued by each succeeding government. The tempo of deregulation and the reduction of tariffs (figure 2.13) picked up in the early 1990s, following a severe macroeconomic crisis fed by public sector deficits and exacerbated by the Gulf War, which forced India to seek the assistance of an International Monetary Fund program (Panagariya 2008). However, the catalytic event that significantly improved India's economic fortunes and grouped it with China as one of Asia's emerging giants was the unanticipated success of business process outsourcing (BPO) activities and information technology–enabled services (ITES), initially concentrated in Bangalore but spreading later to Hyderabad, Chennai, the suburbs of Mumbai and Delhi, and recently to

Figure 2.13   Average Tariff Rates, China and India

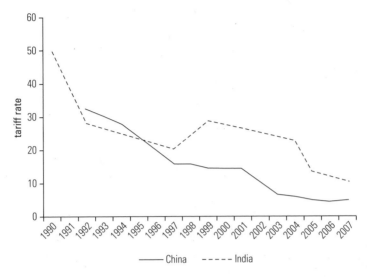

Source: UNCTAD TRAINS database.

Kolkata. Since 2000, India's growth has quickened and the share of manufacturing has edged upward; but how closely India's future industrialization will approximate China's in terms of pace and scale is far from obvious. A look backward can provide a perspective on India's industrial dynamic and how the country is positioned vis-à-vis China.

India's planners, much like their counterparts in China, adopted an import-substituting industrial strategy which favored heavy industry—preferably under state control[19]—when the country embarked on its first five-year plan in 1955 (Kochhar and others 2006). But they also were highly protective of small-scale rural (and urban) cottage-industry production of textiles, garments, household products, farm implements, and other items.[20] Strict licensing of formal and larger-scale industrial activities, a highly protective trade regime, regulations inhibiting the growth of firms, the acquisition of land for industrial purposes, and the laying off of workers by larger firms all discouraged industrial development

---

[19]There were frequent references in planning documents to the desirability of the state maintaining its grip on the "commanding heights of the economy," meaning the producers of ferrous metals and capital equipment.

[20]India was the world's largest exporter of cotton cloth in 1950. But after Nehru reoriented production toward the domestic market, Japan quickly displaced India as the leading exporter.

Figure 2.14   Composition of GDP (Supply Side), India

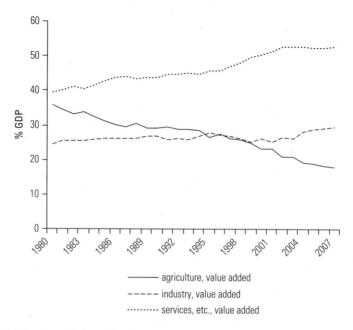

Source: World Development Indicators Database.

(see figure 2.13). A burgeoning state apparatus seemingly devoid of development ambition tightened its suffocating grip on the industrial economy, drowning India in a sea of red tape that came to be known as the "License Raj."[21]

In China, the reform and opening of the economy, starting in 1978, signaled a decisive break from the past. The limited and tentative pro-business reform efforts[22] by the Indian government in the 1980s were by no means as decisive; as a result, India sacrificed a decade or more of growth. India's fractious democratic process, keyed to the interests and frequently conflicting demands of many communities, could not readily focus on a single overarching development objective. The tenacious, process-oriented bureaucracy could not be motivated to adopt a regulatory stance consistent with the rapid growth of industry. The economy grew faster, but it did not enter a period of decisive structural change. The impression emerges of slow change lacking an industrial imperative, as is apparent in figure 2.14 on sectoral shares, and rein-forced by movement in the shares of manufacturing subsectors between 1981 and 2002 (see figure 2.15). Food products gained, as did chemicals, petrochemicals, and

---

[21]On the reach and tenacity of the "License Raj," see Luce (2007) and Khanna (2007).
[22]See Rodrik and Subramanian (2004).

Figure 2.15   Industrial Composition by Type of Manufactures of India, 1981, 1990, and 2002

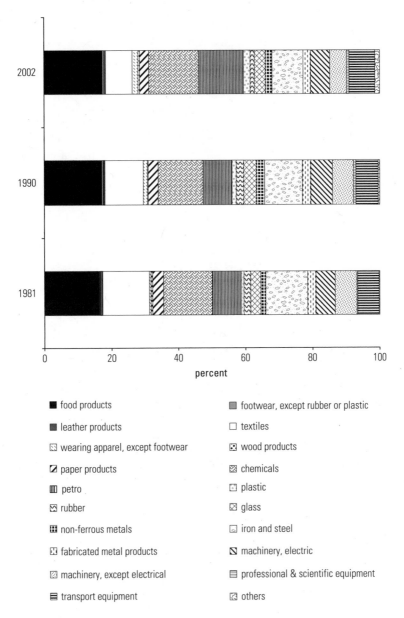

food products

leather products

wearing apparel, except footwear

paper products

petro

rubber

non-ferrous metals

fabricated metal products

machinery, except electrical

transport equipment

footwear, except rubber or plastic

textiles

wood products

chemicals

plastic

glass

iron and steel

machinery, electric

professional & scientific equipment

others

Source: UNIDO INDSTAT3.

transport. Subsectors that lost ground were textiles, iron, and steel. Unlike the situation in China, the changes were modest; and there was no clear trend toward technology-intensive products.

During India's phase of slow growth, from 1960 to 1980, output grew by 3.4 percent per year, with physical capital contributing 1 percent per year and TFP just 0.2 percent. Between 1980 and 2004, the pace of GDP growth rose to 5.8 percent, with capital contributing 1.4 percent and TFP 2.0 percent (see table 2.17). Strikingly, in the earlier period, industry and manufacturing grew at 4.7 and 4.6 percent, respectively; manufacturing TFP rose 0.2 percent, and that of industry as a whole actually declined by 0.4 percent. The performance improved only a little in the high-growth era from 1980 through 2004. Growth was 2 percentage points higher, but manufacturing TFP rose only by 1.5 percent and that of industry as a whole by 1 percent.

The picture is almost unchanged during 1999–2004 for industrial growth and growth of manufacturing, except that the increase in TFP slowed fractionally. From 2004 through 2008, manufacturing output rose faster than in the first half of the decade and made the largest contribution to the growth of GDP (16 percent, as shown in figure 2.16). However, the contribution of TFP dropped to 1.4 percent in 2007–08 (Virmani 2009).

The indicators of labor productivity and value added for industry point to improvement; but overall, the gains are modest, generally less than the gains achieved by China. Figure 2.17 shows that output per worker had a gentle upward slope starting in the mid-1980s, but this began to flatten out 10 years later, with

Table 2.17   Sources of Economic Growth: Total Economy, India, 1960–2005
annual rate of change (%)

Period	Output	Employment	Output per worker	Contribution of Physical capital	Land	Education	Factor productivity
Total economy							
1960–2004	4.7	2.0	2.6	1.2	−0.1	0.3	1.2
1960–80	3.4	2.2	1.3	1.0	−0.2	0.2	0.2
1980–2004	5.8	1.9	3.8	1.4	0.0	0.4	2.0
Selected subperiods							
1960–73	3.3	2.0	1.3	1.1	−0.2	0.1	0.2
1973–83	4.2	2.4	1.8	0.9	−0.2	0.3	0.6
1983–93	5.0	2.1	2.9	0.9	−0.1	0.3	1.7
1993–99	7.0	1.2	5.8	2.4	−0.1	0.4	2.8
1999–2004	6.0	2.4	3.6	1.2	0.1	0.4	2.0

Source: Bosworth, Collins, and Virmani 2007.

Figure 2.16   Contribution of Leading Sectors to Growth, India, 2002–03 through 2007–08

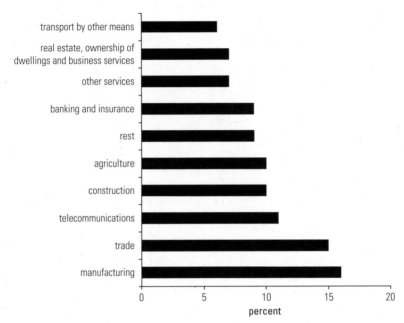

Source: Virmani 2009.

Figure 2.17   Output per Worker by Sector, India, 1978–2004

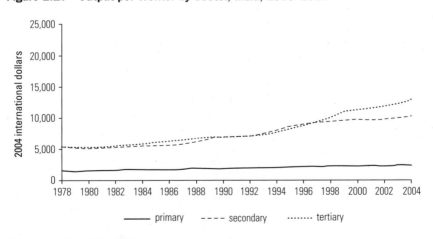

Source: Bosworth and Collins 2007.

little increase from then onward. Value added in secondary industry was half the level in China in 1978. Fifteen years later, in 1993, it was only 4 percentage points higher. It remained unchanged through 2004, whereas value added in services went from 32 percent in 1978 to half of the total for the economy in 2004 (see table 2.6). The share of employment also rose faster in services. When sectoral output growth data are placed alongside the other indicators, it is apparent that— unlike the case for China—tertiary industry has performed better than secondary (including manufacturing) industry in India. In the high-growth period from 1993 through 2004, the contribution of output growth per worker was greater in services (2.1 percent) than in secondary industry (0.9 percent) (see table 2.7). This is in tune with extensive qualitative and empirical evidence highlighting the considerable strides made by the IT-based, financial, and business services in India since the mid-1990s, and it is mirrored in India's exports of goods and services. Between 1995 and 2004, exports of services increased annually by 21 percent, whereas those of goods increased at half that rate. As a consequence, the share of goods in India's total exports declined from 82 percent in 1995 to 67 percent in 2004 (see table 2.18).

Given India's smaller size and moderate pace of growth, manufacturing and other industrial activities have had a lesser influence on its aggregate economic performance relative to China. Nevertheless, the contribution of industry has paralleled—and sometimes marginally exceeded—that of services. In 2007, it was higher than services by 0.6 percentage points. Whether this larger contribution is sustained will depend upon the changing weight and competitiveness of

Table 2.18   Annual Growth in Exports: China and India, 1995–2004
percent

	1995–2004	1995–2000	2000–04
China			
Total exports	18.1	13.7	23.8
Goods	18.6	14.2	24.2
Services	14.0	9.7	19.7
India			
Total exports	12.6	9.5	16.6
Goods	10.1	6.7	14.5
Services	20.6	19.8	21.6

	Memo: Share of goods in total exports		
	1995	2000	2004
China	87.0	89.1	90.5
India	82.2	72.2	67.1

Source: Bosworth and Collins 2007.

Figure 2.18   Contribution to Growth (Demand Side), India

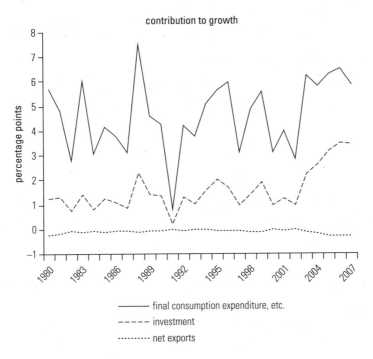

contribution to growth

final consumption expenditure, etc.
----- investment
.... net exports

Source: World Development Indicators Database.

technology-intensive subsectors with robust market prospects. India's engineering, chemicals, pharmaceuticals, iron and steel, and automotive industries have nurtured world-class firms producing competitively priced, quality products.[23] However, these still account for a small part of GDP and of exports. India has yet to establish a significant presence in the export market and derives limited growth benefits from trade, although the negative stimulus provided by net exports indicated in figure 2.18 surely understates the role exports play.

India's Trade

Total exports of goods and services rose fourfold between 2000 and 2007 (in comparison, China's exports were in excess of five times larger), but the composition

_____

[23]See the discussion of Indian companies by Roy (2005) and Chaze (2006). Kumar (2009) explains the success of India's leading firms such as Bharat Forge, Suzlon, Mahindra and Mahindra, and the Tata Group. Van Agtmael (2007) describes the emergence and growth of Indian firms such as Ranbaxy and Infosys. He also examines success stories from China; Taiwan, China; Mexico; and other emerging economies.

Figure 2.19   Export Composition of India by Technology Class

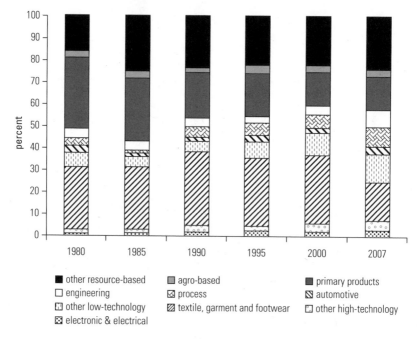

Source: Authors' calculations using UN Comtrade data.

of India's exports does not resemble that of an industrializing economy (see figure 2.19). In 1980, 51 percent of commodity exports consisted of primary products and agriculture- or resource-based products. Less than 14 percent were high-technology or engineering and automotive products. By 2007, the category of low-tech items accounted for 41 percent of exports, while the share of medium- and higher-tech products had risen to 27 percent. The share of textiles and garments had dropped from 29 percent to about 18 percent, but that of other low-tech items doubled from 6.5 percent to nearly 13 percent. As a share of world production, India's manufacturing activities are of significance in subsectors such as food products, textiles and apparel, leather products and footwear, (petro) chemicals, and, more recently, iron and steel. Even in these industries, India's share is a fraction of China's. In other industrial subsectors, India's production is a small—sometimes trivial—part of global production. Its share of global exports presents a comparable picture (see table 2.19).

Urban Development in India

Compared with China, which has been urbanizing at a rapid clip since 1980, India has lagged far behind; the urban population is less than one-third of the

Table 2.19 Global Share of Exports of Goods and Services
percent

Country	1980	1985	1990	1995	2000	2005	2007
China	0.86	1.31	1.56	2.61	3.50	6.44	7.71
India	0.49	0.53	0.52	0.61	0.76	1.24	1.44

Source: World Development Indicators Database.

total.[24] Moreover, many of India's cities have been slow to reform a business environment that subjects industry to numerous obstructive rules and statutes. The country's labor laws and assertive unions discourage hiring because layoffs are problematic and can be expensive. Land use and the real estate market in general are highly inefficient. Acquiring a large block of land composed of contiguous parcels for industry or infrastructure is a major challenge. Even a single landowner can hold a major deal hostage ("India: Land Acquisition" 2009). An amalgam of laws and ownership disputes are to blame, and the Land Acquisition Act and the overburdened courts have persistently failed to penetrate the inherited morass of problems that hobble every city. Limited access to land interferes with the entry of new firms and the growth of existing ones. In short, Indian cities have not made haste to embrace industrialization, seek agglomeration and urbanization economies, or actively pursue industrial clusters. The partial exceptions are cities such as Bangalore and Hyderabad, which have (rather haphazardly) gone about creating IT parks in response to the demands of the business community.

Urban industrialization is further hamstrung by India's notoriously inadequate physical infrastructure, a legacy of insufficient investment, and poor or nonexistent urban planning. Energy shortages and transport bottlenecks have severely curtailed industrial development in strategic urban locations. Even the iconic city of Bangalore has struggled to build the infrastructure it urgently needs, and its traffic jams remain the stuff of legend.[25] In addition, housing shortages and the ramshackle water and sanitation facilities are a brake on urban development. The infrastructure deficit in major Indian cities is vast; reducing this deficit while accommodating the anticipated growth in urban populations poses an enormous challenge for city administrators and will absorb a huge volume of resources. Moreover, the payoff from this investment will depend upon price and

---

[24]Nevertheless, the urban sector accounts for 60 percent of GDP ("India: Urban Development," 2010).

[25]It took years to expand the city's airport and put it on par with international standards. Unfortunately, its location relative to the economic hub makes it highly inconvenient for the business traveler.

Figure 2.20   Gross School Enrollment, 2006

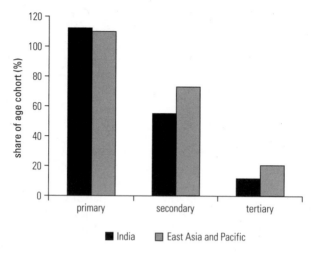

Source: World Development Indicators Database.

regulatory reforms that reduce the risks for investors and combat dysfunctional legacies. Farsighted planning in the areas of land use and public transport is also needed to build compact and resilient cities with smaller carbon footprints. India and China need to anticipate and accommodate global warming concerns and resource constraints as they urbanize. With so much urbanization ahead, both countries have an opportunity to avoid costly mistakes and maximize the gains from urban development.

The urban development gap in India coexists with a human capital gap. The problem arises from a shortage of tertiary-level and technical skills and from the overall low quantity (and quality) of basic and secondary education. Once again, underinvestment in tertiary education and vocational training to increase the number of schools and enhance the quality of instruction are to blame. Furthermore, unlike the case in East Asian countries, enrollment rates in primary and secondary education in India are low, constraining India's efforts to rapidly ramp up human capital formation in post-secondary and tertiary education (see figure 2.20). Manufacturing competes for talented engineers and other knowledge workers with software, IT, and consulting firms,[26] which are able to offer more attractive salaries. India's financial sector has also enticed away some of the most able graduates; this is commonplace in industrialized countries but probably not advantageous at India's current stage of industrial development.

---

[26]Overseas migration of knowledge workers further drains the pool of candidates with high-level skills.

As a result of these institutional, infrastructure, urban, and skill constraints, India's manufacturing sector, which could have been a star performer and the driver of growth, has underperformed over the past decade and accounts for too small a share of GDP and of exports. In particular, the inadequacy of the electronics and electrical engineering industries, which have aided growth elsewhere in East Asia, is conspicuous.

The Role of FDI

The very same factors that have restrained manufacturing overall have also, until recently, discouraged FDI in Indian manufacturing,[27] whereas weak export incentives[28] may account for the absence of dominant homegrown electronics firms comparable to Samsung and LG in Korea, another country that shunned FDI.

Both China and India attracted small amounts of FDI in 1980. But whereas FDI in Chinese industry—in particular, the manufacturing industry—began rising sharply in the 1990s, FDI in India began climbing only after 2000, with just a small percentage initially finding its way into manufacturing.[29] As recently as 2007, FDI in China was $138.4 billion; in India, it was $23 billion. Chinese producers of a wide range of tradables (many of which are joint ventures or subsidiaries of foreign companies) are now among the main suppliers, if not the largest suppliers, to international production networks. Indian manufacturers, other than for textiles, garments, and leather goods, are only now gaining a significant foothold in industries such as auto parts.

Relative to China, India is at an earlier stage of industrialization, even though some Indian firms are manufacturing state-of-the-art products using the most advanced technologies. India is only the world's 16th largest exporter; manufactures constitute only 40 percent of its exports, which puts it a long distance behind China. India has thus far made little difference, if any, in the industrial geography of Asia. It is a tiger that has been slumbering. Many believe that the tiger is now awake, that it can grow at nearly double-digit rates, and that its future industrialization will have major consequences for other countries. In the meantime, China has a lead of almost two decades, and its industrial and trading presence is widely felt.[30] In the following chapter, we will examine the industrial strengths of the two countries and how these could affect others.

---

[27]Until recently, government policy toward FDI by multinational corporations remained relatively cool.

[28]Including incentives provided by exchange rate policies.

[29]Wenhui Wei (2005) ascribes the differences in flows of FDI to China and India to a number of factors. China's great attraction has been the size of its domestic market and the strength of its trading links with the United States and the EU. India, by comparison, has somewhat lower labor costs, lower country risks, and greater cultural affinity with some of the investing countries.

[30]China is now India's foremost trading partner.

References

Asian Development Bank. 2009. *Asian Development Outlook 2009: Rebalancing Asia's Growth.* Mandaluyong City, Philippines: ADB.

Badunenko, O., D. J. Henderson, and V. Zelenyuk. 2008. "Technological Change and Transition: Relative Contributions to Worldwide Growth Dring the 1990s." *Oxford Bulletin of Economics and Statistics* 70(4): 461–92.

Bloom, Nicholas, and John Van Reenen. 2010. "Why Do Management Practices Differ across Firms and Countries?" *Journal of Economic Perspectives* 24(1): 203–24.

Bloomberg. 2010. www.bloomberg.com.

Bosworth, Barry, and Susan M. Collins. 2007. "Accounting for Growth: Comparing China and India." NBER Working Paper Series 12943, National Bureau of Economics, Cambridge, MA.

Bosworth, Barry, Susan M. Collins, and Arvind Virmani. 2007. "Sources of Growth in the Indian Economy." NBER Working Paper 12901, National Bureau of Economic Research, Cambridge, MA.

Chaze, Aaron. 2006. *India: An Investor's Guide to the Next Economic Superpower.* Singapore: John Wiley & Sons (Asia) Pte Ltd.

Chen, Hongyi, and Scott Rozelle. 1999. "Leaders, Managers, and the Organization of Township and Village Enterprises in China." *Journal of Development Economics* 60: 529–57.

Chen, Weixing. 1998. "The Political Economy of Rural Industrialization in China: Village Conglomerates in Shandong Province." *Modern China* 24(1): 73–96.

China Daily. 2010. "China Overtakes U.S. as World's Largest Auto Market." January 11.

Chinability.com. 2009. *Chinability.* http://www.chinability.com.

"China's Other Face." 2009. *Economist*, October 3.

Coe, David T., Elhanan Helpman, and Alexander W. Hoffmaister. 2008. "International R&D Spillovers and Institutions." NBER Working Paper Series 14069, National Bureau of Economic Research, Cambridge, MA.

Ding, Sai and John Knight. 2008. "Why Has China Grown so Fast? The Role of Structural Change." Economic Series Working Paper 415, University of Oxford, Department of Economics, Oxford, UK.

Donnithorne, Audrey. 1967. *China's Economic System.* London: George Allen and Unwin Ltd.

Findlay, Christopher, Andrew Watson, and Harry X. Wu. 1994. *Rural Enterprises in China.* New York: Macmillan Press Ltd.

Gordon, Robert J. 2003. "Hi-Tech Innovation and Productivity Growth: Does Supply Create Its Own Demand?" NBER Working Paper 9437, National Bureau of Economic Research, Cambridge, MA.

Haddock, Ronald, and John Jullens. 2009. "The Best Years of the Auto Industry Are Still to Come." *Strategy + Business* 55: 1–12.

Haltmaier, Jane T., Shaghil Ahmed, Brahima Coulibaly, Ross Knippenberg, Sylvain Leduc, Mario Marazzi, and Beth Anne Wilson. 2007. "The Role of China in Asia: Engine, Conduit, or Steamroller?" International Finance Discussion Papers 904, Board of Governors of the Federal Reserve System, Washington, DC.

He, Jianwu, and Louis Kuijs. 2007. "Rebalancing China's Economy: Modeling a Policy Package." World Bank China Research Paper 7, World Bank, Beijing.

"India: Land Acquisition Problems Obstruct Industry." 2009. *Oxford Analytica,* Oct. 5.

"India: Urban Development Is Crucial But Contested." 2010. *Oxford Analytica,* May 15.

Jorgenson, Dale W., Mun S. Ho, and Kevin J. Stiroh. 2007. "The Sources of Growth of U.S. Industries." In *Productivity in Asia: Economic Growth and Competitiveness,* ed. Dale W. Jorgenson, Masahiro Kuroda, and Kazuyuki Motohashi. Northampton, MA: Edward Elgar Publishing.

Khanna, Tarun. 2007. *Billions of Entrepreneurs: How China and India Are Reshaping Their Futures—and Yours* . Boston, MA: Harvard Business Press.

Kochhar, Kalpana, Utsav Kumar, Raghuram Rajan, and Arvind Subramanian. 2006. "India's Patterns of Development: What Happened, What Follows." NBER Working Paper Series 12023, National Bureau of Economic Research, Cambridge, MA.

Kuijs, Louis. 2010. "China Through 2020: A Macroeconomic Scenario." World Bank China Research Working Paper 9. Beijing: World Bank.

Kumar, Nirmalya. 2009. *India's Global Powerhouses: How They Are Taking On the World.* Boston, MA: Harvard Business Press.

Lall, Sanjaya. 2000. "The Technological Structure and Performance of Developing Country Manufactured Exports, 1985–98." *Oxford Development Studies* 28(3): 337–69.

Lin, Justin Yifu. 2009. *Economic Development and Transition.* Newyork: Cambridge University Press.

Luce, Edward. 2007. *In Spite of the Gods: The Rise of Modern India.* New York: Anchor Books.

McKinsey Global Institute. 2010. *How to Compete and Grow: A Sector Guide to Policy.* Washington, D.C.: McKinsey & Company.

Manion, Melanie. 2004. *Corruption by Design: Building Clean Government in Mainland China and Hong Kong.* Cambridge, MA: Harvard University Press.

National Statistical Bureau of China. 2007. *China Labour Statistical Yearbook 2007.* Beijing: China Statistics Press.

National Statistical Bureau of China. 2008. *China Statistical Yearbook 2008.* Beijing: China Statistics Press.

National Statistical Bureau of China. 2009. *China Statistical Yearbook 2009.* Beijing: China Statistics Press.

Naughton, Barry. 1988. "The Third Front: Defense Industrialization in the Chinese Interior." *China Quarterly* 115: 351–86.

Oi, Jean C. 1999. *Rural China Takes Off: Institutional Foundations of Economic Reform.* Berkeley: University of California Press.

Panagariya, Arvind. 2008. *India: The Emerging Giant.* New York: Oxford University Press.

Pei, Minxin. 2008. *China's Trapped Transition: The Limits of Developmental Autocracy.* Cambridge, MA: Harvard University Press.

Pei, Xiaolin. 1996. "Township-Village Enterprises, Local Governments and Rural Communities: The Chinese Village as a Firm During Economic Transition." *Economics of Transition* 4(1): 43–66.

Perotti, Enrico C., Laixiang Sun, and Liang Zou. 1999. "State-Owned versus Township and Village Enterprises in China." *Comparative Economic Studies* 41(2–3): 151–79.

Prasad, Eswar. 2009. "Rebalancing Growth in Asia." NBER Working Paper Series 15169, National Bureau of Economic Research, Cambridge, MA.

Rodrik, Dani, and Arvind Subramanian. 2004. "From 'Hindu Growth' to Productivity Surge: The Mystery of the Indian Growth Transition." NBER Working Paper 10376, National Bureau of Economic Research, Cambridge, MA.

Roy, Subir. 2005. *Made in India: A Study of Emerging Competitiveness.* New Delhi: Tata McGraw Hill.

"Secret Sauce." 2009. *The Economist,* November 14.

Syverson, Chad. 2010. "What Determines Productivity?" NBER Working Paper 15712, National Bureau of Economic Research, Cambridge, MA.

Urel, B., and Harm Zebregs. 2009. "The Dynamics of Provincial Growth in China: A Nonparametric Approach." *IMF Staff Papers* 56(2): 239–62.

Van Agtmael, Antoine. 2007. *The Emerging Markets Century: How a New Breed of World-Class Companies Is Overtaking the World.* New York: Free Press.

Virmani, Arvind. 2009. *The Sudoku of India's Growth.* New Delhi: Business Standard Books.

Wang, Y., and Y. Yao. 2003. "Sources of China's Economic Growth, 1952–99: Incorporating Human Capital Accumulation." *China Economic Review* 14: 32–52.

Wei, Wenhui. 2005. "China and India: Any Difference in Their FDI Performances?" *Journal of Asian Economics* 16: 719–36.

Womack, James P., and D. T. Jones. 1994. "From Lean Production to Lean Enterprise." *Harvard Business Review* (March–April).

World Bank. 2009. "Quarterly Update: March 2009." Beijing: World Bank.

Yusuf, Shahid. 2009. "Off to the City." *China Business Review 3.* Washington, DC: US-China Business Council.

Yusuf, Shahid, and Weiping Wu. 1997. *The Dynamics of Urban Growth in Three Chinese Cities.* Washington, DC: Oxford University Press.

3

Trade Dynamics in China and India

No observer of China in the 1980s or even in the mid-1990s foresaw how rapidly China would industrialize, the scale of the industrialization, and the market penetration of China's manufactured exports. In the mid-1990s, even those observers who noted the acceleration of India's growth over the preceding decade did not anticipate that India would become the poster child of business process outsourcing (BPO), or that it would turn into a powerhouse of information technology–enabled services (ITES). Now the conventional wisdom is that China could become the preeminent economy within two decades, and India could be in third or fourth place a decade later. All such forecasts must be treated with skepticism, because extrapolation based on a reading of the recent past—and "recent" could capaciously embrace 20 to 30 years—can be highly questionable. It was virtually unimaginable in the 1970s that the Soviet Union would be economically crippled and begin unraveling just a few years later. When Japan was viewed as "Number One,"[1] when Japan's manufacturing firms seemed invincible and Japanese banks towered over their Western counterparts, informed observers were convinced that the Japanese century was about to dawn. By the same token, in the early 1960s, informed observers favored Ghana and Pakistan over Korea. Now, following the hobbling of the United States by wars, indebtedness, industrial hollowing,[2] and a financial

---

[1] The title of a widely cited book by Ezra Vogel (1979).

[2] Almost 55 percent of industrial production in the United States is accounted for by manufacturing. This sector produced less in 2008 than it did a decade earlier, highlighting the retreat of manufacturing. Even as industry recovers from the financial crisis and attempts to ramp up exports, auto and machinery manufacturers are making plans to transfer production abroad, where labor costs are lower and markets more likely to expand.

crisis,[3] the economic optimists are pinning their hopes on the world's two most populous countries and banking on their becoming the engines of growth for the global economy. However, some soothsayers, aware of missteps by earlier divines, are hedging their bets. They doubt that China can maintain its breakneck rate of growth, pointing to resource and environmental constraints, rising wages, the likely waning of U.S. and global demand for Chinese exports, higher energy prices, the declining potential contribution of capital to growth, and the challenge of attempting to make China into a highly innovative economy in a short time. A few go farther and claim that without an overhaul of the political system, China is headed toward an upheaval precipitated by endemic corruption, worsening income inequality, and the suppression of civil liberties by an authoritarian one-party state.

India's naysayers—conscious of India's infrastructural frailties, the shortages and uneven quality of labor skills, the still-powerful remnants of the "License Raj," and the tortuousness of the reform process—are skeptical that the country can push ahead forcefully with urban and industrial development. The worldwide economic crisis of 2008–10, external account imbalances, and the deadlocked Doha Round[4] have also reduced the likelihood of another spell of export-led growth for industrializing countries. All too often, analysts are drawn toward polar extremes. Either the prospects of China and India are painted in the rosiest of hues, or the future for both countries is presented in bleak terms as if their best economic times were behind them.

Our intention is to explore the middle ground and extract what insight we can from a close analysis of the information—quantitative and qualitative—on industry and trade. This information is "noisy"; but many trends, patterns, behaviors, and developments do persist and provide a window on a plausible future. Leavening speculation about the future industrial geography of Asia with a searching analysis of relevant past information perhaps is more likely to identify potential outcomes than is speculation loosely tethered to the empirical past.

In chapters 1 and 2, we examined the contrasting experiences of China and India with regard to industrial development and compared them with those of Japan, Germany, and the Republic of Korea. We also presented indicators to illuminate the performance of China and India and to situate the industrial capacity

---

[3]Sharp commentaries on the humbling of the overextended superpower, seemingly unable to respond adequately to a major crisis, are reminiscent of similar commentaries in the mid-1970s and again in the first half of the 1980s. This time around, the situation might be more desperate.

[4]The likelihood of a ratification of the Doha Round of Trade negotiations remains distant because the Organisation for Economic Co-operation and Development (OECD) countries want greater access to the markets for services in developing countries, which in turn are seeking a reduction in the barriers to imports of agricultural commodities imposed by developed countries (Hoekman 2010).

of the two countries and their trade in an international context. In this chapter, we assess the indicators of industrial competitiveness and trade, which can reveal how China and India are affecting each other's industrial development and those of neighboring Asian economies.

Asian Intraregional and Intra-industrial Trade

Casual empiricism based upon the growth statistics of industry and exports would suggest that China, if not India, is beginning to exert intensifying competitive pressures on Asian countries, both in their domestic markets and in the global market. But to date, the casual impression has proven to be deceptive. Competitive pressure exerted by China, and to a lesser degree by India, has increased; however, the pressure on the exports of other Asian countries has thus far proven tolerable and has been counterbalanced by China's imports of raw materials, components, and capital equipment.[5] Global production networks have continued sourcing from Southeast Asian countries even as the participation of Chinese firms in these networks has risen. Reflecting this, intraregional trade (including exports and imports) within East Asia now accounts for 60 percent of the total trade of the region—of which China accounts for 20 percentage points (see table 3.1) as compared to 3.8 percent in 1980. In contrast, Japan's share has diminished during this period, even though its trade with East Asia has increased—mainly as a result of growing trade with China. The intraregional trade data also show that China's trade with East Asia (and Japan) as a share of its total has decreased between 1985 and 2006, suggesting that Japan and other East Asian countries are supplying intermediate inputs to China to be assembled there and exported from China to the rest of the world.

An examination of intra-industry trade within East Asia, South Asia, and Asia as a whole also sheds light on the interrelationship among these countries.[6] Since 1980, intra-industry trade within Asia (East and South Asia) has been on a rising trend.[7]

---

[5]A number of studies have estimated the impact of China on the trade of other Asian countries during the recent past and arrived at reassuring results. Overall, the diversion of trade to Chinese exporters was limited. Asian exporters of labor-intensive light manufactures have suffered more than others, while suppliers of sophisticated components and equipment have gained from import demand triggered by China's processing exports. See Haltmaier and others (2007); Hanson and Robertson (2008); Ravenhill (2006); Asian Development Bank (2009); and Roland-Holst and Weiss (2005).

[6]In this section, the Grubel-Lloyd Index (GLI) of intra-industry trade is calculated at the bilateral level. See Brülhart (2009) for an extensive review of the intra-industry trade methodologies and the global trend since 1962.

[7]Zebregs (2004) also notes the increase in intra-industry trade in East Asia as production has dispersed geographically under the pull of cost gradients, although the United States and the European Union remain the primary destinations of final products.

Table 3.1   Intraregional Trade in East and South Asia, 1980–2006

Country/region	Year	Share of East Asia, including China and Japan (%)	Share of China (%)	Share of Japan (%)	Share of South Asia, including India (%)	Share of India (%)
East Asia (excluding China and Japan)	1980	44.4	3.8	22.0	1.5	0.7
	1985	46.6	7.7	19.6	1.8	0.9
	1990	47.9	8.4	18.9	1.3	0.7
	1995	53.8	11.1	17.4	1.3	0.8
	2000	54.9	13.0	14.9	1.4	0.9
	2006	59.0	20.4	11.3	2.0	1.6
Japan						
	1980	24.0	3.5		1.3	0.7
	1985	24.8	6.2		1.5	0.9
	1990	28.4	3.5		1.2	0.7
	1995	39.1	7.4		1.1	0.7
	2000	40.2	10.0		0.9	0.6
	2006	44.4	17.2		1.0	0.7
China						
	1985	53.3		30.5	0.8	0.2
	1990	59.4		14.4	0.8	0.2
	1995	55.7		20.5	1.1	0.4
	2000	50.7		17.5	1.1	0.6
	2006	43.9		11.8	2.0	1.4
South Asia						
	1980	30.6	5.1	10.8	9.0	3.9
	1985	27.8	2.6	11.8	3.8	1.4
	1990	28.9	3.2	9.6	3.9	1.7
	1995	31.9	4.0	7.9	4.6	2.7
	2000	27.6	5.0	4.5	4.1	2.7
	2006	25.4	9.1	4.1	5.9	4.8
India						
	1980	12.4	0.2	6.7	0.9	
	1985	16.8	0.6	9.6	0.9	
	1990	17.9	0.1	8.3	1.3	
	1995	22.0	1.7	6.8	2.5	
	2000	19.5	2.5	3.8	2.1	
	2006	25.5	8.3	2.4	2.0	

Source: Authors' calculations based on UN Comtrade data.
Note: Blank cell = not applicable.

Figure 3.1 Changes in Intra-industry Trade of East Asian Economies

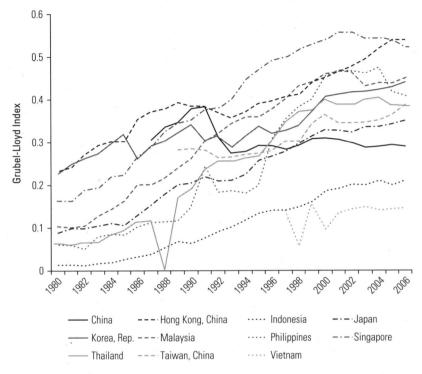

Source: Authors' calculations using UN Comtrade data.

Intra-industry trade rose rapidly among the East Asian economies but then plateaued after 2000 (see figure 3.1). Among the South Asian countries, only India experienced a growth in intra-industry trade (see figure 3.2). Even so, participation of India in intra-industry trade is considerably lower than that of all but two East Asian countries—Indonesia and Vietnam.

Consistent with the industrialization of East Asian economies, the fragmentation of production,[8] and an increase in vertical specialization, the composition of goods with higher intra-industry trade is shifting from primary products and resource-based products toward medium- and high-tech products (see table 3.2). In South Asia, meanwhile, commodities with the highest intra-industry trade ratios are resource-based and low-tech products (see table 3.3). Since 2000, products and machinery related to information and communication technology (ICT) have entered the list of the top five traded commodities.

---

[8]See Deardorff (2001) on fragmentation and production networking.

Figure 3.2   Intra-industry Trade by South Asian Economies

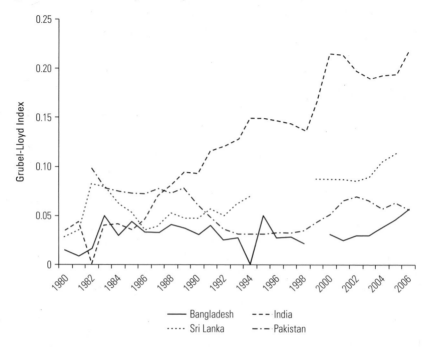

Source: Authors' calculations using UN Comtrade data.

Given the differing stages of development and industrialization, trade within Asia is dominated by East Asia. This is reflected in the data for intra-industry trade in Asia as a whole and is apparent from a comparison of table 3.4 with table 3.2. They are identical except for 1980, when more primary products were among the top five products for all of Asia than for East Asian economies alone.

For the East and South Asian regions combined, intra-industry trade is most active in auto parts, electronics and electronic equipment, furniture, and garments and textiles. Auto parts are traded mostly among the East Asian economies (see figure 3.3).

The same goes for electronics and electrical machinery although, since the late 1990s, intra-industry trade in electronics within South Asia has increased (see figure 3.4).

Intra-industry trade in furniture was on a declining trend between 1980 and 2002 but has been on an upswing since. In South Asia, intra-industry trade in furniture increased from the late 1990s but slumped after 2004 (figure 3.5).

Intra-industry trade in garments and textiles in East Asia peaked in 1986 and has oscillated between a GLI of 0.12 and 0.14 since 1988. Starting from a lower

Table 3.2   Commodities with the Highest Intra-industry Trade in East Asia

Year	Rank	GLI	Description	Technology class
1980	1	0.63	Furskins, Raw (Including Furskin Heads, Tails, and Other Pieces or Cuttings Suitable for Furriers' Use)	PP
	2	0.56	Thermionic, Cold Cathode, or Photocathode Valves and Tubes; Diodes, Transistors, and Similar Semiconductor Devices; Integrated Circuits, etc.; Parts	HT1
	3	0.54	Alcohols, Phenols, Phenol-Alcohols, and Their Halogenated, Sulfonated, Nitrated, or Nitrosated Derivatives	MT2
	4	0.44	Pearls, Precious and Semiprecious Stones, Unworked or Worked	RB2
	5	0.43	Engines and Motors, Nonelectric (Other Than Steam Turbines, Internal Combustion Piston Engines, and Power-Generating Machinery); Parts Thereof, N.E.S.	MT3
1990	1	0.71	Electric Power Machinery (Other Than Rotating Electric Plant of Power-Generating Machinery) and Parts Thereof	HT1
	2	0.66	Furskins, Tanned or Dressed (Including Pieces or Cuttings), Assembled or Unassembled without the Addition of Other Materials, Other Than Apparel, etc.	LT1
	3	0.62	Watches and Clocks	MT3
	4	0.60	Parts and Accessories Suitable for Use Solely or Principally with Office Machines or Automatic Data Processing Machines	HT1
	5	0.59	Barley, Unmilled	PP
2000	1	0.67	Furskins, Tanned or Dressed (Including Pieces or Cuttings), Assembled or Unassembled without the Addition of Other Materials, Other Than Apparel, etc.	LT1
	2	0.67	Telecommunications Equipment, N.E.S.; Parts, N.E.S., and Accessories of Apparatus Falling within Telecommunications, etc.	HT1
	3	0.66	Rotating Electric Plant and Parts Thereof, N.E.S.	HT1
	4	0.66	Electric Power Machinery (Other Than Rotating Electric Plant of Power-Generating Machinery) and Parts Thereof	HT1
	5	0.63	Parts and Accessories Suitable for Use Solely or Principally with Office Machines or Automatic Data Processing Machines	HT1
2006	1	0.69	Rotating Electric Plant and Parts Thereof, N.E.S.	HT1
	2	0.65	Electric Power Machinery (Other Than Rotating Electric Plant of Power-Generating Machinery) and Parts Thereof	HT1
	3	0.64	Parts and Accessories Suitable for Use Solely or Principally with Office Machines or Automatic Data Processing Machines	HT1
	4	0.64	Manufactures of Base Metal, N.E.S.	LT2
	5	0.63	Equipment for Distributing Electricity, N.E.S.	MT3

Source: Authors' calculations using UN Comtrade data. Technology classification is based on Lall (2000).
Note: N.E.S. = not elsewhere specified; HT1 = electronic and electrical products; HT2 = other high-technology products; LT1 = textiles, garments, and footwear; LT2 = other low-technology products; MT1 = automotive products; MT2 = process industry; MT3 = engineering products; PP = primary products; RB1 = agro-based products; RB2 = other resource-based products.

Table 3.3 Commodities with the Highest Intra-industry Trade in South Asia

Year	Rank	GLI	Description	Technology class
1980	1	0.55	Aircraft and Associated Equipment; Spacecraft (Including Satellites) and Spacecraft Launch Vehicles; and Parts Thereof	HT2
	2	0.53	Spices	PP
	3	0.40	Essential Oils, Perfume, and Flavor Materials	RB2
	4	0.30	Paper and Paperboard, Cut to Size or Shape, and Articles of Paper or Paperboard	LT2
	5	0.19	Textile Yarn	LT1
1990	1	0.65	Petroleum Oils and Oils from Bituminous Minerals (Other Than Crude), and Products Thereof Containing 70% (By Wt) or More of These Oils, N.E.S.	RB2
	2	0.57	Electrical Apparatus for Switching or Protecting Electrical Circuits or for Making Connections to or in Electrical Circuits (Excluding Telephone, etc.)	MT3
	3	0.47	Metal Containers for Storage or Transport	LT2
	4	0.35	Essential Oils, Perfume, and Flavor Materials	RB2
	5	0.26	Materials of Rubber, Including Pastes, Plates, Sheets, Rods, Thread, Tubes, etc.	RB1
2000	1	0.60	Fish, Fresh (Live or Dead), Chilled or Frozen	PP
	2	0.59	Aircraft and Associated Equipment; Spacecraft (Including Satellites) and Spacecraft Launch Vehicles; and Parts Thereof	HT2
	3	0.52	Pulp and Waste Paper	RB1
	4	0.51	Crude Vegetable Materials, N.E.S.	PP
	5	0.50	Ships, Boats (Including Hovercraft), and Floating Structures	MT3
2006	1	0.86	Copper	PP
	2	0.81	Electrical Machinery and Apparatus, N.E.S.	HT1
	3	0.71	Floor Coverings, etc.	LT1
	4	0.71	Lime, Cement, and Fabricated Construction Materials, Except Glass and Clay Materials	RB2
	5	0.69	Paper and Paperboard, Cut to Size or Shape, and Articles of Paper or Paperboard	LT2

Source: Authors' calculations using UN Comtrade data. Technology classification is based on Lall (2000).
Note: See the note to table 3.2.

base, South Asia's intra-industry trade has climbed since 2000, pointing to greater participation of producers from the region in global value chains (see figure 3.6).

The overall impression from these figures confirms the information from industry sources indicating that intra-industry trade in major product groups is more active in East Asia than in South Asia. Evidence of production networking is most apparent in electronics and electrical machinery, rising in auto parts, and

Table 3.4   Commodities with the Highest Intra-industry Trade in Asia

Year	Rank	GLI	Description	Technology class
1980	1	0.63	Furskins, Raw (Including Furskin Heads, Tails and Other Pieces or Cuttings Suitable for Furriers' Use)	PP
	2	0.56	Thermionic, Cold Cathode, or Photocathode Valves and Tubes; Diodes, Transistors and Similar Semiconductor Devices; Integrated Circuits, etc.; Parts	HT1
	3	0.52	Alcohols, Phenols, and Phenol-Alcohols; and Their Halogenated, Sulfonated, Nitrated, or Nitrosated Derivatives	MT2
	4	0.42	Parts and Accessories Suitable for Use Solely or Principally with Office Machines or Automatic Data Processing Machines	HT1
	5	0.42	Lead	PP
1990	1	0.70	Electric Power Machinery (Other Than Rotating Electric Plant of Power Generating Machinery) and Parts Thereof	HT1
	2	0.66	Furskins, Tanned or Dressed (Including Pieces or Cuttings), Assembled or Unassembled without the Addition of Other Materials, Other Than Apparel, etc.	LT1
	3	0.61	Watches and Clocks	MT3
	4	0.60	Parts and Accessories Suitable for Use Solely or Principally With Office Machines or Automatic Data Processing Machines	HT1
	5	0.59	Barley, Unmilled	PP
2000	1	0.67	Furskins, Tanned or Dressed (Including Pieces or Cuttings), Assembled or Unassembled without the Addition of Other Materials, Other Than Apparel, etc.	LT1
	2	0.66	Telecommunications Equipment, N.E.S.; and Parts, N.E.S., and Accessories of Apparatus Falling Within Telecommunications, Etc.	HT1
	3	0.65	Electric Power Machinery (Other Than Rotating Electric Plant of Power Generating Machinery) and Parts Thereof	HT1
	4	0.65	Rotating Electric Plant and Parts Thereof, N.E.S.	HT1
	5	0.63	Parts and Accessories Suitable for Use Solely or Principally with Office Machines or Automatic Data Processing Machines	HT1
2006	1	0.67	Rotating Electric Plant and Parts Thereof, N.E.S.	HT1
	2	0.64	Electric Power Machinery (Other Than Rotating Electric Plant of Power Generating Machinery) and Parts Thereof	HT1
	3	0.63	Parts and Accessories Suitable For Use Solely or Principally with Office Machines or Automatic Data Processing Machines	HT1
	4	0.61	Manufactures of Base Metal, N.E.S.	LT2
	5	0.60	Equipment for Distributing Electricity, N.E.S.	MT3

Source: Authors' calculations using UN Comtrade data. Technology classification is based on Lall (2000).
Note: See the note to table 3.2.

Figure 3.3   Intra-industry Trade in Auto Parts by Asia Region

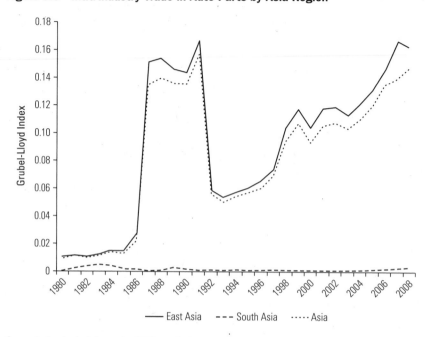

Source: Authors' calculations using UN Comtrade data.

moderately intense in garments and textiles. From among the South Asian countries, India is engaging in auto parts trade as well as in electronics trade, thereby distancing itself from its neighbors and beginning to position itself as an industrial economy that—in time—could resemble China's (figure 3.7 and figure 3.8).[9]

East Asian economies can be divided into two groups. One group comprises Hong Kong, China; Japan; Korea; Malaysia; the Philippines; Singapore; and Thailand. A sizable portion of their trade in electronics can be classified as intra-industry trade, and, until recently, the trend has been upward. A second group consists of China and Vietnam, whose engagement in intra-industry trade appears to be waning. Most notable are the changes in China's intra-industry trade. It was increasing until 1999 and has declined rapidly since. Given that China is now the largest exporter of electronics, the diminishing import intensity of its products suggests that backward integration is gathering momentum through the multiplication of local suppliers (although some or most of these may be foreign-owned). Increasingly, China's intra-industry trade is with Japan and Korea, countries that

_____

[9]A brief spurt of intra-industry trade in electronics between India and Sri Lanka dissipated after 1990 (see figure 3.8).

Figure 3.4   Intra-industry Trade in Electronics and Electrical Machinery by Asia Region

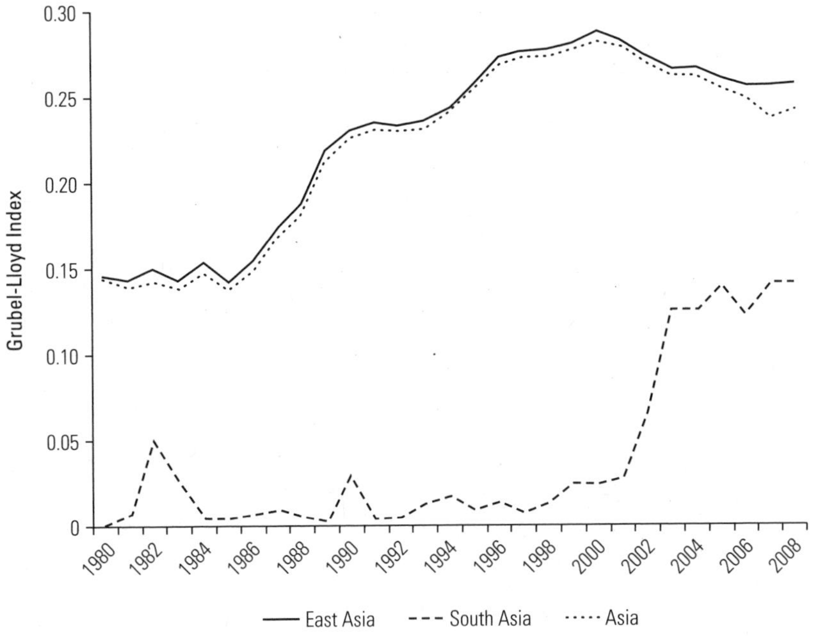

Source: Authors' calculations using UN Comtrade data.

supply sophisticated components and production equipment.[10] Other parts and components are being sourced from within China (see Haltmaier and others 2007). The persistence of such a trend would spell trouble for other economies in East Asia, especially for Southeast Asian economies that rely on exports of electronic parts to China to balance their trade (see also Ravenhill 2006).

The inability of South Asian economies to sustain the trade in furniture was a setback for the region, and the East Asian countries have been quick to seize the opportunities this has presented (figure 3.9). Several countries have been riding an upward trend since 2000, although Hong Kong, China; Indonesia; Japan; and Vietnam do not engage in intra-industry trade in this particular product group.

Pakistan and Bangladesh are participating more actively in the intra-industry trade in garments and textiles. Participation by India has stabilized, but that of Sri

---

[10]China's rising intra-industry trade with Japan, primarily in the machinery and electrical engineering and electronics subsectors, is linked to Japan's foreign direct investment (FDI) in China. Growth of such trade with the United States is seemingly unrelated to U.S. FDI in China and is mainly in food products and chemicals (Xing 2007).

Figure 3.5 Intra-industry Trade in Furniture by Asia Region

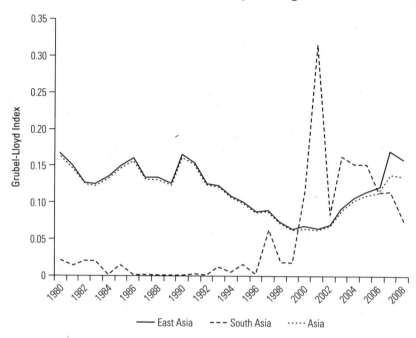

Source: Authors' calculations using UN Comtrade data.

Lanka remains low (see figure 3.10). Among East Asian economies, Hong Kong, China; Thailand; Malaysia; Korea; Singapore; and Indonesia are also active. China; Taiwan, China; Vietnam; Japan; and the Philippines saw the proportion of their trade in garments and textiles classified as intra-industry trade decrease. This is expected for Japan and Taiwan, China, as they have largely exited from this industrial segment and now are mainly importers of these goods (some produced by multinational corporations (MNCs) in other East Asian countries). What is striking is the large trade balance in textiles favoring China, reflecting the rapid decline in China's intra-industry trade in garments and textiles and, since global quotas were abolished in 2005, China's export success in the United States, where it now holds a one-third share. This shows that China is deepening the domestic supplier base for this industry and relying less on other Asian suppliers—most notably those in Association of Southeast Asian Nations (ASEAN) countries, which are being squeezed between Chinese exporters and those from low-income South Asian countries ("South-East Asia: Shake-up Looms" 2009).

Investing to Export

A better understanding of the industrial realities underlying the intra-industry trade statistics can be garnered from data on investment in manufacturing capacity in the

Figure 3.6   Intra-industry Trade in Garments and Textiles by Asia Region

Source: Authors' calculations using UN Comtrade data.

Asian countries. Unfortunately, information on subsectoral investment is not readily available. One indicator, admittedly a crude one, is gross investment. Ideally, one would want a time series of investment disaggregated by manufacturing subsectors, but e ven the aggregate data can provide insights on growth and competitiveness. First, the data point to market expectations regarding returns from investment. Second, the volume of expenditure on productive assets is a gauge of entrepreneurship and access to financing from various sources. Third, investment in productive assets introduces new embodied technology. The higher the level of investment, the younger the vintage of the capital stock in the manufacturing sector[11] and the more modern the infrastructure. In other words, countries with high rates of investment are likely to have more advanced and productive technologies in place.

(continued on page 86)

---

[11]This is vital in industries subject to rapid turnover of technologies. The production of DRAMs (dynamic random access memory) and thin-film transistor LCDs (liquid crystal displays) evolves in cycles of two years or less, and to remain competitive, producers must continuously be investing in the latest generation of product design and process technologies. Taiwanese producers may have lost ground to Korean ones by cutting investment during 2009, when demand briefly slumped.

Figure 3.7 Intra-industry Trade in Auto Parts within the Region by Asian Economy

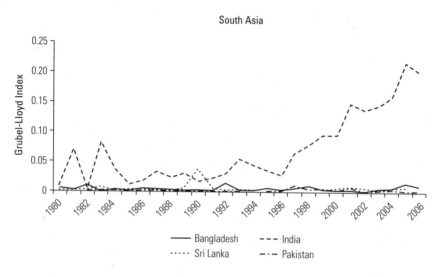

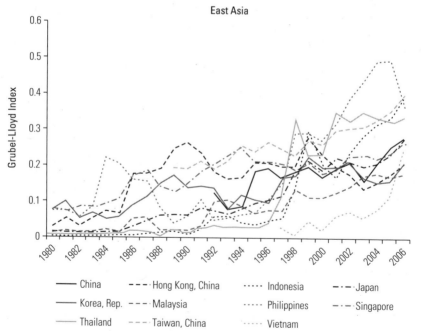

Source: Authors' calculations using UN Comtrade data.

Figure 3.8   Intra-industry Trade in Electronics within the Region by Asian Economy

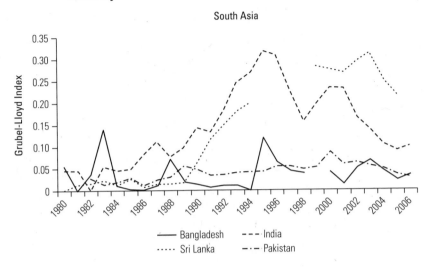

South Asia

Legend:
— Bangladesh   --- India
····· Sri Lanka   -··- Pakistan

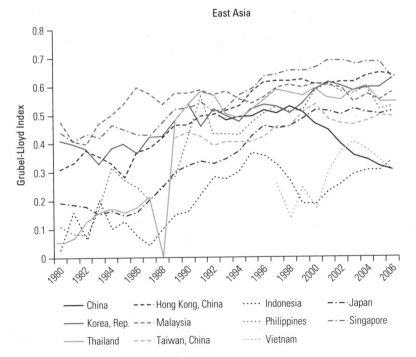

East Asia

Legend:
— China   --- Hong Kong, China   ····· Indonesia   -··- Japan
— Korea, Rep.   --- Malaysia   ····· Philippines   -··- Singapore
— Thailand   --- Taiwan, China   ····· Vietnam

Source: Authors' calculations using UN Comtrade data.

Figure 3.9 **Intra-industry Trade in Furniture within the Region by Asian Economy**

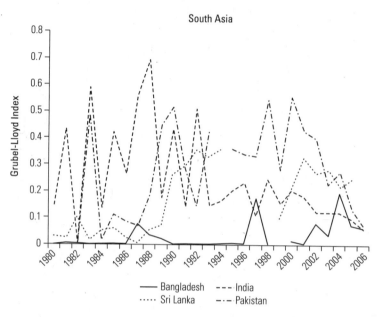

South Asia

Bangladesh --- India
..... Sri Lanka --.-- Pakistan

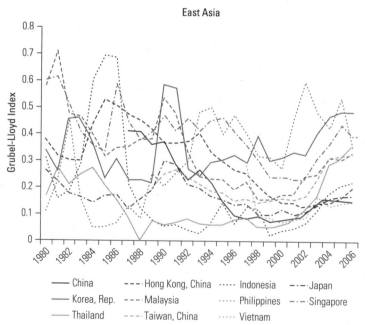

East Asia

— China --- Hong Kong, China ..... Indonesia --.-- Japan
— Korea, Rep. --- Malaysia ..... Philippines --.-- Singapore
— Thailand --- Taiwan, China ..... Vietnam

Source: Authors' calculations using UN Comtrade data.

Figure 3.10 **Intra-industry Trade in Garments within the Region by Asian Economy**

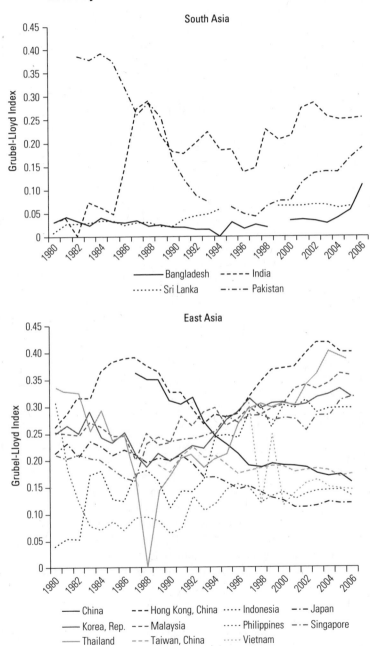

Source: Authors' calculations using UN Comtrade data.

Fourth, investment builds capacity and positions producers to respond quickly to market opportunities while exploiting scale economies, if present, to quote lower prices. When demand from the United States rose after 2005 as the consequence of a policy-induced demand shock, investment in productive capacity by China in the preceding years allowed a matching supply response that massively increased exports to the United States. Fifth, investment not only can serve as a transmission mechanism for the latest technologies and as a means of achieving optimal scale—which is a big advantage in industries where technological change is rapid and production units must be of a certain minimum size in order to be cost competitive—but also is a good proxy for learning by doing. Learning is one of the key sources of productivity gains and represents the accumulation of tacit knowledge, the intangible asset that underpins productivity in complex industries. Sixth, high investment also supports the growth and quality of business services such as finance and insurance, which are among the biggest users of ICT. Finance, insurance, and real estate (FIRE), engineering, and consulting services contribute substantially to the growth and upgrading of manufacturing.[12]

Table 3.5 shows how investment-to-GDP ratios have trended in Asian countries since 1995. In China, the ratio has averaged 42 percent. In several of the formerly high-investing countries in Southeast Asia—such as Singapore, Malaysia, and Thailand—investment ratios declined following the 1997–98 crisis. Investment rates have also diminished in Japan and Korea. Only Vietnam has bucked the trend. Its investment rose from 27 percent in 1995 to 42 percent in 2007. In South Asia, the level of investment re mains modest or moderate, with the exception of India. This is the one instance where investment has risen sharply since the late 1990s—from 24 to 39 percent of GDP in 2008.

Countries with high levels of investment, such as China, India, and Vietnam, are sinking significant resources into manufacturing; the shares range from one-quarter to one-third of the total. In countries where investment has been shrinking, the share of manufacturing has declined, and more of the investment is in real estate, infrastructure, and services. This is also the case in the low-investing South Asian economies. These trends are likely to reinforce China's industrial strength and could add to the relative industrial heft of India and Vietnam, if higher levels of investment in these two countries are sustained and favor manufacturing. The three countries stand to benefit from the gains associated with rapid industrialization via exports, productivity, and technological change, the latter two being related to export competitiveness. Moreover, this practice of

---

[12]See Jorgenson, Ho, and Stiroh (2007) on the role of capital in promoting the growth of FIRE in the United States.

Table 3.5 Gross Capital Formation
share of GDP (%)

Country/economy	1995	2000	2005	2007
China	41.9	35.1	44.0	43.3
Vietnam	27.1	29.6	35.6	41.7
India	26.6	24.2	34.8	38.7
Korea, Rep.	37.7	31.0	30.1	29.4
Sri Lanka	25.7	28.0	26.1	27.2
Thailand	42.1	22.8	31.4	26.9
Indonesia	31.9	22.3	25.1	24.9
Bangladesh	19.1	23.0	24.5	24.5
Japan	28.4	25.4	23.6	24.1
Pakistan	18.6	17.2	19.1	22.9
Singapore	34.5	33.3	19.9	22.6
Malaysia	43.6	26.9	20.0	21.9
Taiwan, China	25.2	23.3	21.4	21.1
Philippines	22.5	21.2	14.6	15.3

Source: World Development Indicators Database.

investment by deepening industrial capacity should also steadily raise domestic value added. There remains, however, the looming problem of excess capacity in many industries worldwide, which we will address in chapter 5.

Wages and Labor Productivity

All of the successful East Asian economies have relied to varying degrees on export-led growth, and cost has been one of the key determinants of competitiveness. The cost advantage weighed more heavily during the early stages of industrialization, when the countries concerned were mainly producing and exporting standardized light manufactures that were labor-intensive, generally low-cost items. They competed on the basis of price, meeting specifications set by buyers, measuring up to a variety of international production and product standards, and building the capacity to fulfill volume and delivery requirements. For standardized manufactures that are assembled or processed, price can be decisive; where these products are labor intensive, labor costs are a prime consideration. Such costs are a function of wages adjusted for productivity. The former is relatively straightforward. The latter, however, is the product of a number of factors, including the organization and management of

Table 3.6 Average Annual Wages
constant 2000$

Country/economy	1981	1990	2002
China	478	423	—
India	853	1,155	1,363
Japan	31,091	36,012	31,255
Korea, Rep.	5,508	10,054	17,472
Philippines	1,713	2,287	2,510
Singapore	8,503	13,078	22,134
Taiwan, China	5,323	10,222	13,366
Thailand	2,534	2,328	2,542
Vietnam	—	—	802
Pakistan	1,320	2,214	2,139
Bangladesh	654	656	447
Sri Lanka	729	741	756

Source: UNIDO INDSTAT3.
Note: China (1981, 1986); Indonesia (1981, 1990, 2003); Philippines (1981, 1990, 1997); Singapore (1981, 1990, 2003); Taiwan, China (1981, 1990, 1997); Thailand (1982, 1990, 1994); Vietnam (2000); Pakistan (1981, 1990, 1996); Bangladesh (1981, 1990, 1998); Sri Lanka (1981, 1990, 2001). — = not available.

production;[13] the level of education and training; advances in communication; teamwork and noncognitive skills; acculturation, which predisposes the worker to adapt quickly to the discipline of factory work routines; minimum wage and labor laws, which can impose requirements that increase the costs for employers (including the costs of laying off workers); and unionization, which also can put upward pressure on wage rates. Virtually all of the East Asian countries adopted exchange rate policies, especially in the earlier stages of industrialization, to enhance their competitiveness—although the benefits these conferred are not easy to disentangle. Wage rates in constant dollars are the most convenient and readily available metric, but not for all countries or for all years.

In table 3.6, we can see one reason why China established such a commanding lead over other Asian countries. China's low wage rates relative to other Asian countries (with the exception of Bangladesh), reinforced by the trainability and discipline of the workforce, meant that factories operating in China could quote a price for labor-intensive standardized products that other producers in Asia had difficulty matching, much less undercutting. When China moved into the assembly

---

[13]The role of management and the importance of well-structured organizations and efficient work routines have been stressed by Nick Bloom. See Bloom and Van Reenen (2010).

Table 3.7   Chinese Productivity, Wages, and RULC Compared to Selected Countries, 2002

as a share of comparator country levels (%)

	Relative productivity	Relative wage	RULC
a. UNIDO-based estimates (narrow definition of manufacturing)			
United States	7.9	3.4	42.8
Japan[a]	10.3	4.3	41.6
India	160.3	100.3	62.6
Indonesia	107.9	118.0	109.3
Malaysia[a]	43.6	27.5	62.9
Korea, Rep.[a]	12.2	8.6	70.2
Singapore[a]	17.5	6.3	35.9
b. World Bank/Chinese/BLS–based estimates (broad definition of manufacturing)			
United States	7.7	2.1	27.0
Japan	8.7	2.6	30.3
India	152.1	61.8	40.6
Indonesia	102.4	72.6	70.9
Malaysia[a]	41.4	16.9	40.8
Korea, Rep.[a]	11.6	5.3	45.5
Singapore[a]	16.6	3.9	23.3

Source: Ceglowski and Golub 2007.
a. 2001.

and testing of high-tech electronic products—and more recently into the assembly of autos—the lower wages and high productivity of Chinese workers have translated into a solid competitive advantage.[14] The so-called China price[15] (see Harney 2008) became the competitive benchmark by 2005; together with aggressive marketing, it explained the penetration of Chinese goods into markets throughout Asia and the rest of the world. Table 3.7, on relative wages and relative unit labor costs (RULC),[16] provides additional evidence of China's cost advantage relative to East Asian comparators.

---

[14]These firms are able to offer customers a wide range of choices at prices their competitors are unable to match. Chinese firms prefer a cost innovation high volume strategy preferring to target the lower tiers of a product market—which is the approach of most disruptive innovators—before attacking the higher tiers (Williamson and Zeng 2008).

[15]China has competed on the basis of cost innovation rather than product innovation.

[16]Relative unit labor costs are the ratio of relative wages to relative labor productivity. RULC values reflect currency fluctuations as well as differences in wages and labor productivity, and provide a compact measure of international competitiveness (Ceglowski and Golub 2007).

With low labor costs being juxtaposed with heavy investment in up-to-date plant and equipment, and manufacturers making every effort to achieve scale economies, it is little wonder that China moved to the forefront. Other producers in South Asia such as Pakistan, Bangladesh, and Sri Lanka also had relatively low wage rates; but Chinese firms enjoyed a lead in manufacturing capacity combined with a large domestic market. They also integrated much faster and more fully with Pacific-spanning global value chains, initially through their overseas Chinese connections and later also through the avenues opened by FDI.

As demand for workers has risen in China's principal industrial regions from 2001 onward, wages have also risen; however, productivity also has generally climbed faster than wages, and this has largely offset the increase in labor costs. Wages have trended upward in other Asian countries as well without a commensurate increase in productivity, so the competitiveness of China's labor-intensive manufactures is not necessarily eroding relative to its competitors in South and Southeast Asia.[17] Only India, Bangladesh, and Vietnam can compete on equal or better terms with respect to efficiency and wage rates in certain labor-intensive industries.

The crisis of 2008–09 could make the competition more fierce by curtailing trade flows, forcing the closure of factories in China and throughout Asia, and easing the demand for factory labor. Slower-growing domestic and international markets will ease the upward pressure on wages.[18] Most likely, though, it will favor the bigger, more capital-intensive firms with deeper pockets and a longer presence in the global value chains.[19] More Chinese and Indian firms fit this profile than

---

[17]With China's labor productivity growing at close to 9 percent in the aggregate and at higher rates in the manufacturing sector (well in excess of China's competitors), most industries, including relatively labor-intensive ones, are able to absorb the demand for higher wages and make decent profits in the industrialized coastal regions. Looking ahead, labor productivity should continue growing at these rates for at least the next five years and, with aggregate employment in manufacturing virtually flat, it is unlikely that wage pressures could become so acute that Chinese firms would be forced to move out of textiles, garments, footwear, leather goods, and other light manufactures (Kuijs 2010 and "China: New Generation" 2010). Some of the labor-intensive manufacturing in the Pearl River Delta (PRD) and the Changjiang Basin urban regions is beginning to migrate in two directions: shifting to lower-cost urban regions in interior provinces such as Jiangxi and Henan, and moving to neighboring Asian countries with cost structures and longer-term trends in costs more favorable than in the PRD (see, for instance, Cheung and Qian 2009, on China's FDI and exports).

[18]This remains to be seen, as reservation wages in China have been rising; and some of the workers who left Guangdong in 2009 appear reluctant to return, which will lead to localized shortages.

[19]European experience indicates that exporters compose a small subset of firms—on average those that are larger, more skill- and capital-intensive, and more productive (Mayer 2007).

firms from the lower-middle- and low-income Asian countries. Looking ahead, cost competition could be complemented by greater competition in the areas of design, process innovation, and quality, among others. Larger firms with ties to the MNCs could widen their advantage over others, because they enjoy more technology spillovers and are better prepared to introduce process improvements and to ascend product quality ladders. China has the greatest concentration of such firms—particularly in consumer durables, electronics, telecommunications equipment, and electrical equipment—clustered in a few urban regions. India is strong in textiles and apparel, pharmaceuticals, petrochemicals, and engineering products. Other Asian countries have fewer firms in this category, and their cluster densities and technological capabilities are lower.[20]

Competitive Advantage and Its Evolution

What is the likely direction of industrial change in China and India, and how will it affect the industrial geographies of these countries and that of the region? One factor that will influence change is the competitive advantage of various products and how this manifests itself by way of export performance relative to other countries. One frequently employed indicator of product competitiveness is revealed comparative advantage (RCA). This mechanically identifies products whose share in the country's export mix is greater than their share in global exports. The higher the ratio, the greater the RCA. By itself, the RCA casts a narrow beam of light on comparative advantage, but it can usefully complement other indicators that illuminate additional facets of industry and trade. The group of export commodities with the highest RCAs in China has remained fairly constant since the 1980s: raw silk, plaited products, and pyrotechnic articles have always been near the top (see table 3.8). India, on the other hand, has seen a shift in its high-ranking commodities. Textiles and leather products were topmost in the 1980s; since then, castor oil has moved ahead and has consistently been the commodity with the highest RCA (see table 3.9).

The trouble with the RCA measure is that it can identify only products in which a country has a static comparative advantage; it overlooks other important products and products with high growth potential in the future. Therefore, in table 3.10 we list the 10 fastest-growing manufacturing industries in China and India, and in table 3.11 we list the 10 fastest-growing manufactured exports between 2000 and 2007. These tables together provide a better sense of how the composition of industry is changing and point toward commodities with the most promising growth prospects. Data on the largest manufactured exports by value for the two countries (see tables 3.12 and 3.13) offer another perspective,

---

[20]See, for instance, Yusuf and Nabeshima (2010) on the state and capabilities of industrial clustering in the Bangkok urban region.

Table 3.8   **Top 10, Four-Digit-Level Commodities with the Highest RCA in China, 1985 and 2006**

Short description	RCA	PRODY	Technology class
1985			
Raw silk (not thrown)	218.83	826	PP
Plaits, plaited products for all uses; straw envelopes for bottles	150.05	1,343	LT1
Goat and kid skins, raw, whether or not split	121.74	2,541	PP
Sheep's or lambs' wool, or of other animal hair, carded or combed	114.74	2,188	PP
Articles of leather for use in machinery or mechanical appliances, etc.	114.01	1,210	LT1
Pile and chenille fabrics, woven, of man-made fibers	109.13	1,191	MT2
Pyrotechnic articles	91.77	3,347	MT2
Yarn of regenerated fibers, put up for retail sale	85.08	2,387	LT1
Fabrics, woven, of silk, noil, or other waste silk	79.03	3,189	LT1
Natural honey	66.20	4,784	RB1
2006			
Raw silk (not thrown)	8.70	5,554	PP
Personal adornments and ornaments; articles of plastic	8.23	9,348	LT2
Pyrotechnic articles	7.92	4,658	MT2
Plaits, plaited products for all uses; straw envelopes for bottles	7.89	1,858	LT1
Umbrellas, canes, and similar articles and parts thereof	7.15	9,697	LT2
Silk yarn and yarn spun from noil or waste; silkworm gut	6.76	4,387	LT1
Traveling rugs, blankets (nonelectric), not knitted or crocheted	6.61	4,709	LT1
Silkworm cocoons and silk waste	6.31	3,145	PP
Complete digital data processing machines	6.26	11,648	HT1
Baby carriages and parts thereof, N.E.S.	5.91	12,150	LT2

Source: Authors' calculations using UN Comtrade data. Technology classification is based on Lall (2000).
Note: PRODY is calculated by taking a weighted average of the GDP per capita of countries exporting that product; Commodities with larger PRODY are thought as more "sophisticated" goods. See the note to table 3.2.

while tables 3.14 and 3.15 show the fastest-growing global exports during 1997–2007 and the most rapidly expanding exports for the Asia region. By comparing these tables, we are able to see the intersection between the high-flying global exports and the fastest-growing and most significant exports of China and India. The production data indicate how manufacturing capacity is evolving in the two countries in relation to the trends in global exports.

From tables 3.10 and 3.13, transport equipment, electrical equipment, chemicals, and machinery emerge as the leading industries that are also contributing the largest exports, although the fastest-growing exports (table 3.11)

Table 3.9   Top 10, Four-Digit-Level Commodities with the Highest RCA in India, 1985 and 2006

Short description	RCA	PRODY	Technology class
1985			
Fabrics woven of jute or other textile bast fibers of heading 2640	57.69	278	LT1
Leather of other hides or skins	51.47	852	LT1
Pepper; pimento	42.90	1,824	PP
Tea	40.55	536	PP
Natural gums, resins, lacs, and balsams	35.73	1,236	PP
Carpets, carpeting, and rugs, knotted	35.33	1,256	LT1
Parts of footwear of any material, except metal and asbestos	35.13	3,866	LT1
Manganese ore and concentrates	31.72	2,455	RB2
Bags, sacks of textile materials, for the packing of goods	26.61	603	LT1
Spices, except pepper and pimento	25.85	1,272	PP
2006			
Castor oil	79.71	2,246	RB1
Coal gas, water gas, and similar gases	41.14	11,166	PP
Fabrics, woven of jute or other textile bast fibers of heading 2640	38.55	842	LT1
Vegetable textile fibers, N.E.S., and waste	31.29	2,518	RB1
Organic chemicals, N.E.S.	30.16	13,085	RB2
Sesame seeds	27.52	443	PP
Goat and kid skins, raw, split or not	25.30	1,190	PP
Building and monumental (dimension) stone, roughly squared, split	22.55	5,518	PP
Carpets, rugs, mats of wool or fine animal hair	22.48	7,651	LT1
Carpets, rugs, mats, of other textile materials, N.E.S.	21.68	8,567	LT1

Source: Authors' calculations using UN Comtrade data. Technology classification is based on Lall (2000).
Note: See the note to table 3.2.

are a heterogeneous mix, including some transport equipment, equipment for power plants,[21] food products, chemicals, and newsprint.

India's industrial mix is shifting mainly toward low- and medium-tech products, including chemicals and plastics, furniture, textiles and footwear, and industrial raw materials. The top exports in 2006 were mostly industrial materials, diamonds, and jewelry, and the fastest-growing ones were food products and industrial materials. From these results, it appears that China as a

---

[21]China and Korea have acquired the capacity and specialized skills to build nuclear power plants because of their large homegrown programs.

Table 3.10   Fastest-Growing Manufacturing Industries, China and India
percent

China, 1996–2003		India, 1996–2002	
Industry	Average growth rate	Industry	Average growth rate
Transport equipment	505.3	Furniture, except metal	49.0
Iron and steel	496.4	Petroleum refineries	20.0
Industrial chemicals	476.8	Other manufactured products	14.0
Machinery, except electrical	474.0	Footwear, except rubber or plastic	9.2
Food products	464.8	Beverages	8.3
Machinery, electrical	352.8	Plastic products	7.9
Professional and scientific equipment	17.6	Professional and scientific equipment	6.9
Petroleum refineries	16.0	Glass and products	6.2
Furniture, except metal	14.4	Wearing apparel, except footwear	6.0
Non-ferrous metals	14.1	Iron and steel	5.7

Source: UN Comtrade.

Table 3.11   Fastest-Growing Manufactured Exports, China and India

China Exports, 2000–06		India Exports, 2000–07	
Product name	Average growth rate	Product name	Average growth rate
Other rail locomotives; tenders	342.7	Barley, unmilled	399.9
Other wheat and meslin, unmilled	200.3	Gold, nonmonetary	342.1
Nuclear reactors and parts	188.3	Ash & residues, contain metals/	286.2
Lard, other pig fat & poultry, rendered	147.5	Coal gas, water gas, producer gas & similar gases	249.1
Newsprint	126.1	Other fresh, chilled, frozen meat or other edible meat	211.9
Coin (other than gold) not being legal tender	123.0	Petroleum gases and other gaseous hydrocarbons	189.2
Road tractors and semi-trailers	122.9	Zinc and zinc alloys, unwrought	179.1
Copolymers of vinyl chloride and vinyl acetate	115.5	Ground nut (peanut) oil	173.4
Steam & other vapor power units	110.4	Tugs, special purpose vessels, floating structures	167.3
Wire rod of iron or steel	110.1	Mineral tars and products	155.1

Source: UN Comtrade.

Table 3.12   India's Top 10 Exports, 2006

Short description of export	Trade value (in millions of dollars)
Diamonds (nonindustrial), not mounted or set	10,573
Precious jewelry, goldsmiths' or silversmiths' wares	4,948
Iron ore and concentrates, not agglomerated	3,860
Medications (including veterinary medications)	2,934
Undergarments, knitted or crocheted; of cotton, not elastic or rubberized	2,115
Copper and copper alloys, refined or not, unwrought	1,866
Organic chemicals, N.E.S.	1,830
Other sheets and plates, of iron or steel, worked	1,778
Cotton yarn	1,676
Rice, semimilled or wholly milled	1,546

Source: UN Comtrade.

Table 3.13   China's Top 10 Exports, 2006

Short description of export	Trade value (in millions of dollars)
Complete digital data processing machines	43,384
Peripheral units, including control and adapting units	37,594
Television, radio broadcasting; transmitters, etc.	35,776
Parts, N.E.S. of and accessories for machines of headings 7512 and 752	32,786
Parts, N.E.S. of and accessories for apparatus falling in heading 76	31,474
Electronic microcircuits	21,306
Other sound recording and reproducer, N.E.S.; video recorders	21,266
Footwear	21,015
Children's toys, indoor games, etc.	18,011
Outerwear, knitted or crocheted, not elastic nor rubberized; other clothing accessories, nonelastic, knitted or crocheted	14,892

Source: UN Comtrade.

competitive trading nation is advancing much more than India, which has been slow to wean itself from a variety of low-tech primary products and processed commodities.

Further insight into the relative comparative advantage of China and India can be gleaned from measures of dynamic revealed competitiveness (DRC), which indicate how their exports are faring relative to those of competitors in third-country markets (Gallagher, Moreno-Brid, and Porzecanski 2008). DRC is based

Table 3.14   Fastest-Growing Global Manufactured Exports, 1997–2007

Product name	Average growth rate (%)
Optical instruments and apparatus	77.0
Platinum and other metals of the platinum group	74.0
Glycosides; glands or other organs	50.7
Other nitrogen-function compounds	49.0
Other articles of precious metal	48.4
Nickel and nickel alloys, unwrought	46.4
Nickel and nickel alloys, worked	40.3
Cyclic hydrocarbons	40.0
Orthopedic appliances	39.2
Medicaments (including veterinary	39.2

Source: UN Comtrade.

Table 3.15   Fastest-Growing Manufactured Exports in Asia, 1997–2007

Product name	Average growth rate (%)
Dishwashing machines, household	1,703.0
Other articles of precious metal	198.7
Radiotelegraphic and radiotelephonic	147.8
Cellulose acetates	135.5
Silver, unwrought, unworked, or semimanufactured	135.1
Aircraft	126.1
Optical instruments and apparatus	122.1
Reaction engines	111.4
Nickel and nickel alloys, unwrought	109.5
Drawn or blown glass, unworked	104.6

Source: UN Comtrade.

on the changing market (import) shares of a commodity i between two time periods. Using this measure, we can examine the changing import share of Chinese and Indian products in three important markets: the United States, Japan, and the EU15. These represent the major importing markets globally. A positive DRC means that the share of Chinese (or Indian) products has increased in the importing country/region. Furthermore, by comparing the DRC measures for two countries, it is possible to determine which products are in direct competition. For instance, if the DRC is negative for a commodity exported by India but is positive for China, then the commodity is said to be in "direct threat." However, if the DRC is positive for both India and China, then it is in "partial threat."

Table 3.16   DRCP by Technology Level in U.S. Market: China and India

	China			India		
	1991–96	1997–2000	2001–07	1991–96	1997–2000	2001–07
HT1	3.54	3.04	23.75	0.08	−0.08	0.25
HT2	2.29	0.16	0.55	0.04	0.04	0.70
LT1	4.80	−1.11	18.31	0.70	0.17	1.11
LT2	9.46	4.58	12.97	0.31	0.18	0.95
MT1	0.23	0.32	1.76	0.04	0.01	0.13
MT2	0.32	2.46	6.63	0.31	0.58	0.97
MT3	3.46	2.97	8.28	0.07	0.01	0.40
PP	−0.36	−0.21	0.26	0.18	−0.05	−0.30
RB1	0.83	1.04	6.66	0.11	0.02	0.09
RB2	1.48	0.41	0.25	0.12	0.23	−0.46

Source: Authors' calculations using UN Comtrade data. Technology classification is based on Lall (2000).
Note: See the note to table 3.2. DRCP = dynamic revealed competitiveness position.

Looking at the changing market share of Chinese and Indian products in the United States during three different time periods reveals that China has increased its U.S. market share in the majority of technology classes. China enlarged its market share in the United States in low-technology products by 18 and 13 percentage points during the 2001 and 2007 period, respectively, and in electronics and electrical products by 24 percentage points (see table 3.16). India also increased its market share in several technology classes; but compared to China, the increase is much smaller. The largest increase was in textiles, garments, and footwear.

A similar trend is apparent in the Japanese market—China's market share in Japan has risen consistently for most technology classes. The only product groups in which China is losing market share are primary products and resource-based products (see table 3.17). In low-technology products, China increased its market share by 47 and 35 percentage points between 1990 and 2007, while India's market share in Japan barely grew.

The European Union (EU) market is where the competitive pressure from exporters in China is rather muted. Even though China has raised its market share in a broad spectrum of products, the magnitudes of the increase are smaller than those in the Japanese and U.S. markets. For instance, China's market share in electronics and electrical products increased by 13 percentage points during 2001–07—small compared to its 24 and 20 percentage point increases in the U.S. and Japanese markets, respectively (see table 3.18). India also increased its market share in most products in the EU market, although by smaller magnitudes than for China. A glance at the changes in market shares of Chinese and Indian exports suggests that for Chinese firms, U.S. and Japanese markets have been the major

Table 3.17 DRCP by Technology Level in Japan's Market: China and India

	China			India		
	1990–96	1997–2000	2001–07	1990–96	1997–2000	2001–07
HT1	6.32	1.79	19.92	0.03	0.03	0.07
HT2	2.64	1.35	3.93	0.00	0.00	−0.01
LT1	28.92	11.76	6.42	−0.04	−0.08	−0.12
LT2	12.87	5.52	16.49	0.00	−0.08	0.00
MT1	1.49	2.38	8.13	0.01	0.00	0.23
MT2	1.99	−0.48	8.84	0.46	−0.23	0.68
MT3	9.35	4.88	15.61	0.04	0.02	0.11
PP	0.21	−0.60	−2.39	0.24	−0.18	−0.25
RB1	6.07	3.24	5.26	0.04	0.06	0.08
RB2	4.95	1.03	−0.34	−0.74	−0.30	−0.82

Source: Authors' calculations using UN Comtrade data. Technology classification is based on Lall (2000).
Note: See the note to table 3.2. DRCP = dynamic revealed competitiveness position.

Table 3.18 DRCP by Technology Level in EU15 Countries' Markets: China and India

	China			India		
	1990–96	1997–2000	2001–07	1990–96	1997–2000	2001–07
HT1	1.41	2.22	12.76	0.04	0.00	0.14
HT2	0.54	0.04	−0.04	0.09	−0.06	0.23
LT1	1.91	3.05	11.40	0.74	0.18	0.81
LT2	1.74	2.66	5.69	0.21	0.11	0.42
MT1	0.00	0.10	0.47	0.09	−0.02	0.16
MT2	0.16	0.55	1.56	0.14	0.03	0.40
MT3	1.02	1.44	4.15	0.16	0.01	0.19
PP	0.11	0.05	0.07	0.21	−0.09	−0.03
RB1	−0.04	0.30	1.30	0.17	0.03	0.12
RB2	0.73	−0.18	0.69	0.77	−0.11	0.36

Source: Authors' calculations using UN Comtrade data. Technology classification is based on Lall (2000).
Note: See the note to table 3.2. DRCP = dynamic revealed competitiveness position.

targets; they have had somewhat less success in penetrating the EU market.[22] India, by comparison, has made greater headway in the U.S. and EU markets than in the Japanese market. These differences partly reflect differences in FDI flows to India and China and in their trade orientation. China's exports have been facilitated

---

[22]The EU is China's largest export market but should the Euro remain weak, market penetration by Chinese exports could become even tougher.

by large inflows of FDI from the United States and Japan. Hence, exports from China are geared toward the U.S. and Japanese markets through production networks managed by lead firms from these countries and by contract manufacturers. So far, India has not attracted as much FDI in manufacturing from these two sources, and this is reflected in the smaller increase in its market shares in the United States and Japan.

Apart from competing in third-country markets, China and India are also actively trading with each other. In fact, China is now India's biggest trading partner. Chinese producers have penetrated Indian markets in a broad range of products, primary products being the exception. China has commanding shares in electronics and electrical products, textiles, garments, and footwear in the Indian market (see table 3.19). In contrast, India has not been able to expand its market share in China, except in resource-based products (see table 3.20).

From India's standpoint, competitive pressures from China are greatest in the EU market, where 95 percent of its products are either directly or partially threatened by Chinese imports. The Japanese market is where Indian firms are not facing much competitive pressure from China (see table 3.21) because of differences in the composition of exports.

Among other Asian countries, Bangladesh, an exporter of textiles and garments, is feeling the competitive pressure from China. However, compared to the situation in 1990, the degree of competition seems to have abated. Nonetheless, more than half of all commodities exported by Bangladesh are threatened by Chinese exports in the EU market (see table 3.22). The distribution between

Table 3.19   DRCP of China in India's Market, by Technology Level

	China		
	1990–96	**1997–2000**	**2001–07**
HT1	3.28	2.22	29.46
HT2	5.05	1.00	3.18
LT1	9.12	1.09	29.00
LT2	1.47	0.00	6.26
MT1	—	1.56	13.25
MT2	2.32	−0.35	17.88
MT3	1.39	1.33	11.56
PP	1.06	0.09	−1.45
RB1	0.29	0.25	5.22
RB2	2.22	0.57	4.54

Source: Authors' calculations using UN Comtrade data. Technology classification is based on Lall (2000).
Note: See the note to table 3.2. DRCP = dynamic revealed competitiveness position; — = not available.

Table 3.20 DRCP of India in China's Market, by Technology Level

	India		
	1992–96	1997–2000	2001–07
HT1	0.02	0.03	0.03
HT2	−0.03	0.09	−0.25
LT1	0.79	0.32	0.06
LT2	0.56	0.01	0.03
MT1	0.01	−0.02	0.03
MT2	0.08	0.38	0.25
MT3	0.01	0.05	0.18
PP	1.06	−0.93	0.66
RB1	0.27	0.07	0.17
RB2	0.41	−0.93	4.55

Source: Authors' calculations using UN Comtrade data. Technology classification is based on Lall (2000).
Note: See the note to table 3.2. DRCP = dynamic revealed competitiveness position.

Table 3.21 The Degree of Competition between Indian and Chinese Exports
    percent

	Country/region	1990–91	2000–01	2006–07
Direct threat	EU15	23.1	38.2	44.2
Partial threat	EU15	20.1	33.9	50.7
Total	EU15	43.2	72.1	94.9
Direct threat	Japan	9.0	15.9	18.2
Partial threat	Japan	8.2	12.9	14.0
Total	Japan	17.2	28.8	32.2
Direct threat	U.S.	19.7*	28.7	35.8
Partial threat	U.S.	19.8*	26.7	32.7
Total	U.S.	39.5*	55.4	68.5

Source: Authors' calculation. Data are from the UN Comtrade database.
Note: * = 1991–92.

direct and partial threat is almost even. In the U.S. market, the proportion of goods threatened by Chinese products is lower (23 percent); and it is lower still in the Japanese market, where the competitive pressure from China is least, again because of the low-tech mix of products exported by Bangladesh. The threat posed by India's exports to Bangladeshi exports mirrors that of China. Bangladeshi producers are under the greatest threat in the EU market, followed

Table 3.22   The Degree of Competition between Bangladeshi and Chinese Exports
percent

	Country/region	1990–91	2000–01	2006–07
Direct threat	EU15	23.0	29.2	27.4
Partial threat	EU15	37.0	26.6	27.9
Total	EU15	60.0	55.8	55.3
Direct threat	Japan	9.3	10.2	4.3
Partial threat	Japan	5.8	9.2	3.9
Total	Japan	15.1	19.4	8.2
Direct threat	U.S.	18.1*	17.3	13.1
Partial threat	U.S.	25.8*	10.6	9.8
Total	U.S.	43.9*	27.9	22.9

Source: Authors' calculation. Data are from the UN Comtrade database.
Note: * = 1991–92.

by the U.S. market; whereas in Japan, Bangladesh is not facing much challenge from Indian exports (see table 3.23). It appears, however, that the competitive pressure on Bangladeshi exports from Chinese and Indian producers are generally decreasing over time. This is suggestive of product upgrading by both China and India and stagnation in the product quality and product mix of the low-income Asian countries and a widening wage gap between Bangladesh and China.[23]

Among the middle-income countries in Southeast Asia, Malaysia is a typical case. Its export structure is dominated by electronics and resource-based products owing to its rich natural resource endowment. Unlike Bangladesh, Malaysia (like other Southeast Asian economies) faces much stiffer competition from China in all three markets. In the EU market, 70 percent of Malaysia's exports are threatened, and in the U.S. and Japanese markets, 43 percent and 33 percent, respectively (table 3.24). The competition Malaysian products confront in the European Union is comparable to what Bangladeshi exporters are encountering, but in the U.S. and Japanese markets, Malaysian producers are under intense pressure, mainly from Chinese producers. Relative to the pressure exerted by Chinese manufacturers, India's exports are less of a threat to Malaysia's exports (see table 3.25). Unlike Bangladesh, Malaysia is subject to intensifying pressures from China and India in the EU and U.S. markets, but competition is diminishing in the Japanese market. This decrease can be explained with reference to

---

[23] As in China, Bangladeshi workers are also demanding higher minimum wages ("China: New Generation" 2010).

Table 3.23 **The Degree of Competition between Bangladeshi and Indian Exports**
percent

	Country/region	1990–91	2000–01	2006–07
Direct threat (%)	EU15	13.0	26.4	22.0
Partial threat (%)	EU15	22.2	21.9	21.3
Total (%)	EU15	35.2	48.3	43.3
Direct threat (%)	Japan	8.2	7.3	3.4
Partial threat (%)	Japan	7.1	5.3	3.3
Total (%)	Japan	15.3	12.6	6.7
Direct threat (%)	U.S.	20.7*	14.9	7.6
Partial threat (%)	U.S.	16.1*	7.5	6.5
Total (%)	U.S.	36.8*	22.4	14.1

Source: Authors' calculation. Data are from the UN Comtrade database.
Note: * = 1991–92.

Table 3.24 **The Degree of Competition between Malaysian and Chinese Exports**
percent

	Country/region	1990–91	2000–01	2006–07
Direct threat	EU15	10.0	28.6	35.7
Partial threat	EU15	12.9	22.2	33.7
Total	EU15	22.9	50.8	69.4
Direct threat	Japan	8.3	22.9	19.3
Partial threat	Japan	10.0	12.7	14.1
Total	Japan	18.3	35.6	33.4
Direct threat	U.S.	12.7*	20.0	22.4
Partial threat	U.S.	11.8*	15.5	20.2
Total	U.S.	24.5*	35.5	42.6

Source: Authors' calculation. Data are from the UN Comtrade database.
Note: * = 1991–92.

Malaysia's place in the production network spanning East Asia. Malaysia is transitioning from being a final assembler to becoming a supplier of intermediate products[24] within East Asia, to networks associated with Japanese multinational corporations (MNCs).

---

[24]Rising costs of production in Malaysia are responsible for this shift away from assembly (see Yusuf and Nabeshima 2009).

Table 3.25   The Degree of Competition between Malaysian and Indian Exports
percent

	Country/region	1990–91	2000–01	2006–07
Direct threat	EU15	7.5	23.6	29.0
Partial threat	EU15	7.8	16.1	20.3
Total	EU15	15.3	39.7	49.3
Direct threat	Japan	6.5	15.8	15.7
Partial threat	Japan	9.2	10.4	9.8
Total	Japan	15.7	26.2	25.5
Direct threat	U.S.	10.3*	16.4	15.4
Partial threat	U.S.	8.0*	8.5	11.6
Total	U.S.	18.3*	24.9	27.0

Source: Authors' calculation. Data are from the UN Comtrade database.
Note: * = 1991–92.

Among the three country income groupings (low, middle, and high), higher-income countries are exposed to the most competitive pressure from China and India. Korea, for instance, faces competitive pressure from China in 93 percent of the products that it exports to the EU market. Corresponding figures for the Japanese and U.S. markets are 69 percent and 78 percent, respectively (see table 3.26). Even India, which is by no means in the same league as China, is starting to exert pressure on Korea in all three major markets; the E.U. market is the one most contested, followed by the U.S. and Japanese markets (see table 3.27). And the evidence suggests that Korean manufacturers will have more to worry about from their competitors in China and India in the future.

Competition faced by exporters from high-income East Asian countries is intensifying in the EU market and, to a lesser extent, in the U.S. market. Many MNCs from Western and East Asian economies now produce and export similar products from China—as well as from other Southeast Asian economies—to the EU15. For example, MNCs in Malaysia and China are both exporting to the EU15 market. Similarly, the competition in the United States is most likely competition among MNCs located in East Asia.[25]

Close inspection of the data reveals that Korea is facing direct competition from India mainly in textiles, garments, and footwear (LT1); other low-technology

---

[25] In this, we include indigenous MNCs located in their own country, such as Samsung in Korea. For instance, the degree of competition between Korea and China can be high in television sets in the EU or U.S. market because of the exports by Samsung in Korea and Sony in China, or when Samsung in Korea exports higher-quality products and Samsung in China exports similar lower-quality products to the same market.

Table 3.26 **The Degree of Competition between Korean and Chinese Exports**
percent

	Country/region	1990–91	2000–01	2006–07
Direct threat	EU15	29.2	43.0	51.0
Partial threat	EU15	21.6	26.8	42.4
Total	EU15	50.8	69.8	93.4
Direct threat	Japan	39.8	46.4	46.7
Partial threat	Japan	20.0	23.3	22.4
Total	Japan	59.8	69.7	69.1
Direct threat	U.S.	39.2*	38.4	47.3
Partial threat	U.S.	18.5*	27.3	30.9
Total	U.S.	57.7*	65.7	78.2

Source: Authors' calculation. Data are from the UN Comtrade database.
Note: * = 1991–92.

Table 3.27 **The Degree of Competition between Korean and Indian Exports**
percent

	Country/region	1990–91	2000–01	2006–07
Direct threat	EU15	21.9	37.8	40.7
Partial threat	EU15	16.1	18.6	26.2
Total	EU15	38.0	56.4	66.9
Direct threat	Japan	30.4	34.9	36.8
Partial threat	Japan	21.9	22.8	20.7
Total	Japan	52.3	57.7	57.5
Direct threat	U.S.	31.2*	32.2	36.4
Partial threat	U.S.	15.7*	17.7	17.7
Total	U.S.	46.9*	49.9	54.1

Source: Authors' calculation. Data are from the UN Comtrade database.
Note: * = 1991–92.

products (LT2); process industry (MT2); and engineering products (MT3) (see figure 3.11). Similarly, Korea is facing partial threat from India in primary products (PP) and resource-based products (RB2) in addition to the goods facing direct threat (see figure 3.12). To a certain degree, facing more competition from India in the light manufactures is understandable, given the fact that Korea's comparative advantage is shifting away from them. What could be more troublesome in the future is the competition in the medium-tech products. While Korea is not threatened by India in the automotive sector (MT1), it is starting to feel the pressure in other medium-tech products, reflecting the emerging comparative advantage of India in these areas.

Figure 3.11   Trends in Direct Threat Faced by the Republic of Korea in EU15 Market from India

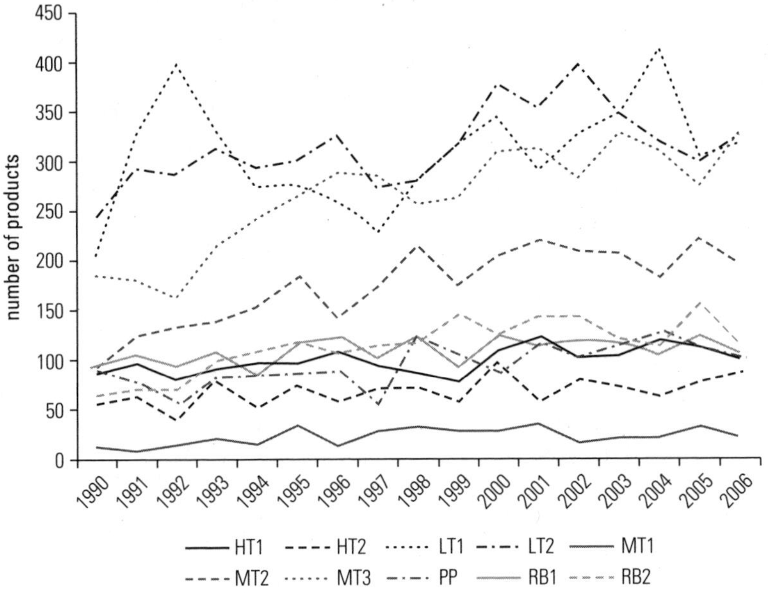

Source: Authors' calculation. Technology classification is based on Lall (2000).
Note: The vertical axis measures the number of products at the 6-digit level. See the note to table 3.2.

The preceding analysis suggests that China and India will remain competitive producers of labor-intensive light manufactures, as well as assembled or processed medium- and high-tech manufactures for which market share depends upon price competitiveness (although other factors also count). For the next decade and beyond, both countries will benefit from a relatively elastic supply of rural labor for labor-intensive manufacturing. It is worth noting that because of ongoing capital- and skill-based technological change, manufacturing is absorbing small numbers of workers, and new technologies are skill biased. Hence, it is unlikely that the anticipated growth in manufacturing activities in China will absorb more than a small fraction of the workforce, and—except in one or two urban regions such as the Pearl River Delta—labor demand from the manufacturing sector will not be driving the wages of semiskilled or unskilled workers. In India also, employment in manufacturing will most likely peak at between 25 percent and 30 percent of GDP and involve a smaller fraction of the labor force, assuming (somewhat optimistically) that industry is the leading sector with double-digit growth rates over the next two decades. The scope for productivity gains in all manufacturing activities (which are between 40 and 60 percent of U.S. levels),

Figure 3.12 Trends in Partial Threat Faced by the Republic of Korea in EU15 Market from India

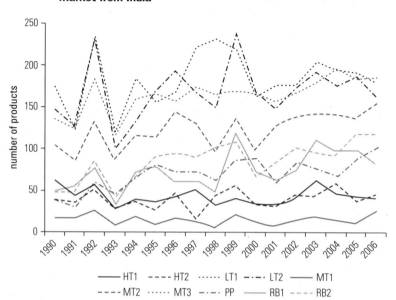

Source: Authors' calculation. Technology classification is based on Lall (2000).
Note: The vertical axis measures the number of products at the 6-digit level. See the note to table 3.2.

including labor-intensive ones, means that both countries would be able to accommodate rising wages without compromising their competitiveness relative to other Asian countries (barring unforeseen changes in exchange rates).[26]

Comparative advantage in cost-sensitive manufacturing will be complemented in India and China by continuous diversification into technology, skill- and design-intensive products, and product differentiation in a variety of product groups. Peter Schott has shown that China's exports already span the entire spectrum of products traded by the OECD countries (Schott 2006). The only difference is that, on average, the unit value of China's exports is less because many of the products are of lower quality (see Edwards and Lawrence 2010), although this finding has been questioned (see Feenstra and Wei 2010; Wang and Wei 2010). Overall, China will lead; but India also is poised to become an active competitor in the automotive, engineering, and resource-based industries.

---

[26]An appreciation of China's real effective exchange rate would most directly affect the fortunes of its labor-intensive exports—in particular, clothing, footwear, and furniture, all of which have been stimulated in recent years by the depreciation of the renminbi with

(*continued on next page*)

Prospects for Export Diversification

Export diversification to enhance revenue growth and profitability is an important objective for developing countries. A number of studies show that countries with a narrow range of exports typically experience slower overall growth (Hesse 2009; Lederman and Maloney 2009).[27] Methodologies developed by Hausmann and Klinger (2006) and Hausmann, Hwang, and Rodrik (2007) enable us to map a country's potential for progressing up the value chain and identify the scope for product diversification. By comparing the product maps for China and India with those of other countries, it is possible to take the analysis of evolving competitive advantage of Asian countries vis-à-vis China and India a step further. Their methodology assumes that each commodity produced gives rise to specific opportunities for future diversification based on its technological complexity and its input-output relationships. That is, some products offer easier (and multiple) diversification paths to related products compared with others. In general, primary and resource-based products offer fewer opportunities for diversification. Manufactured goods—such as electronics and auto parts—generate skills, technological competencies, and assets that are similar to those required for the production of other manufacturing commodities; hence, they are classified as high-value products. Thus, the product space–mapping technique notionally identifies the potential diversification opportunities arising from each of a country's exports.[28] The

---

(*continued from previous page*)

respect to the euro. As the European Union is a major exporter of products in each of these categories, China's enhanced competitive position has tended to crowd out European exports. An appreciation of the renminbi, while arguably constraining low-value, labor-intensive exports, would most likely induce Chinese producers to emphasize high-value items. Furthermore, the implications even for the low-end exports of light manufactures by China will depend upon how the exchange rates of its Asian competitors adjust relative to the renminbi. That China will lose its advantage in certain types of apparel and footwear is by no means a given (Thorbecke and Zhang 2009).

[27]Lederman and Maloney (2009) find that it is not the dependence on resource-based exports (such as oil) that is detrimental per se, but the concentration of such commodities in the export basket.

[28]Brenton, Pierola, and von Uexkull (2009) find that while developing countries search for and discover new exports and new overseas markets, they struggle to sustain exports, and many of them exit these new export markets quickly. They offer a number of reasons as to why this is the case, such as the higher-than-expected fixed costs of exporting, high search costs of potential buyers (or suppliers from the importing countries' point of view), and erratic business climate and policy inconsistency. Their analysis suggests that exporters starting out with large export volumes have a higher probability of surviving. This suggests that larger firms have better prospects when it comes to exporting than small firms. In addition, an existing trading relationship between the exporting and importing

(*continued on next page*)

measure of each commodity's density gives the probability that a country will export two separate goods, conditional on its already exporting at least one of the goods. The more a country specializes in high-value goods (with the highest densities), the greater is its potential for diversification into other high-value products. The x-axis is the inverse of the density (that is, a value closer to the origin indicates higher density); the y-axis measures the difference between PRODY and EXPY. PRODY is a measure calculated by taking a weighted average of the GDP per capita of countries exporting that product; the underlying assumption is that products exported mainly by high-income countries are of higher quality and more sophisticated technology. EXPY is calculated as a weighted sum of PRODY and signifies the sophistication of a country's export basket. Table 3.28 lists the changes in EXPY for selected economies in East and South Asia. It shows that middle-income countries in East Asia and China doubled their EXPY over a period of 20 years, and the average level of sophistication of their exports is approaching that of high-income countries in East Asia. Relative to East Asia, the average sophistication of exports from countries in South Asia is lower, although Bangladesh was able to increase the sophistication of its exports faster than many others starting from the lowest base. Pakistan, by comparison, has upgraded the least. The difference between PRODY and EXPY signifies whether a commodity is an "upgrade"; that is, a positive difference means "upgrading" in the sense of exporting more sophisticated commodities relative to the overall export basket.

Figures 3.13 and 3.14 show the product spaces for China in 1987 and 2006, respectively. In 20 years, China has significantly expanded its production capabilities and export competitiveness and, compared to the product mix in 1987, there are more commodities located closer to the origin (signifying ease of diversifying), with approximately half of all products classified as "upgrades."

Similarly, India's product mix has shifted closer to the origin, and the distribution of products tightened between 1987 and 2006, suggesting that India also is strengthening its manufacturing capabilities (see figures 3.15 and 3.16).

Upon closer inspection of the products in China's export basket with the highest densities that are upgrades, the degree of China's rapid industrial progress becomes clear. In 1987, the top 10 commodities with the highest densities (implying more sophistication) were mainly low-tech items offering minimal opportunities for diversification (see table 3.29). By 2006, the composition of the high-density products had altered radically. China was now presented with

---

(*continued from previous page*)
countries is conducive to sustaining exporting activities. However, it is still the case that developing countries export to fewer countries compared to developed countries, and that much of export growth comes from intensive margin (increase in exports to existing markets) (Brenton and Newfarmer 2009).

Table 3.28   EXPY by Economy

Exporter	1980	1985	1990	1995	2000	2006
Bangladesh	1,483	2,772	3,347	4,097	3,773	5,927
China	—	5,009	8,231	8,152	9,296	11,743
Indonesia	4,897	4,721	6,481	6,242	8,543	8,291
India	5,783	6,337	7,028	6,335	6,694	9,329
Japan	14,019	14,689	14,449	12,842	13,484	14,532
Korea	9,803	10,180	10,258	10,557	11,681	13,719
Malaysia	4,433	5,137	7,912	9,577	10,875	11,897
Pakistan	—	4,181	4,084	3,944	4,480	5,323
Philippines	5,242	5,093	6,317	7,457	11,297	11,813
Singapore	8,311	9,113	11,248	12,449	12,912	15,079
Thailand	4,954	5,673	7,660	8,559	9,666	11,099
Taiwan, China	—	—	10,874	11,107	12,364	14,481
Vietnam	—	—	—	—	5,806	7,190
Sri Lanka[a]	2,888	3,423	4,261	4,561	4,749	5,148

Source: Authors' calculations
a. Data are for 1980, 1985, 1990, 1994, 1999, and 2005.
Note: — = not available

Figure 3.13   Product Space of China, 1987

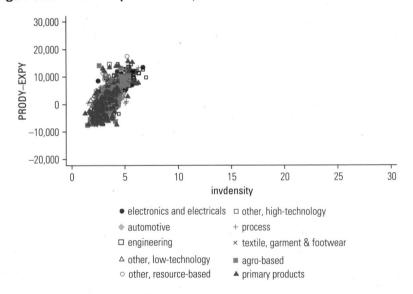

Source: Authors' calculations based on UN Comtrade data.

Figure 3.14   Product Space of China, 2006

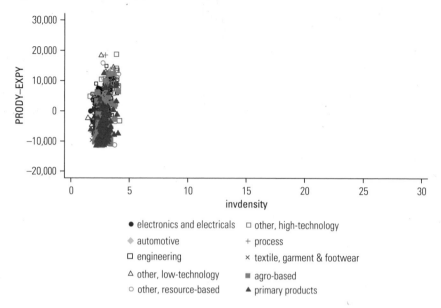

Source: Authors' calculations based on UN Comtrade data.

Figure 3.15   Product Space of India, 1987

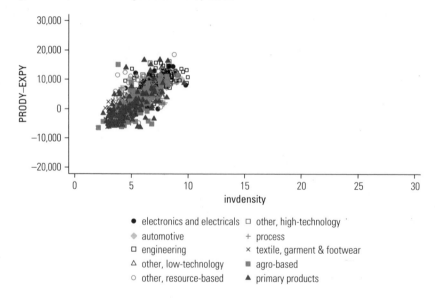

Source: Authors' calculations based on UN Comtrade data.

Figure 3.16   Product Space of India, 2006

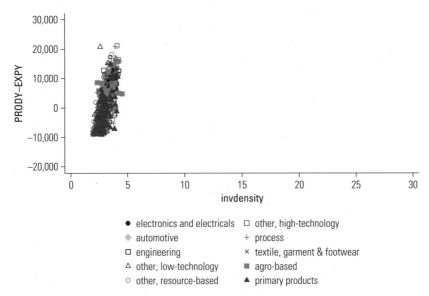

Source: Authors' calculations based on UN Comtrade data.

Table 3.29   Top 10 "Upscale" Commodities with the Highest Density in China, 1987

Short description	Density	Technology class	PRODY–EXPY
Pyrotechnic articles	0.655046	MT2	451
Manufactured goods, N.E.S.	0.558615	LT2	1,325
Children's toys, indoor games, etc.	0.474168	LT2	3,163
Traveling rugs, blankets (nonelectric), not knitted or crocheted	0.461357	LT1	1,934
Umbrellas, canes, and similar articles, and parts thereof	0.458874	LT2	891
Base metal domestic articles, N.E.S., and parts thereof, N.E.S.	0.455813	LT2	981
Other materials of animal origin, N.E.S.	0.451113	PP	447
Fabrics, woven, of sheep's or lambs' wool or of fine hair, N.E.S.	0.449691	LT1	4,309
Soybeans	0.439272	PP	534
Hydrocarbon derivatives, nonhalogenated	0.436489	RB2	4,983

Source: Authors' calculations based on UN Comtrade data. Technology classification is based on Lall (2000).
Note: See the note to table 3.2.

opportunities for upgrading into far more technologically advanced products with greater market prospects, and a higher potential for increased sophistication (see table 3.30). Thus, China's capacity to compete with higher-income countries was growing.

Table 3.30 **Top 10 "Upscale" Commodities with the Highest Density in China, 2006**

Short description	Density	Technology class	PRODY–EXPY
Optical instruments and apparatus	0.607906	HT2	4,818
Portable radio receivers	0.542989	MT3	5,612
Children's toys, indoor games, etc.	0.528838	LT2	4,149
Other radio receivers	0.525168	MT3	3,470
Printed circuits, and parts thereof, N.E.S.	0.523646	MT3	3,574
Knitted, not elastic or rubberized, of fibers other than synthetic	0.510308	LT1	1,775
Pins, needles, etc. of iron or steel; metal fittings for clothing	0.509124	LT2	219
Peripheral units, including control and adapting units	0.506912	HT1	506
Fabrics, woven, of continuous synthetic textile materials	0.497133	MT2	2,840
Pearls, not mounted, set, or strung	0.49101	RB2	5,397

Source: Authors' calculations based on UN Comtrade data. Technology classification is based on Lall (2000).
Note: See the note to table 3.2.

The baseline for India was lower; however, it too is on an ascending trend. In 1987, India could easily upgrade only into low-tech products, mainly garments (see table 3.31). By 2006, the composition of products within reach included more medium-tech, textile, engineering, and resource-based items (see table 3.32), enabling India to eventually compete across a broader range of products.

Role of FDI and Processing Trade

An important facet of China's industrialization and its trade relates to the contribution of FDI in building its processing and assembly activities. These are mostly located in special industrial zones or technology parks that provide access to serviced land and a variety of incentives. Table 3.33 shows how the stock of FDI in China between 1990 and 2008 rose from $20 billion to $378 billion. Figure 3.17 compares China with other East Asian countries. Although the increase is breathtaking, a careful analysis suggests that China's share of FDI is not unusually large, given its market size and the low base from which it started. Relatively little FDI was diverted to China from elsewhere in East Asia (Eichengreen and Tong 2005).[29]

---

[29]Branstetter and Foley (2007) find that FDI in China by American MNCs was not displacing investment elsewhere; instead firms increasing investment in China were also raising employment in other places.

Table 3.31   Top 10 "Upscale" Commodities with the Highest Density in India, 1987

Short description	Density	Technology class	PRODY–EXPY
Undergarments of textile fabrics, not knitted or crocheted; men's, boys' undergarments other than shirts	0.36857	LT1	221
Kelem, Schumacks, and Karamanie rugs and the like	0.334449	LT1	2,450
Outerwear, knitted or crocheted, not elastic or rubberized; jerseys, pullovers, slipovers, cardigans, etc.	0.33149	LT1	597
Other materials of animal origin, N.E.S.	0.299071	PP	1,443
Traveling rugs, blankets (nonelectric), not knitted or crocheted	0.297307	LT1	2,930
Base metal domestic articles, N.E.S., and parts thereof, N.E.S.	0.291553	LT2	1,977
Sheep- and lambskin leather	0.287327	LT1	729
Other natural abrasives	0.283956	PP	4,902
Women's, girls,' infants outerwear, textile, not knitted or crocheted; coats and jackets	0.28179	LT1	197
Hydrocarbon derivatives, nonhalogenated	0.276444	RB2	5,979

Source: Authors' calculations based on UN Comtrade data. Technology classification is based on Lall (2000).
Note: See the note to table 3.2.

Table 3.32   Top 10 "Upscale" Commodities with the Highest Density in India, 2006

Short description	Density	Technology class	PRODY–EXPY
Iron ore and concentrates, not agglomerated	0.456043	RB2	1,843
Fabrics, woven, of continuous synthetic textile materials	0.433029	MT2	5,254
Crustaceans and mollusks, prepared or not prepared, N.E.S.	0.430432	RB1	8,600
Outerwear, knitted or crocheted, not elastic or rubberized; jerseys, pullovers, slipovers, cardigans, etc.	0.42895	LT1	861
Yarn, 85% synthetic fibers, not for retail; monofil, strip, etc.	0.412938	LT1	835
Discontinuous synthetic fibers, not carded or combed	0.410214	MT2	1,108
Tires, pneumatic, new, for motorcycles and bicycles	0.409602	RB1	5,753
Coal gas, water gas, and similar gases	0.409145	PP	1,837
Machinery for the grain milling industry; working cereals, parts	0.409017	MT3	5,143
Tulle, lace, embroidery, ribbons, trimmings, and other small wares	0.407986	LT1	702

Source: Authors' calculations based on UN Comtrade data. Technology classification is based on Lall (2000).
Note: See the note to table 3.2.

Table 3.33 Inward FDI

Country/economy	1980	1990	2000	2008
Hong Kong, China	177,755.3	201,652.9	455,469.0	835,764.0
China	1,074.0	20,690.6	193,348.0	378,083.0
Singapore	5,350.7	30,468.0	110,570.3	326,142.4
Japan	3,270.0	9,850.0	50,322.0	203,371.9
India	451.8	1,656.8	17,517.1	123,288.0
Thailand	980.6	8,242.2	29,915.0	104,849.5
Korea, Rep.	1,138.6	5,185.6	38,109.8	90,693.0
Malaysia	5,168.7	10,318.0	52,747.5	73,262.1
Indonesia	—	—	—	67,044.0
Vietnam	1,415.7	1,649.6	20,595.6	48,325.3
Taiwan, China	2,405.0	9,735.0	19,521.0	45,458.0
Pakistan	691.3	1,891.7	6,918.6	31,059.0
Philippines	914.2	4,528.2	18,156.2	21,470.0
Bangladesh	461.1	477.5	2,162.0	4,817.0
Sri Lanka	230.5	679.3	1,596.2	4,282.6

Source: UNCTAD.
Note: — = not available

Many of the manufacturing activities that have migrated from the advanced industrial countries to East and Southeast Asia are labor-intensive, low-value-added activities. China has been a major attractor of such migratory activities since the 1980s, and its processed exports have risen steeply. By 1992, 47 percent of total commodity exports were processed goods, mostly low-tech, such as textiles, leather goods, and toys. Processed exports climbed to a peak of 57 percent in 1997 before falling to 53 percent in 2007. However, during this period the composition of the exports changed; electronics parts, office equipment, computers, and telecommunications equipment displaced some of the low-tech light manufactures. Processed exports generated demand for imports of raw materials and intermediate products. These peaked at 49 percent in 1998 before settling at 41 percent in 2007. Trade in processed goods (exports plus imports) in 2007 accounted for 45 percent of total trade (see table 3.34). It is the processing industry in China that has been responsible for much of the export growth from Southeast Asian countries.

Foreign-invested enterprises inevitably dominate the processing trade, accounting for 55 percent of imports and approximately the same share of exports, but Chinese producers are rising fast. Indigenous firms in particular are making determined efforts to upgrade their products and raise the domestic share

Figure 3.17   East Asia Inward FDI

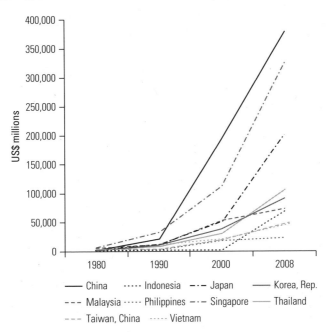

Source: UNCTAD.

Table 3.34   Share and Value of Trade by Customs Regime, China, 2007

Customs regime	Share (%)	Total value (US$ 100 millions)
Processing	45.4	9,860.36
Ordinary	44.5	9,670.69
Other	10.1	2,206.21

Source: National Statistical Bureau of China 2008.

of value added. This ongoing effort to break out of the "processing" end of the value chain and to design and produce more complex items domestically is reflected in the findings from the product space analysis and from the trends in intra-industry trade noted in chapter 2. A few Chinese firms such as Huawei, BYD, Geely, ZTE, CIMC, and Wanxiang are also building the potential to innovate through in-house research, supplemented by collaboration and the acquisition of technology from providers throughout the world, taking full advantage of the 'open innovation' system that spans the globe.

The preceding empirical rendition of the manufacturing and trading sectors casts light on how recent trends in capacity building and the acquisition of capabilities are shaping industrial development and the international competitiveness of China and India. Although some observers hold the view that services deserve more attention—and that the weaknesses of the financial sector undermine allocative efficiency and threaten macroeconomic stability—we maintain that lower- and middle-income countries must give primacy to the real sector, and that a premature financialization of an economy can be disadvantageous for growth. Advanced economies might also be forced to reconsider their own growth strategies, which lately have leaned heavily on finance, real estate, and business and IT-related services, to the neglect of manufacturing.[30]

What we surmise from these results is that China has constructed an exceedingly broad manufacturing base. With the help of FDI, it has built up a strong competitive advantage in the processing industries, ranging from textiles to electronics to chemicals to pharmaceuticals. It has embarked on the process of industrial deepening and is achieving mastery in the design and production of complex capital goods and high-tech components. This will help raise domestic value added as well as the returns from exporting. This stage could take a decade or more, but it is a necessary achievement if China is to realize its ambition to become a world-class industrial nation combining sophisticated manufacturing with innovation capabilities. How China is attempting to achieve these objectives—and the implications for other Asian countries—is the topic of chapter 5. This could ratchet up the pressure on other Asian countries, which thus far have been able to sustain an uneasy symbiosis with China in the sphere of global trade. We will discuss this in the following chapter.

India's industrial base is smaller and narrower, and this is partly because India attracted only a trickle of FDI until almost 2000. Between 2000 and 2008, FDI rose dramatically and far in excess of investment in other South Asian countries (see table 3.33 and figure 3.18). As observed earlier, India is less export oriented, and the bulk of its exports are primary products or low-tech manufactures. However, the Indian industrial establishment also includes firms that can boast manufacturing excellence in the engineering, automotive, petrochemical, pharmaceutical, green energy, and ferrous metal industries (Kumar 2009). There is a vast scope for industrialization in India, and the domestic market potentially can soak up a major chunk of the growth in output. If past experience of manufacturing development is a guide, however, India's future industrialization will be a function of exports—not only of engineering and resource-based products, but also of light and processed manufactures as with China. The likelihood of this in

---

[30]There is an increasing awareness in the United States and the United Kingdom that the declining role of manufacturing and the salience of services may have gone too far and that some reversal is desirable in the interests of rebalancing, growth, and employment.

Figure 3.18 South Asia Inward FDI

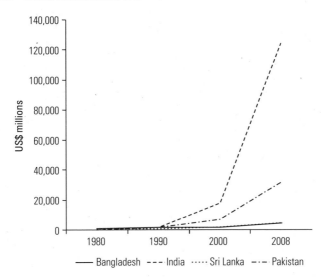

Source: UNCTAD.

view of the slower growth of the U.S. and EU markets and the implications for the rest of Asia are covered in chapter 5.

India has a processing industry as well, but it is largely homegrown because very little FDI flowed into export-oriented light manufacturing and, until recently, virtually none found its way into medium- and high-tech activities. Primarily for this reason, India's imports of raw material and of parts and components for processing are far smaller than China's, and domestic value added in light manufacturing is higher. This situation will change if there is another surge of FDI, but at present it appears that this is not in the cards. It would take a decade or more to create a processing sector on the scale of China's, even if India should attempt to do so, MNCs were prepared to invest, and the global economy could absorb this additional capacity.

China and India as Importers

A focus on exports needs to be complemented by a closer look at China and India's imports. Imports must be given due consideration for a number of important reasons. Although mercantilist policies are attractive to governments of industrializing countries pursuing export-led growth, globally trade must balance. Exports must equal imports. The trade surpluses of some countries must be offset by the deficits of others. That is, if some countries consume more than they produce, others must consume less. A few countries, including China, could run large export surpluses because the United States could consume far more than it produces and could accumulate huge deficits by virtue of its unique status as the supplier of a reserve currency, the attractiveness of U.S. government paper as a gilt-edged, interest-bearing store of value, and the scale and liquidity of its financial system. Other, less fortunate countries cannot do so—and looking ahead, the United States will also be forced to adjust, and its adjustment will reverberate through the global trading system. But to return to China and India, sustaining the demand for their exports has depended in part on the volume of their imports from other countries, especially their neighbors in Asia. The rising intraregional trade reported in table 3.1 vividly underscores the increasing interdependence in the region and the importance of China and Japan in the regional trading regime.

This multiplying of trade linkages, which has been mutually fruitful for the countries in the East Asian region more than in South Asia, has been significantly facilitated by the dismantling of trade barriers as a result of the Uruguay (and earlier) Rounds[31] and the free trade agreements (FTAs) that proliferated starting in the mid-1990s (Desker 2004; "Free Trade Pacts" 2006; "Asia: Bilateralism to Trump 'Alphabet Soup' Diplomacy" 2010). Falling tariff and nontariff barriers, by further promoting production networking in Asia, pushed the growth of trade to double-digit rates between 1995 and 2007. The expanding appetite for imports—not just in the United States, but in the EU and Asia as well—is the flip side of the export-led growth phenomenon for which East Asia is famous.

Imports have a wider economic significance that is sometimes obscured by the emphasis given to exports. A part of China's technological progress and rising productivity is traceable to its greater openness relative to India. Imports of plant and equipment are the leading channel for transferring technology to late-industrializing countries.[32] Of course, importers have to learn how to use the technology, but that is the easy part; the hard work of inventing, innovating, developing, testing, debugging, refining, and codifying is mostly already done. Imports are one of the keys to catching up to the leaders and compressing the stages of development. Some countries have been more adept at extracting the growth potential from imports by deepening their manufacturing capability through more effective business leadership, organizational skills, and human capital; but in principle, the lever of imports has been available to all comers. In this respect, China and other East Asian countries are the stars, and South Asian countries the laggards.

Imports do more than just transfer codified technologies; they also diffuse the findings of research and upgrade technology in the importing countries

---

[31]Following the signing of the General Agreement on Tariffs and Trade in 1948, the eight rounds of trade negotiations reduced the average tariff level on industrial products levied by industrial countries from 40 percent to 4 percent and contributed to the gains in trade related globalization (Baldwin 2010).

[32]See Ding and Knight (2008) on the contribution of imports to China's growth.

(Coe, Helpman, and Hoffmaister 2008). This confers two advantages: it can enhance productivity if the new technology is fully utilized through local adaptation and the effort of assimilation; and when it brings a country closer to the technological frontier, this raises the returns to domestic R&D—which in turn feeds productivity down the road.[33] How best to access R&D via imports, and from which countries, continues to be debated. Current evidence suggests that imports are an effective mechanism of research and development (R&D) transfer from the United States, but not necessarily from other countries. From Germany, for example, FDI is a more efficacious means of achieving such a transfer.

The transformative power of imports does not stop here. By exposing domestic producers to competition from imports, a country can initiate a cycle of productivity enhancement and innovation. Firms that can compete survive and grow. Less productive and technologically weaker firms are driven out of business. Apart from raising the average level of productivity for industries subjected to competition, this also frees up resources to be absorbed by activities generating higher returns (Lawrence and Weinstein 2001). Imports also identify opportunities for local producers by delineating markets. This challenges firms to go the extra mile by inventing better substitutes through a careful analysis of the imports, their clientele, and the requirements of that clientele.

Having made the case for imports, it is important to temper it with a dose of East Asian experience. Borrowing from infant industry–strategic trade theories, the success stories in the region, including China, have proven to be selective in liberalizing imports—preferring to start with capital equipment, intermediate products, and raw materials, which fueled their industrial development but did not compete against nascent domestic firms. It was only when domestic industries were demonstrating their competitiveness that tariff and, even more critically, nontariff barriers were scaled down (see figure 2.13, figure 3.19, and figure 3.20) (see Amsden 1989; Chang 2003). What differentiates the East Asian economies from the South Asian economies is the speed with which they were able to develop a competitive export sector. This helped diffuse manufacturing skills through to the rest of the economy and bolstered productivity throughout the industrial system.

China and India are both large countries, and their size creates the conditions for industries that can span the entire spectrum. China already exports a diverse basket of goods, similar to other large advanced countries. India, with a less developed manufacturing industry, exports a much narrower range of goods; but in the future, it is not inconceivable that India will start to export a

---

[33] Aghion (2006) shows that R&D intensity increases the closer an industry is to the technological frontiers, because once the gains from catching up are nearing exhaustion, one's own innovation becomes increasingly important as the basis for competitiveness and profitability.

Figure 3.19 Average Tariff Rates, East Asia

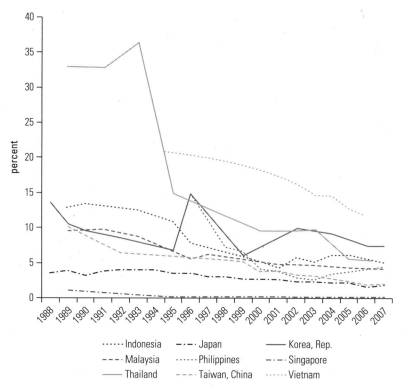

Source: UN Comtrade.

variety of products similar to the case for China. Although no country can have comparative advantages in all the products it exports, the integration of these two large economies into the global trade will exert substantial pressures on other countries.

Indeed, the review of the recent trade performance of China and India in this chapter showed that it is in fact putting pressure on other countries in Asia. China's impact is felt most in the U.S. and Japanese markets, while India's presence is more pronounced in the EU15 and U.S. markets. In addition, China and India are still at intermediate stages of development in terms of their domestic manufacturing capabilities, although China is well ahead of India in this regard. Both are investing heavily in infrastructure and manufacturing capabilities. This domestic investment is complemented by a large inflow of FDI. Even as they ramp up their manufacturing output, China and India could maintain their cost

Figure 3.20   Average Tariff Rates, South Asia

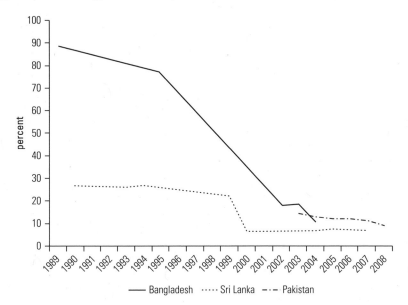

Source: UN Comtrade.

competitiveness for a few more decades, owing to the ample supply of unskilled and semiskilled workers[34] and the increased productivity that would partially mitigate the potential rise in wages.

So far, countries in Asia have been able to cope with the emergence of these two giants. East Asian economies had a head start, and they have used their participation in the global production network judiciously to accommodate the rise of China. These economies in East Asia are key network participants in many industrial products. Economies in South Asia were less prepared for the rise of China and India, but they are holding their ground in their traditional low-skill manufactured and resource-based products so far. However, what about the future, when China and India have deepened manufacturing capabilities sufficiently to span the entire product chain domestically? Which manufactured goods offer the best prospects for these economies in Asia to sustain their export momentum? These are the questions that we explore in the next chapter.

---

[34]Half of China's workforce and two-thirds of India's are largely engaged in rural production activities, and at least half or more of these workers will be available for urban-industrial employment.

References

Aghion, Philippe. 2006. "A Primer on Innovation and Growth." Bruegel Policy Brief, Brussels, June.

Amsden, Alice H. 1989. *Asia's Next Giant: South Korea and Late Industrialization.* New York and Oxford: Oxford University Press.

"Asia: Bilateralism to Trump 'Alphabet Soup' Diplomacy." 2010. *Oxford Analytica,* January 7.

ADB (Asian Development Bank). 2009. *Asian Development Outlook 2009: Rebalancing Asia's Growth.* Mandaluyong City, Philippines: ADB.

Baldwin, Robert E. 2010. "The World Trading System Without American Leadership." VoxEU.org.

Bloom, Nicholas, and John Van Reenen. 2010. "Why Do Management Practices Differ across Firms and Countries?" *Journal of Economic Perspectives* 24(1): 203–24.

Branstetter, Lee, and C. Fritz Foley. 2007. "Facts and Fallacies about U.S. FDI in China." NBER Working Paper 13470. National Bureau of Economic Research, Cambridge, MA.

Brenton, Paul, and Richard Newfarmer. 2009. "Watching More Than the Discovery Channel: Export Cycles and Diversification in Development." In *Breaking into New Markets: Emerging Lessons for Export Diversification,* ed. Richard Newfarmer, William Shaw, and Peter Walkenhorst, 111–24. Washington, DC: World Bank.

Brenton, Paul, Martha Denisse Pierola, and Erik von Uexkull. 2009. "The Life and Death of Trade Flows: Understanding the Survival Rates of Developing-Country Exporters." In *Breaking into New Markets: Emerging Lessons for Export Diversification,* ed. Richard Newfarmer, William Shaw, and Peter Walkenhorst, 127–44. Washington, DC: World Bank.

Brülhart, Marius. 2009. "An Account of Global Intra-Industry Trade, 1962–2006." *World Economy* 32(3): 401–59.

Ceglowski, Janet, and Stephen Golub. 2007. "Just How Low Are China's Labour Costs?" *World Economy* 30(4): 597–617.

Chang, Ha-Joon. 2003. "Kicking Away the Ladder: Infant Industry Promotion in Historical Perspective." *Oxford Development Studies* 31(1): 21–32.

Cheung, Yin-Wong, and Xingwang Qian. 2009. "The Empirics of China's Outward Direct Investment." CESifo Working Paper 2621, Insitute for Economic Research, Munich, Germany.

"China: New Generation of Labour Makes its Demands." 2010. *Oxford Analytica,* June 25, 2010.

Coe, David T., Elhanan Helpman, and Alexander W. Hoffmaister. 2008. "International R&D Spillovers and Institutions." Working Paper 14069, National Bureau of Economic Research, Cambridge, MA.

Deardorff, Alan V. 2001. "International Provision of Trade Services, Trade, and Fragmentation." Policy Research Working Paper 2548, World Bank, Washington, DC.

Desker, Barry. 2004. "In Defence of FTAs: From Purity to Pragmatism in East Asia." *Pacific Review* 17(1): 3–26.

Ding, Sai, and John Knight. 2008. "Why Has China Grown so Fast? The Role of Structural Change." Economic Series Working Paper 415, University of Oxford, Department of Economics, Oxford, UK.

Edwards, Lawrence, and Robert Z. Lawrence. 2010. "Do Developed and Developing Countries Compete Head to Head in High-Tech?" Working Paper 16105, National Bureau of Economic Research, Cambridge, MA.

Eichengreen, Barry, and Hui Tong. 2005. "Is China's FDI Coming at the Expense of Other Countries?" Working Paper 11335, National Bureau of Economic Research, Cambridge, MA.

Feenstra, Robert C., and Shang Jin Wei. 2010. *China's Growing Role in World Trade.* Chicago: University of Chicago Press.

Gallagher, Kevin P., Juan Carlos Moreno-Brid, and Roberto Porzecanski. 2008. "The Dynamism of Mexican Exports: Lost in (Chinese) Translation?" *World Development* 36(8): 1365–80.

Haltmaier, Jane T., Shaghil Ahmed, Brahima Coulibaly, Ross Knippenberg, Sylvain Leduc, Mario Marazzi, and Beth Anne Wilson. 2007. "The Role of China in Asia: Engine, Conduit, or Steamroller?" International Finance Discussion Paper 904, Board of Governors of the Federal Reserve System, Washington, DC.

Hanson, Gordon H., and Raymond Robertson. 2008. "China and the Manufacturing Exports of Other Developing Countries." Working Paper 14497, National Bureau of Economic Research, Cambridge, MA.

Harney, Alexandra. 2008. *The China Price: The True Cost of Chinese Competitive Advantage.* New York: Penguin Group.

Hausmann, Ricardo, Jason Hwang, and Dani Rodrik. 2007. "What You Export Matters." *Journal of Economic Growth* 12(1): 1–25.

Hausmann, Ricardo, and Bailey Klinger. 2006. *Structural Transformation and Patterns of Comparative Advantage in the Product Space.* Cambridge, MA: Harvard University Center for International Development.

Hesse, Heiko. 2009. "Export Diversification and Economic Growth." In *Breaking into New Markets: Emerging Lessons for Export Diversification,* ed. Richard Newfarmer, William Shaw, and Peter Walkenhorst, 55–80. Washington, DC: World Bank.

Hoekman, Bernard. 2010. "The Doha Round Impasse and the Trading System." *VoxEU.org.*

"International: Free Trade Pacts Are Bad for Business." 2006. *Oxford Analytica,* March 23.

Jorgenson, Dale W., Mun S. Ho, and Kevin J. Stiroh. 2007. "The Sources of Growth of U.S. Industries." In *Productivity in Asia: Economic Growth and Competitiveness,* ed. Dale W. Jorgenson, Masahiro Kuroda, and Kazuyuki Motohashi. Northampton, MA: Edward Elgar Publishing.

Kuijs, Louis. 2010. "China Through 2020: A Macroeconomic Scenario." World Bank China Research Working Paper 9, World Bank, Beijing.

Kumar, Nirmalya. 2009. *India's Global Powerhouses: How They Are Taking On the World.* Boston, MA: Harvard Business Press.

Lall, Sanjaya. 2000. "The Technological Structure and Performance of Developing Country Manufactured Exports, 1985–98." *Oxford Development Studies* 28(3): 337–69.

Lawrence, Robert Z., and David E. Weinstein. 2001. "Trade and Growth: Import-Led or Export-Led? Evidence from Japan and Korea." In *Rethinking the East Asian Miracle,* ed. Joseph E. Stiglitz and Shahid Yusuf. New York: Oxford University Press.

Lederman, Daniel, and William F. Maloney. 2009. "Trade Structure and Growth." In *Breaking into New Markets: Emerging Lessons for Export Diversification,* ed. Richard Newfarmer, William Shaw, and Peter Walkenhorst, 39–54. Washington, DC: World Bank.

Mayer, Thierry. 2007. "The Internationalization of European Firms: New Facts Based on Firm-Level Evidence." EFIM Report, Bruegel, Brussels.

National Statistical Bureau of China. 2008. *China Statistical Yearbook 2008.* Beijing: China Statistics Press.

Ravenhill, John. 2006. "Is China an Economic Threat to Southeast Asia?" *Asian Survey* 46(5): 653–674.

Roland-Holst, David, and John Weiss. 2005. "People's Republic of China and Its Neighbors: Evidence on Regional Trade and Investment Effects." *Asia-Pacific Economic Literature* 19(2): 18–35.

Schott, Peter K. 2006. "The Relative Sophistication of Chinese Exports." Working Paper 12173, National Bureau of Economic Research, Cambridge, MA.

"South-East Asia: Shake-up Looms in Textiles Sector." 2009. *Oxford Analytica,* August 28.

Thorbecke, Willem, and Hanjiang Zhang. 2009. "The Effect of Exchange Rate Changes on China's Labor-Intensive Manufacturing Exports." *Pacific Economic Review* 14(3): 398–409.

Vogel, Ezra. 1979. *Japan as Number One: Lessons for America.* Lincoln, NE: iUniverse .com, Inc.

Wang, Zhi, and Shang Jin Wei. 2010. "What Accounts for the Rising Sophistication of China's Exports?" In *China's Growing Role in World Trade,* ed. Robert C. Feenstra and Shang Jin Wei. Chicago: University of Chicago Press.

Williamson, Peter and Ming Zeng. 2008. "How to Meet China's Cost Innovation Challenge." *Ivey Business Journal* (November/December).

Xing, Yuqing. 2007. "Foreign Direct Investment and China's Bilateral Intra-Industry Trade with Japan and the US." *Journal of Asian Economics* 18(4): 685–700.

Yusuf, Shahid, and Kaoru Nabeshima. 2009. *Tiger Economies under Threat: Comparative Analysis of Malaysia's Industrial Prospects and Policy Options.* Washington, DC: World Bank.

Yusuf, Shahid, and Kaoru Nabeshima. 2010. *Industrial Change in the Bangkok Urban Region.* Washington, DC: World Bank.

Zebregs, Harm. 2004. "Intraregional Trade in Emerging Asia." Policy Discussion Paper PDP/04/1, International Monetary Fund, Washington, DC.

4

Unfolding Industry Dynamics in East and South Asia

Since 2001, developments including the ascent of China, the improved long-term potential of the Indian economy, the growth of intraregional trade in Asia, and the declining share of the United States in the exports of East Asian economies induced many to believe that, in spite of ongoing globalization, the Asian countries were decoupling from the United States. This view gained adherents, although the growth of the U.S. economy and the expanding U.S. trade deficit meant that in 2005 the United States absorbed close to 16 percent of total world imports, against 18.4 percent in 2000 and 14.2 percent in 1995. With more than a third of the global growth contributed by China and India between 2005 and 2007, China came to be viewed as an economic force comparable to the United States. Initial worries that Chinese firms would erode the exports of other Asian countries eased somewhat once other East and Southeast Asian countries found that their exports to China were growing. The threat from China's textile exports following China's accession to the World Trade Organization (WTO) also proved to be less acute than other Asian countries—particularly South Asian ones—had anticipated.[1] China's textile exports rose steeply after 2003, but worldwide demand and product diversification by other exporters enabled firms in Pakistan, Bangladesh, and Sri Lanka to cushion the shock. The emergency protections against Chinese imports provided by the United States and European Union also helped to create some breathing room for these countries. Southeast Asian countries found that they were able to achieve mutually acceptable trading relations with China,

---

[1]Yang (2006) observed that following China's accession to the WTO, China's impact on other Asian countries would be mainly with respect to trade in textiles, garments, and electronics. Writing in 2004, Eichengreen, Rhee, and Tong stated that export competition from China would be strongest in light manufactures and processed commodities. But China's growth would generate strong demand for capital equipment and components from high-income countries, principally Japan, the Republic of Korea, and the United States.

thanks to the intermediation of production networks dominated by multinational corporations (MNCs). While China focused more on final assembly of electronics, electrical engineering, telecommunications, and office equipment,[2] the Southeast Asian countries concentrated on producing and exporting assembled, packaged, and tested electronic components to China. Primary producers such as Malaysia and Indonesia also benefited from the demand for wood products, minerals, and tree crops. Japan, the Republic of Korea, and Taiwan, China, exported capital equipment, high-value components, and transport equipment. All of these countries also gained from the import of low-priced final goods from China, courtesy of China's productivity gains and competitive suppliers.

With the global economy and trade growing by 3.8 and 7.5 percent, respectively, in 2007 (see table 4.1)—rates without precedent—there were few clouds on the horizon, and those few appeared distant. Worries over the subprime mortgage market in the United States, which began surfacing in late 2007 and spread in early 2008, did not dispel the optimism about the basic health of the global economy until almost the middle of 2008. According to a *World Economic Outlook* (WEO) forecast in the summer of 2008, the International Monetary Fund still pegged global growth at 3.7 percent. By the fourth quarter of 2008, when the full magnitude of the global recession became apparent, forecasters quickly realized that their recent projections for 2008 and 2009 were wildly optimistic and based on questionable assumptions.

First and foremost was the convenient assumption that rapid economic growth could be sustained indefinitely by bubbles in key sectors in major economies. Warnings of the threat of asset bubbles had been aired since 2005, but policy makers in Western countries pinned their hopes on the efficiency of markets, capitalized on the benefits, and bravely underplayed the risks—as did financial institutions. Across much of Asia, governments felt confident that they could easily cope with a temporary squall, because in reaction to the crisis of 1997–98, several East Asian countries had accumulated vast reserves of foreign exchange.[3] Most

Table 4.1   Global GDP and Trade Growth
% annual growth

	2004	2005	2006	2007
World GDP	4.1	3.5	4.0	3.8
World trade	10.4	7.8	9.8	7.5
Low- and middle-income countries' GDP	7.5	6.9	7.7	8.1

Source: World Development Indicators Database; World Bank 2009.

---

[2]Steinfeld (2004) refers to the shallow integration of Chinese firms in production networks.
[3]The accumulation of resources by Asian countries which extend credit to foreign buyers to purchase Asian exports raises tradable output and can have a positive effect on productivity gains from technology absorption and learning by doing. However, it has a cost in terms of deferred consumption (Korinek and Serven 2010).

also were comfortable with their macroeconomic circumstances and growth momentum, and downplayed concerns over the likelihood of a major financial meltdown in the United States.

Second, policy makers had lulled themselves into believing that they could gently deflate bubbles and achieve a soft landing with the help of tested policy instruments. The advanced countries were more confident than the industrializing economies because their markets were supposedly deeper, more resilient, and inherently self-equilibrating. Thus, it was widely believed in 2007–08 that the subprime mortgage problem could be contained. When it began to spread and to take on crisis proportions in the United States, other countries continued to pin their hopes on the decoupling hypothesis, underestimating their dependence on trade with the United States and exposure to its financial markets.[4] These convenient assumptions were dashed when the numerous overlapping strands of globalization conveyed and magnified the shock from the U.S. financial markets to the rest of the world—and from financial markets to the real sector, first in the United States and then in the European Union and other industrializing economies. Virtually no country or major sector was spared.

Third, the prominence of the U.S. economy in an integrated world environment was reaffirmed. Other economies such as the European Union, Japan, and China were revealed as having neither the growth momentum, the share of trade, nor the economic weight to serve as an adequate counterweight to the United States.[5] China, with 8 percent of world trade in 2008, was not a large enough player; the European Union, although large, was too enmeshed with the U.S. economy, its own banks far too exposed to U.S. housing and real estate markets and overall too fiscally conservative to play an autonomous role in a strongly countercyclical manner.[6]

Fourth, the contribution of financial development and innovation to efficient allocation of resources, productivity, and growth that had been gaining prominence was abruptly called into question. Suddenly, doubts arose as to whether it was healthy for the U.S. economy to derive 8 percent of GDP and 40 percent of corporate profits from the financial sector. The crisis raised questions as to the allocative capabilities of financial entities and the consequences for economies, both advanced and industrializing, of the increasing concentration of highly talented

---

[4]Clearly, trade and financial decoupling lagged far behind the levels assumed in popular belief and casual empiricism. See Dooley and Hutchison (2009); Eichengreen and others (2009); Kose, Otrok, and Prasad (2008); and Levy-Yeyati (2009).

[5]Moreover, East Asia's export dependency on North America and the EU is high—overall 9 percent of East Asian GDP was dependent on exports to the former and 7.4 percent to the latter (Cohen-Setton and Pisani-Ferry 2008).

[6]This fiscal conservatism was reinforced during 2010 by the crisis that engulfed Greece and imperiled the Euro.

people in privately lucrative financial activities with low or negative social returns that could be contributing to widening income disparities. The United Kingdom had 8 percent of GDP originating in finance, Singapore over 11 percent, China 6 percent, and India over 9 percent; all were suddenly alerted to the ambiguous benefits of financialization and the disutility of making financial development a central plank of their growth strategies.[7]

Fifth, Asia's embracing of production networks came under scrutiny as levels of exports began to implode throughout the region. Production networks have been hailed as vehicles that have promoted intra-industry trade in the East Asian region and the participation of firms throughout the region. Production networks have also been associated with the mobilizing of industrial capabilities in East Asia and with buttressing the success of the export-led strategy. The crisis, however, revealed important vulnerabilities and costs. One vulnerability was that intra-industry trade in parts, components, and raw materials had concealed the persistent heavy reliance on the United States and the European Union (EU) for exports of final products that incorporated these intermediates.[8] Hence, when demand in the United States began to crumble in late 2008, this created a ripple effect through the production networks. A related cost was that the pyramidal system of intra-industry trade meant that when demand for final goods went into reverse, networking magnified the effects for suppliers of parts and services and assembly operations, which are sometimes distributed over a number of countries. Just as production networking and associated intra-industry trade was advantageous in generating flows on the upside of the long boom, it increased the severity of the downturn once the bubble-driven growth had abruptly collapsed. This experience has highlighted the costs of production networking straddling regions and countries.

Production networking is an outcome of legacy and choice. Starting in the 1970s, East Asia's efforts to industrialize coincided with the off-shoring of manufacturing from Western countries, with foreign direct investment (FDI) serving as the vehicle. This created a patchwork of production units across the East Asian region.

---

[7]Economic crises rooted in the financial sector cause such major dislocation for the real sector and for consumers that recovery can be a much slower process (Reinhart and Rogoff 2009). Furthermore, deep crises are associated with a permanent decline in the level of output—including a prolonged slowdown of investment (Blanchard 2009; Cerra and Saxena 2008). The findings of Cerra, Panizza, and Saxena (2009) suggest, though, that targeted countercyclical measures can promote recovery (especially in relatively closed economies)—as is apparent from the rebound of activity in India and China. How durable these are likely to be in the absence of globally coordinated actions will become apparent in due course.

[8]Asian Development Bank (2009). Gaulier, Lemoine, and Unal-Kesenci (2004) observe that $10 of Chinese processed exports incorporated $4 of imports from Japan; Korea; Taiwan, China; and Singapore.

Over time, the picture has changed as evolving comparative advantage, national policies, and shifting objectives of MNCs have weeded out producers in some countries and added them in others. But by and large, first-mover advantages have imparted a certain inertia, reinforced by the efforts of MNCs to maintain a portfolio of production units and exploit localized expertise, cost advantages, and market opportunities, as well as local incentives. This overlapping, multicountry assortment of producers provided MNCs, large retailers in industrial countries, and contractors such as Li and Fung and Wal-Mart with the means to engineer production networks that stoked competition among producers, encouraged innovation and new start-ups, duplicated sources of supply for similar products, and melded production capacity in several countries or regions (Fung, Fung, and Wind 2008).

Sixth and finally, the 2008–09 crisis underscores the autonomous growth potential of late-starting industrializers with very large economies and high rates of saving. The two economies that have demonstrated the greatest resilience (and have partially neutralized the effects of the external shock) are China and India. They grew by 9.1 and 6.8 percent, respectively, in 2009 and are forecast to grow by 8.4 and 8.1 percent during 2010–14 (Kuijs 2010; EIU 2010). Four factors linked to their performance during the past decade or so are enabling them to defy the drag exerted by a slower growing global economy. A large backlog of investment in infrastructure and the prospect of decades of urbanization are two enduring sources of demand. A third is the scope for industrial deepening, technological catch-up, and incorporating green technologies into all relevant activities in China. There is similar scope for building a modern, green industry in India.[9] Raising energy efficiency as infrastructure building and industrial development proceed can only augment the demand for capital. That these investment imperatives can be largely satisfied from domestic resources confers a fourth significant advantage and greatly reduces dependence on foreign providers. China's low public indebtedness also facilitates expansion of public investment. India, which has run large public deficits, is more constrained, but it too benefits from being able to finance those deficits mainly from domestic savings—as Japan has done since the 1990s.

In both countries, the share of household consumption in GDP is still fairly low, 35 percent in China and 54 percent in India.[10] This allows room for demand to grow. Thus, the weakening of international trade that circumscribes the growth impetus from exports can be partially compensated for by domestic investment and consumption demand. It is this demand potential in two of the world's growth poles that will induce flows of FDI, which, as we noted earlier, will supplement productivity growth through capital and technology transfer from external sources.

---

[9]On the development of renewable energy resources, see Mathews (2006).

[10]See Prasad (2009). In 2008, household savings in India, at over 30 percent, were the highest in the world—higher than China's (29 percent).

The global crisis of 2008–09 is likely to have macroeconomic implications for the industrial geography of Asia. A number of comfortable certitudes will need to be reappraised, and, as we have indicated above, the prevailing symbiosis between China and India—and between China and other Asian countries—might not persist. What replaces it will depend on the future course of economic relations between India and China, and on the industrial capabilities of other Asian countries and their competitiveness relative to the two Asian giants. We examine these considerations next.

Industrial Trends in the Rest of Asia

The Asian economies affected by China's expanding economic footprint and India's emerging economic presence can be divided into three categories: high-income economies, including Japan, Singapore, Korea, and Taiwan, China; middle-income countries, concentrated in Southeast Asia; and low-income countries, principally in South Asia, but including Vietnam, Cambodia, and the Lao People's Democratic Republic. Each set of countries has benefited from trade with China, and some are seeing their exports to India increase. However, industries in these countries must also compete with Chinese exports in a widening range of goods, and India has likewise stepped up the pressure in services and a narrower range of manufactures (see chapter 3). Here we address the following questions. First, how have the manufacturing economies of other Asian countries evolved over the past decade? Second, what are some of the significant trends in major traded items, and how has the composition of trade changed over time? Third, what light do revealed comparative advantage (RCA) indicators shed on the course of industrial development, and is this consistent with other information on manufacturing capabilities? Fourth, are the lower- and middle-income countries moving up the technology ladder to higher-value items? In addition, what is the direction industrial diversification might take? And what are the options for the high-income economies as their labor-intensive and low-technology products face intensifying competition from imports?

High-Income Economies

As incomes rise, the share of manufacturing in GDP tends to decline for a variety of reasons. One is the tendency of the relative prices of manufactured products to fall. This is both because of higher productivity relative to services and because they are traded in more competitive (global) markets. Another reason is that the income elasticity—and also the price elasticity of demand for most manufactures—may be lower, which pulls down their share. A third reason is that manufacturing is more movable than are services. However, the information and communication technology (ICT) revolution is lowering the odds against (impersonal) services relocating. Also, the more labor-intensive activities tend to migrate to countries where the wage costs are lower. Codified technologies for the more mature products facilitate the process and make it easier for late-starting industrializers to speedily attain levels of productivity comparable to those in the more advanced countries. Aside from labor costs, late-starting developers generally offer other attractions; these may include lower costs of land and cheaper utility rates as well as generous fiscal incentives favoring land-, water-, and energy-intensive activities, some with high up-front fixed costs.[11] With barriers to trade declining and transport costs also falling, buyers of a range of manufactured products have found it cost-effective to purchase from foreign suppliers and, in many instances, to locate their own production overseas as well.

Because manufacturing has long been the principal driver of growth, productivity, and technological change in Japan, in Korea, and in Taiwan, China, these economies have resisted the hollowing of their manufacturing sectors. Nevertheless, market forces are proving irresistible, and each is experiencing a steady contraction in the share of manufacturing. The labor-intensive activities are the most susceptible, although they are not the only ones affected. The huge expansion of resource-based industries such as those producing petrochemicals, cement, ferrous and non-ferrous metals, and bulk pharmaceuticals in neighboring Asian countries has triggered a geographical redistribution of such industries as well.

The outcome is most clearly apparent in the case of Japan, where the ratio of manufacturing to GDP has fallen to 18 percent, compared to 28 percent in 1980. A glance at figure 4.1 shows how the composition of the manufacturing sector has also been altered. Producers of electronics, machinery and transport equipment have enlarged their shares at the expense of iron, steel, and petrochemicals. Similar but less marked changes are apparent in Korea (figure 4.2).

The economy of Taiwan, China, also has undergone a significant sectoral adjustment as large segments of its manufacturing industries have transferred to the mainland to take full advantage of lower costs (see figure 4.3). Most upstream activities in electronics and machinery industries remain in Taiwan, China, but these now constitute 19.5 percent of GDP (National Statistics, Republic of China (Taiwan) 2009).

The pattern of trade for the high-income Asian economies essentially mirrors the change sweeping their industries. All three remain dependent upon the export of manufactures but now face intensifying competition and are struggling to sustain competitiveness by dint of innovation.[12] As can be seen from figures 4.4, 4.5, and 4.6, the weight of medium- and high-tech items has increased. Within these categories, the three economies are specializing in high-value

---

[11]Although labor costs are generally a small—and shrinking—fraction of total manufacturing costs, when profit margins are narrow, lower wages can exert a strong pull.

[12]Only Japan's high-end garments industry survives. Its textile industry is also struggling to remain profitable through innovation and diversification into new synthetic meterials, medical supplies, and materials for the construction and auto industries (figure 4.4).

Figure 4.1 **Industrial Composition by Type of Manufactures of Japan: 1981, 1990, and 2002**

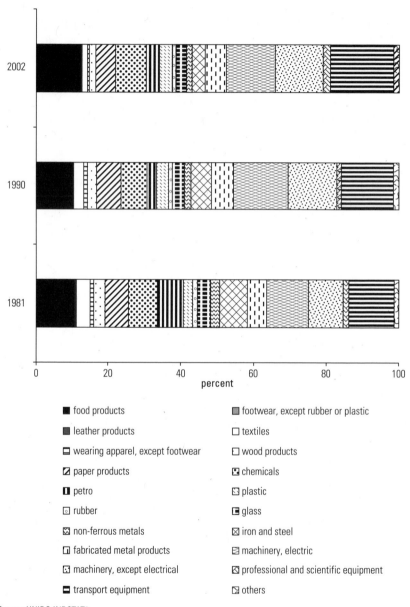

- ■ food products
- ▦ leather products
- ▢ wearing apparel, except footwear
- ▨ paper products
- ▮ petro
- ▣ rubber
- ▨ non-ferrous metals
- ▢ fabricated metal products
- ▣ machinery, except electrical
- ▬ transport equipment

- ▦ footwear, except rubber or plastic
- ▢ textiles
- ▢ wood products
- ▣ chemicals
- ▨ plastic
- ▣ glass
- ▨ iron and steel
- ▨ machinery, electric
- ▨ professional and scientific equipment
- ▨ others

Source: UNIDO INDSTAT3.

Figure 4.2   Industrial Composition by Type of Manufactures of the Republic of Korea: 1981, 1990, and 2002

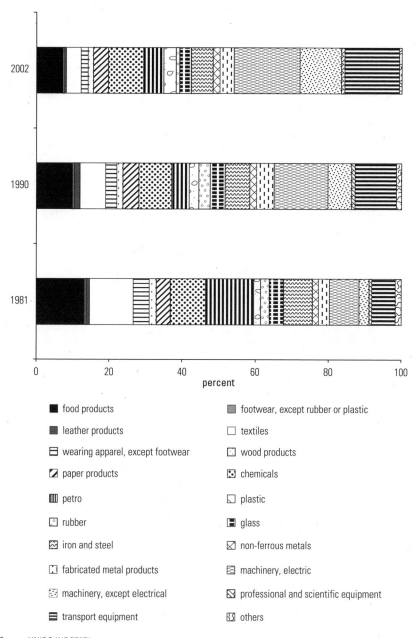

■ food products	▨ footwear, except rubber or plastic
■ leather products	☐ textiles
☰ wearing apparel, except footwear	⬚ wood products
▨ paper products	▨ chemicals
▥ petro	◩ plastic
◔ rubber	▣ glass
▩ iron and steel	⊠ non-ferrous metals
⬚ fabricated metal products	▧ machinery, electric
▨ machinery, except electrical	◩ professional and scientific equipment
☰ transport equipment	▨ others

Source: UNIDO INDSTAT3.

Figure 4.3   Industrial Composition by Type of Manufactures of Taiwan, China: 1981, 1990, and 1996

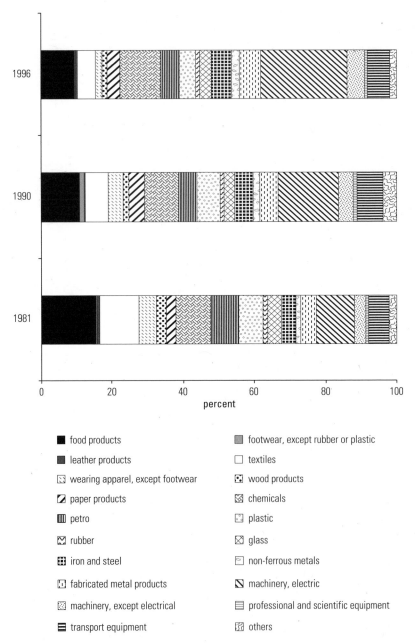

Source: UNIDO INDSTAT3.

Figure 4.4 Export Composition of Japan by Technology Class

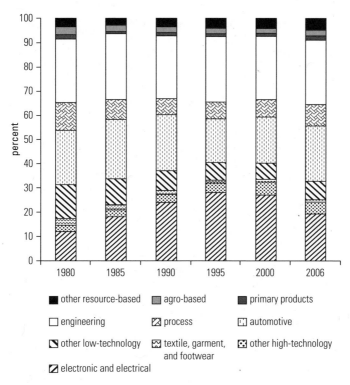

Source: Authors' calculations based on UN Comtrade data.

products—capital and scientific equipment, machinery, and components being the most prominent.

The product space analysis for these three economies also points to the increasing importance of capital goods. For Japan, the scope for diversification and upgrading is fairly narrow, because the average sophistication of its exports is already high (see figure 4.7 and figure 4.8). Among the most promising opportunities for Japan are engineering goods and industrial raw materials. The composition of these areas for diversification has shifted more toward machinery in 2006 compared to 1987 (tables 4.2 and 4.3).

Relative to Japan, Korea's product space in 1987 indicated a broader spectrum of opportunities for upgrading. By 2006 the distribution had tightened (see figures 4.9 and 4.10). The rapid evolution of Korea's export capabilities can be seen from an examination of the commodities listed in tables 4.4 and 4.5. In 1987, opportunities for upgrading and diversification for Korea included a number of low-tech products such as toys, musical instruments, and textiles, in addition to a

Figure 4.5   Export Composition of the Republic of Korea by Technology Class

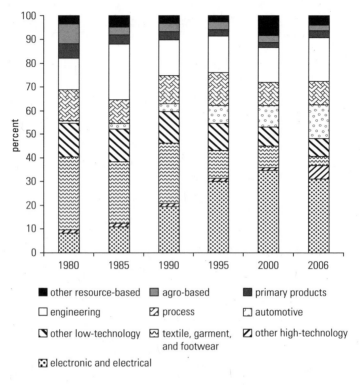

Source: Authors' calculations based on UN Comtrade data.

number of the less complex high-tech items such as picture tubes (used in television screens or monitors). By 2006, the composition had altered radically to include more sophisticated high-tech products such as optical instruments, electronic components, and engineering goods (machinery). This is a reflection of the industrial capabilities acquired by Korea over the course of two decades. Similarly, Taiwan, China's opportunity for upgrading and diversification had narrowed by 2006 compared to the situation in 1995 (see figures 4.11 and 4.12). Like Korea, the composition of Taiwan, China's options for upgrading and diversification are concentrated in medium- and high-tech products (see tables 4.6 and 4.7).

An important development paralleling the evolution of comparative advantage is the rising share of exports from these four high-income economies to China. Since the early 1990s, exports to China from these economies have grown substantially (see figure 4.13). In 2006, more than one-fifth of exports from Korea and Taiwan, China, were shipped to China. The four economies and China are part of a tightly knit production network cemented by FDI, whereby China

Figure 4.6   Export Composition of Taiwan, China, by Technology Class

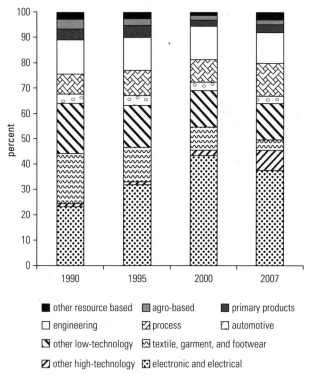

- ■ other resource based   ▨ agro-based   ■ primary products
- □ engineering   ▨ process   ▢ automotive
- ◩ other low-technology   ⊠ textile, garment, and footwear
- ◪ other high-technology   ▦ electronic and electrical

Source: Authors' calculations based on UN Comtrade data.

imports the capital equipment and key intermediate inputs from its three high-income neighbors[13] and exports a part of the output to the rest of the world—a networking arrangement that has strongly influenced the composition and value added of Chinese exports (also see Prasad 2009; Asian Development Bank 2009).

The evolution of product space for Singapore has taken the same direction as in Korea and Taiwan, China. With rising wages, the scope for diversifying its manufacturing activities and upgrading products is becoming restricted (see figures 4.14 and 4.15). As in the other high-income Asian economies, the shift is toward more high-tech (electronic) and medium-tech items such as watch components and optical products (see tables 4.8 and 4.9). Each of these economies is being pushed by competitive pressures (mainly from China) into

(*text continues on page 144*)

---

[13]Exports to China largely explain the rebound in manufacturing activity in Japan and Korea during the second half of 2009.

Figure 4.7 Product Space of Japan, 1987

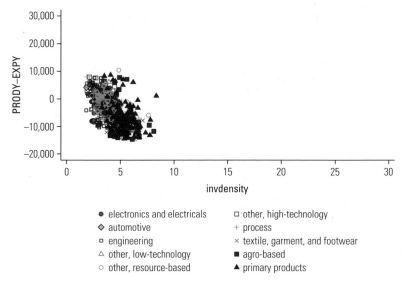

- ● electronics and electricals
- ◆ automotive
- ▫ engineering
- △ other, low-technology
- ○ other, resource-based
- ▫ other, high-technology
- + process
- × textile, garment, and footwear
- ■ agro-based
- ▲ primary products

Source: Authors' calculations based on UN Comtrade data.

Figure 4.8 Product Space of Japan, 2006

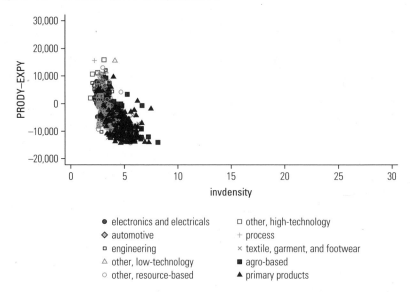

- ● electronics and electricals
- ◆ automotive
- ▫ engineering
- △ other, low-technology
- ○ other, resource-based
- ▫ other, high-technology
- + process
- × textile, garment, and footwear
- ■ agro-based
- ▲ primary products

Source: Authors' calculations based on UN Comtrade data.

Table 4.2   Top 10 "Upscale" Commodities with the Highest Density in Japan, 1987

Short description	Density	Technology class	PRODY–EXPY
Musical instruments, N.E.S.	0.55638	LT2	4,594
Motorcycles, autocycles; sidecars of all kinds, etc	0.532631	MT1	4,129
Rail locomotives, electric	0.525335	MT2	8,060
Photographic cameras, flash apparatus, parts, accessories, N.E.S.	0.523405	HT2	2,957
Printing presses	0.522007	MT3	5,600
Telecommunications equipment, N.E.S.	0.507709	HT1	1,800
Other sound recording and reproducer, N.E.S.; video recorders	0.496983	MT3	1,102
Other rail locomotives; tenders	0.48729	MT2	6,206
Metal-forming machine-tools	0.472177	MT3	5,229
Steam power units (mobile engines but not steam tractors, etc.)	0.46722	HT2	7,972

Source: Authors' calculations using UN comtrade data. Technology classification is based on Lall (2000).
Note: HT1 = electronic and electrical products; HT2 = other high-technology products; LT1 = textiles, garments, and footwear; LT2 = other low-technology products; MT1 = automotive products; MT2 = process industry; MT3 = engineering products; PP = primary products; RB1 = agriculture-based products; RB2 = other resource-based products.

Table 4.3   Top 10 "Upscale" Commodities with the Highest Density in Japan, 2006

Short description	Density	Technology class	PRODY–EXPY
Optical instruments and apparatus	0.53694	HT2	2,030
Printing presses	0.490102	MT3	7,501
Photographic and cinematographic apparatus and equipment, N.E.S.	0.489971	HT2	10,654
Other machines and tools for working metal or metal carbides, N.E.S.	0.458992	MT3	6,544
Weaving, knitting, etc., machines, machines for preparing yarns, etc.	0.450559	MT3	5,195
Cellulose acetates	0.449124	MT2	15,671
Crystals and parts, N.E.S., of electronic components of heading 776	0.44501	HT1	2,225
Machines for extruding manmade textile; other textile machinery	0.443969	MT3	1,380
Metal-cutting machine tools	0.431927	MT3	4,373
Halogen and sulfur compounds of nonmetals	0.428799	RB2	6,420

Source: Authors' calculations using UN Comtrade data. Technology classification is based on Lall (2000).
Note: See the note to table 4.2.

Figure 4.9   Product Space of the Republic of Korea, 1987

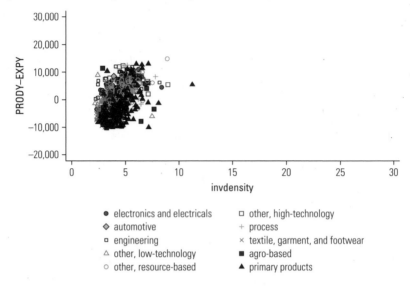

- electronics and electricals
- ◆ automotive
- ▫ engineering
- △ other, low-technology
- ○ other, resource-based

- ▫ other, high-technology
- + process
- × textile, garment, and footwear
- ■ agro-based
- ▲ primary products

Source: Authors' calculations based on UN Comtrade data.

Figure 4.10   Product Space of the Republic of Korea, 2006

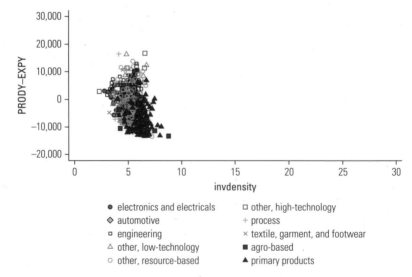

- electronics and electricals
- ◆ automotive
- ▫ engineering
- △ other, low-technology
- ○ other, resource-based

- ▫ other, high-technology
- + process
- × textile, garment, and footwear
- ■ agro-based
- ▲ primary products

Source: Authors' calculations based on UN Comtrade data.

Table 4.4   Top 10 "Upscale" Commodities with the Highest Density in the Republic of Korea, 1987

Short description	Density	Technology class	PRODY–EXPY
Portable radio receivers	0.412405	MT3	680
Musical instruments, N.E.S.	0.410817	LT2	8,967
Other sound recording and reproducer, N.E.S.; video recorders	0.407477	MT3	5,475
Children's toys, indoor games, etc	0.404916	LT2	509
Watches, watch movements, and cases	0.403	MT3	6,928
Microphones; loudspeakers; audio-frequency electric amplifiers	0.37149	HT1	3,451
Tulle, lace, embroidery, ribbons, trimmings, and other small wares	0.361857	LT1	1,643
Television receivers, color	0.361731	HT1	2,160
Television cathode ray tubes	0.349637	HT1	3,348

Source: Authors' calculations using UN Comtrade data. Technology classification is based on Lall (2000).
Note: See the note to table 4.2.

Table 4.5   Top 10 "Upscale" Commodities with the Highest Density in the Republic of Korea, 2006

Short description	Density	Technology class	PRODY–EXPY
Optical instruments and apparatus	0.431612	HT2	2,842
Crystals and parts, N.E.S., of electronic components of heading 776	0.358525	HT1	3,037
Printed circuits and parts thereof, N.E.S.	0.329223	MT3	1,598
Electronic microcircuits	0.318382	HT1	2,745
Portable radio receivers	0.304986	MT3	3,636
Television receivers, monochrome	0.297786	HT1	2,859
Other electrical machinery and equipment, N.E.S.	0.295666	HT1	1,066
Parts, N.E.S., of and accessories for apparatus falling in heading 76	0.294377	HT1	715
Lenses and other optical elements of any material	0.291567	MT3	4,510
Weaving, knitting, etc., machines, machines for preparing yarns, etc.	0.289247	MT3	6,007

Source: Authors' calculations using UN Comtrade data. Technology classification is based on Lall (2000).
Note: See the note to table 4.2.

Figure 4.11 Product Space of Taiwan, China, 1995

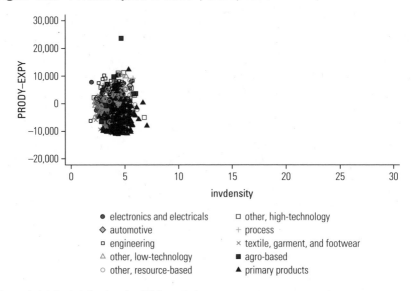

Source: Authors' calculations based on UN Comtrade data.

Figure 4.12 Product Space of Taiwan, China, 2006

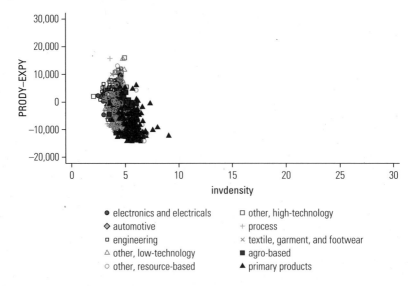

Source: Authors' calculations based on UN Comtrade data.

Table 4.6   Top 10 "Upscale" Commodities with the Highest Density in Taiwan, China, 1995

Short description	Density	Technology class	PRODY–EXPY
Other electronic valves and tubes	0.521362	HT1	7,776
Photographic cameras, flash apparatus, parts, accessories, N.E.S.	0.467948	HT2	2,156
Children's toys, indoor games, etc.	0.45628	LT2	384
Baby carriages and parts thereof, N.E.S.	0.426852	LT2	620
Clocks, clock movements, and parts	0.422245	MT3	1,561
Electronic microcircuits	0.420811	HT1	1,538
Invalid carriages; parts, N.E.S., of articles of heading 785	0.417452	MT1	1,989
Motorcycles, autocycles; sidecars of all kind, etc.	0.414916	MT1	357
Other sound recording and reproducer, N.E.S.; video recorders	0.399394	MT3	161
Calculating, accounting, cash registers, ticketing, et.c, machines	0.396287	HT1	1,222

Source: Authors' calculations using UN Comtrade data. Technology classification is based on Lall (2000).
Note: See the note to table 4.2.

Table 4.7   Top 10 "Upscale" Commodities with the Highest Density in Taiwan, China, 2006

Short Description	Density	Technology Class	PRODY–EXPY
Optical instruments and apparatus	0.484053	HT2	2,081
Crystals and parts, N.E.S., of electronic components of heading 776	0.404476	HT1	2,276
Printed circuits and parts thereof, N.E.S.	0.373448	MT3	836
Electronic microcircuits	0.366439	HT1	1,984
Lenses and other optical elements of any material	0.35053	MT3	3,749
Television receivers, monochrome	0.346917	HT1	2,098
Weaving, knitting, etc., machines, machines for preparing yarns, etc.	0.344998	MT3	5,246
Parts, N.E.S., of and accessories for machines of headings 7512 and 752	0.338037	HT1	2,972
Other electrical machinery and equipment, N.E.S.	0.337847	HT1	305
Other machines or tools for working metal or metal carbides, N.E.S.	0.334271	MT3	6,595

Source: Authors' calculations using UN Comtrade data. Technology classification is based on Lall (2000).
Note: See the note to table 4.2.

Figure 4.13 Share of Exports Destined for China

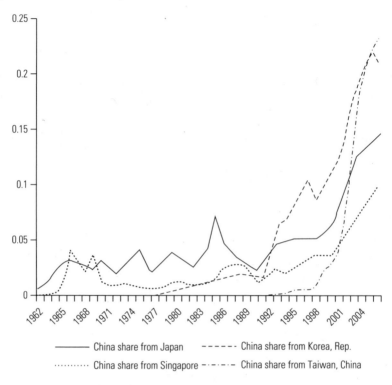

Source: Authors' calculations based on UN Comtrade data.

the upper end of various product categories, including automotive, engineering, other transport, capital equipment, sophisticated components, industrial raw materials, and pharmaceuticals.

Middle-Income Economies

Beginning in the 1970s, the middle-income economies of Southeast Asia transitioned to export-oriented manufacturing—with the help of FDI—in light industries such as textiles, footwear, and consumer electronics. A decade later, they entered into production of electronic components and equipment and automobile manufacturing, also with the help of FDI from the United States and the high-income East Asian economies. Figure 4.16 and table 4.10 present the growing contribution of industry to GDP. It has risen in three countries, with only the Philippines showing a decline. The shift in the composition of manufacturing toward electronics and transport industries in the 1990s is apparent from figures 4.17, 4.18, 4.19, and 4.20. In all four countries, assembly and processing

Figure 4.14   Product Space of Singapore, 1987

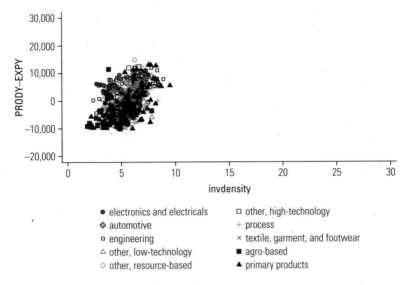

● electronics and electricals   □ other, high-technology
◇ automotive   + process
▫ engineering   × textile, garment, and footwear
△ other, low-technology   ■ agro-based
○ other, resource-based   ▲ primary products

Source: Authors' calculations based on UN Comtrade data.

Figure 4.15   Product Space of Singapore, 2006

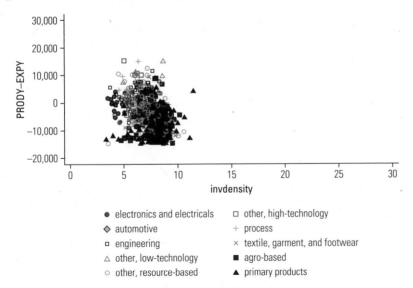

● electronics and electricals   □ other, high-technology
◇ automotive   + process
▫ engineering   × textile, garment, and footwear
△ other, low-technology   ■ agro-based
○ other, resource-based   ▲ primary products

Source: Authors' calculations based on UN Comtrade data.

Table 4.8 Top 10 "Upscale" Commodities with the Highest Density in Singapore, 1987

Short description	Density	Technology class	PRODY–EXPY
Radio receivers for motor vehicles	0.419293	MT3	291
Telecommunications equipment, N.E.S.	0.367705	HT1	6,231
Other sound recording and reproduction, N.E.S.; video recorders	0.342748	MT3	5,533
Portable radio receivers	0.340884	MT3	737
Calculating, accounting, cash registers, ticketing, etc., machines	0.328277	HT1	5,910
Microphones; loudspeakers; audio-frequency electric amplifiers	0.301605	HT1	3,509
Children's toys, indoor games, etc.	0.301335	LT2	567
Crystals and parts, N.E.S., of electronic components of heading 776	0.297748	HT1	2,949
Parts, N.E.S., of and accessories for apparatus falling in heading 76	0.297151	HT1	5,644
Air-conditioning machines and parts thereof, N.E.S.	0.282536	MT3	2,830

Source: Authors' calculations using UN Comtrade data. Technology classification is based on Lall (2000).
Note: See the note to table 4.2.

Table 4.9 Top 10 "Upscale" Commodities with the Highest Density in Singapore, 2006

Short description	Density	Technology class	PRODY–EXPY
Crystals and parts, N.E.S., of electronic components of heading 776	0.287318	HT1	1,678
Watches, watch movements, and cases	0.269138	MT3	5,620
Electronic microcircuits	0.264946	HT1	1,386
Printed circuits and parts thereof, N.E.S.	0.256303	MT3	238
Other radio receivers	0.255811	MT3	134
Parts, N.E.S., of and accessories for machines of headings 7512 and 752	0.243415	HT1	2,374
Parts, N.E.S., of and accessories for machines of headings 7511 and 7518	0.236869	HT1	4,075
Lenses and other optical elements of any material	0.233473	MT3	3,150
Offline data processing equipment, N.E.S.	0.23059	HT1	323
Organo-sulfur compounds	0.221744	RB2	10,490

Source: Authors' calculations using UN Comtrade data. Technology classification is based on Lall (2000).
Note: See the note to table 4.2.

Figure 4.16   Manufacturing, Value Added

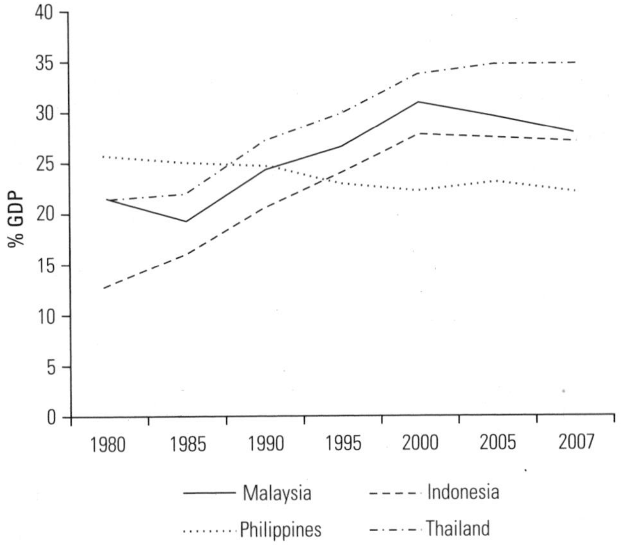

Source: World Development Indicators Database.

Table 4.10   Manufacturing, Value Added
   % GDP

Country	1980	1985	1990	1995	2000	2005	2007
Indonesia	13.0	16.0	20.7	24.1	27.8	27.4	27.0
Malaysia	21.6	19.3	24.2	26.4	30.9	29.6	28.0
Philippines	25.7	25.2	24.8	23.0	22.2	23.2	22.0
Thailand	21.5	21.9	27.2	29.9	33.6	34.7	34.8

Source: World Development Indicators Database.

activities predominate, and as a consequence, value added has remained low—typically less than 30 percent. This can be seen from table 4.10. Unlike Korea and Taiwan, China, which successfully moved upstream, the Southeast Asian economies have failed to graduate from the processing of high-tech standardized commodities produced mainly by MNCs—or for MNCs by joint ventures or local suppliers.

The growth of manufacturing has been matched by the imports of parts and materials and by the exports of assembled products and components. Among the four countries, Malaysia is the most trade dependent. Malaysia and the Philippines are the two relying most heavily on electronic and electrical engineering exports, followed by Thailand and Indonesia. The importance of high-tech assembled exports notwithstanding, these countries' static RCA continues (with all due

(*text continues on page 152*)

Figure 4.17   Industrial Composition by Type of Manufactures of Indonesia: 1981, 1990, and 2003

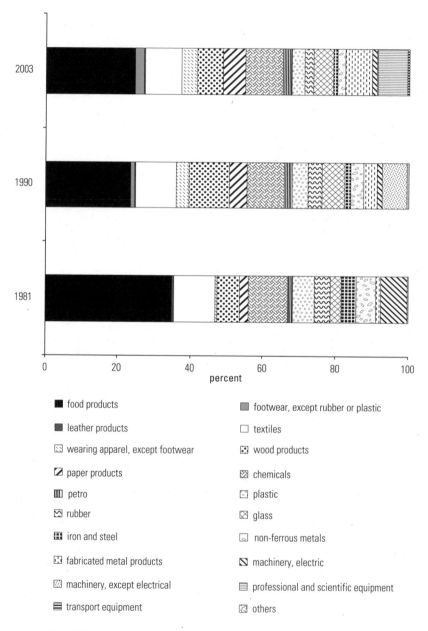

■ food products	■ footwear, except rubber or plastic
■ leather products	□ textiles
◩ wearing apparel, except footwear	◪ wood products
◪ paper products	◪ chemicals
▥ petro	◪ plastic
◪ rubber	◪ glass
▦ iron and steel	◪ non-ferrous metals
◪ fabricated metal products	◪ machinery, electric
◪ machinery, except electrical	▤ professional and scientific equipment
▤ transport equipment	◪ others

Source: UNIDO INDSTAT3.

Figure 4.18 Industrial Composition by Type of Manufactures of Malaysia: 1981, 1990, and 2002

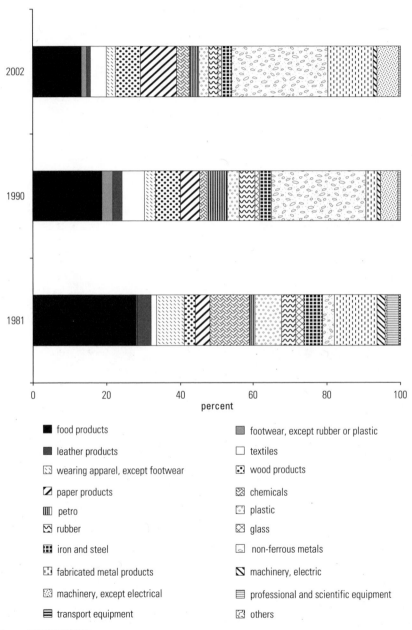

Source: UNIDO INDSTAT3.

Figure 4.19 Industrial Composition by Type of Manufactures of the Philippines: 1981, 1990, and 1997

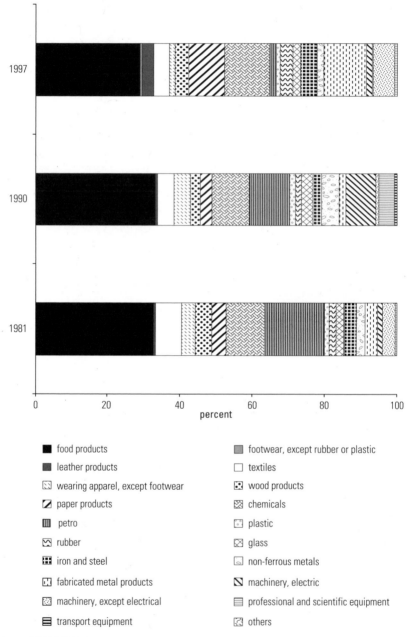

Source: UNIDO INDSTAT3.

Figure 4.20   Industrial Composition by Type of Manufactures of Thailand: 1981, 1990, and 1994

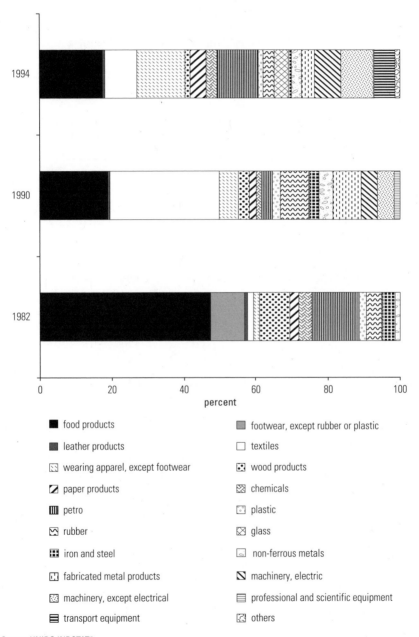

	food products		footwear, except rubber or plastic
	leather products		textiles
	wearing apparel, except footwear		wood products
	paper products		chemicals
	petro		plastic
	rubber		glass
	iron and steel		non-ferrous metals
	fabricated metal products		machinery, electric
	machinery, except electrical		professional and scientific equipment
	transport equipment		others

Source: UNIDO INDSTAT3.

caveats) to reside in a range of primary products, resource-based products, and low- and medium-tech manufactures (see tables 4.11, 4.12, 4.13, and 4.14). The industrial platforms created by FDI have failed to inculcate homegrown technological capability; in spite of numerous incentives, local firms have faced difficulty in carving out a larger industrial role for themselves, establishing a brand name, and becoming innovative (see Yusuf and Nabeshima 2009).

The slow progress in technological upgrading, following decades of industrialization, is constraining the ability of the leading Southeast Asian countries to

Table 4.11 **Top 10 Four-Digit-Level Commodities with the Highest RCA in Indonesia: 1980, 2006**

Short description	RCA	PRODY	Technology class
1980			
Palm nuts and kernels	44.40	500	PP
Saw logs and veneer logs, of nonconiferous species	29.89	917	RB1
Vegetable plaiting materials	25.82	4,154	PP
Petroleum gases, N.E.S., in gaseous state	15.75	8,367	PP
Natural rubber latex; natural rubber and gums	14.12	1,901	PP
Nickel ores and concentrates; nickel mattes, etc.	12.47	9,200	RB2
Pepper; pimento	12.33	1,779	PP
Goat and kid skins, raw, whether or not split	12.18	1,337	PP
Tin ores and concentrates	11.29	1,722	RB2
Pitprops, poles, piling, post and other wood in the rough, N.E.S.	11.12	10,648	RB1
2006			
Calf leather	70.72	1,181	LT1
Palm kernel oil	67.39	2,258	RB1
Typewriters; check-writing machines	47.76	6,099	HT1
Palm oil	45.85	2,321	RB1
Palm nuts and kernels	36.42	1,807	PP
Tin and tin alloys, unwrought	35.96	3,044	PP
Natural rubber latex; natural rubber and gums	32.91	1,781	PP
Knitted or crocheted fabrics, elastic or rubberized	31.69	9,578	LT1
Coconut (copra) oil	25.95	1,417	RB1
Nickel ores and concentrates; nickel mattes, etc.	24.81	12,050	RB2

Source: Authors' calculations using UN Comtrade data. Technology classification is based on Lall (2000).
Note: See the note to table 4.2.

Table 4.12   Top 10 Four-Digit-Level Commodities with the Highest RCA in Malaysia: 1980, 2006

Short description	RCA	PRODY	Technology class
1980			
Palm kernel oil	88.55	2,627	RB1
Palm oil	74.36	2,772	RB1
Tin and tin alloys, unwrought	48.62	1,989	PP
Natural rubber latex; natural rubber and gums	43.26	1,901	PP
Saw logs and veneer logs, of nonconiferous species	41.30	917	RB1
Wood, nonconiferous species, sawn, planed, tongued, grooved, etc.	30.23	2,340	RB1
Diodes, transistors, photocells, etc.	22.36	6,938	HT1
Pepper; pimento	21.34	1,779	PP
Railway or tramway sleepers (ties) of wood	18.85	2,417	RB1
Wood, simply shaped, N.E.S.	17.17	7,176	RB1
2006			
Palm oil	31.70	2,321	RB1
Hydrogenated animal or vegetable oils and fats	23.66	3,511	RB1
Fatty acids, acid oils, and residues; degras	23.65	8,885	RB1
Gramophones and record players, electric	23.58	12,741	MT3
Articles of apparel, clothing accessories of plastic or rubber	20.05	6,158	LT1
Palm kernel oil	20.02	2,258	RB1
Other radio receivers	14.36	15,213	MT3
Plywood consisting solely of sheets of wood	13.71	5,650	RB1
Saw logs and veneer logs, of nonconiferous species	11.25	1,415	RB1
Natural rubber latex; natural rubber and gums	10.96	1,781	PP

Source: Authors' calculations using UN Comtrade data. Technology classification is based on Lall (2000).
Note: See the note to table 4.2.

diversify their product mix. In 1987, the product space for Indonesia showed a wide dispersion. This suggests that underlying industrial capabilities were not conducive to diversification, although there were many upgrading opportunities, because the average sophistication of exports was low at that time (see figure 4.21). By 2006, the distribution had shifted toward the origin, pointing to the scope for diversification of its exports (see figure 4.22). Upgrading opportunities were mainly in low-tech and resource-based products for Indonesia in 1987 (see table 4.15). The opportunity set had not changed much by 2006, except for the addition of

Table 4.13   Top 10 Four-Digit-Level Commodities with the Highest RCA in the Philippines: 1980, 2006

Short description	RCA	PRODY	Technology class
1980			
Castor oil seeds	247.77	730	PP
Coconut (copra) oil	239.39	5,944	RB1
Manila hemp, raw or processed but not spun, its tow and waste	234.90	1,155	RB1
Copra	127.24	2,447	PP
Copper ore and concentrates; copper matte; cement copper	101.73	2,708	RB2
Banana, plantain, fresh or dried	61.37	1,619	PP
Sugars, beet and cane, raw, solid	45.35	2,820	RB1
Fuel wood and wood charcoal	43.45	2,204	PP
Articles and manufacture of carving, molding materials, N.E.S.	37.87	5,476	LT2
Molasses	35.41	2,824	RB1
2006			
Manila hemp, raw or processed but not spun, its tow and waste	143.03	1,527	RB1
Coconut (copra) oil	117.54	1,417	RB1
Diodes, transistors, photocells, etc.	32.42	9,787	HT1
Photographic cameras, flash apparatus, parts, accessories, N.E.S.	23.77	10,515	HT2
Banana, plantain, fresh or dried	15.58	3,535	PP
Glass, N.E.S.	10.48	13,732	RB2
Ceramic plumbing fixtures	9.60	5,013	MT3
Vegetable textile fibers, N.E.S., and waste	8.85	2,518	RB1
Articles and manufacture of carving, molding materials, N.E.S.	8.82	5,133	LT2
Builders' carpentry and joinery (including prefabricated)	7.69	10,113	RB1

Source: Authors' calculations using UN Comtrade data. Technology classification is based on Lall (2000).
Note: See the note to table 4.2.

one high-tech product (see table 4.16). The options lie mainly in resource-based and low-tech products like textiles and food products, although the actual commodities have changed.

The change in the product space for Malaysia resembles that of Indonesia in some respects. Relative to 1987, the distribution has shifted inward, with more commodities closer to the origin (see figures 4.23 and 4.24). The difference is the

Table 4.14   Top 10 Four-Digit-Level Commodities with the Highest RCA in Thailand: 1980, 2006

Short description	RCA	PRODY	Technology class
1980			
Vegetable products roots and tubers, N.E.S., fresh, dried	135.89	1,695	PP
Flour, meals and flakes of potatoes, fruit and vegetables, N.E.S.	107.28	1,792	RB1
Rice, semimilled or wholly milled	81.32	1,946	PP
Castor oil	69.20	1,544	RB1
Vegetable textile fibers, N.E.S., and waste	68.83	543	RB1
Tin and tin alloys, unwrought	48.38	1,989	PP
Sesame seeds	40.82	468	PP
Fabric, woven, of continuous regenerated textile materials	36.50	3,919	MT2
Precious and semiprecious stones, not mounted, set, or strung	34.92	4,656	RB2
Natural rubber latex; natural rubber and gums	25.41	1,901	PP
2006			
Natural rubber latex; natural rubber and gums	32.45	1,781	PP
Rice, semimilled or wholly milled	23.15	2,678	PP
Vegetable products roots and tubers, N.E.S., fresh, dried	23.01	2,039	PP
Hygienic, pharmaceutical articles of unhardened vulcanized rubber	17.46	10,149	RB1
Starches, insulin and wheat gluten	16.83	6,755	RB2
Crustaceans and mollusks, prepared or prepared, N.E.S.	16.11	17,929	RB1
Fruit, fruit-peel, and parts of plants, preserved by sugar	16.08	3,218	RB1
Fish, prepared or preserved, N.E.S.	14.91	5,528	RB1
Tires, pneumatic, new, for aircraft	10.29	7,177	RB1
Articles of apparel, clothing accessories of plastic or rubber	9.70	6,158	LT1

Source: Authors' calculations using UN Comtrade data. Technology classification is based on Lall (2000).
Note: See the note to table 4.2.

change in the composition of upgrading opportunities for Malaysia. In 1987, half of the items that presented upgrading opportunities were primary products or low-tech products (see table 4.17). By 2006, these had been largely replaced by medium- and high-tech products, mostly electronics, demonstrating Malaysia's export-oriented industrial focus (see table 4.18).

Figure 4.21   Product Space of Indonesia, 1987

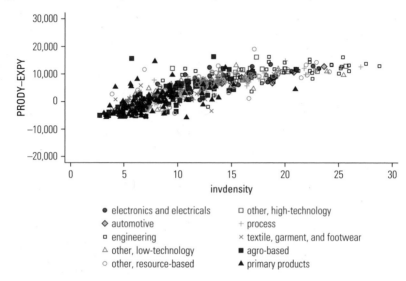

electronics and electricals
automotive
engineering
other, low-technology
other, resource-based

other, high-technology
process
textile, garment, and footwear
agro-based
primary products

Source: Authors' calculations based on UN Comtrade data.

Figure 4.22   Product Space of Indonesia, 2006

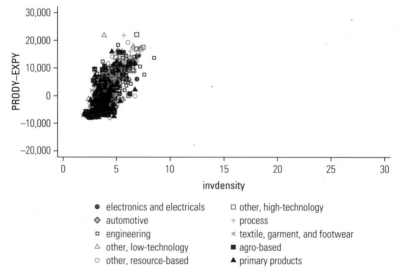

electronics and electricals
automotive
engineering
other, low-technology
other, resource-based

other, high-technology
process
textile, garment, and footwear
agro-based
primary products

Source: Authors' calculations based on UN Comtrade data.

Table 4.15   Top 10 "Upscale" Commodities with the Highest Density in Indonesia, 1987

Short description	Density	Technology class	PRODY–EXPY
Nickel ores and concentrates; nickel mattes, etc.	0.256007	RB2	2,673
Undergarments of textile fabrics, not knitted or crocheted; men's, boys' undergarments, other than shirts	0.23813	LT1	789
Petroleum gases and other gaseous hydrocarbons, N.E.S., liquefied	0.237669	PP	5,299
Crude petroleum and oils obtained from bituminous materials	0.203862	PP	133
Outerwear knitted or crocheted, not elastic nor rubberized; women's, girls', infants' suits, dresses, etc., knitted, crocheted	0.197408	LT1	95
Undergarments, knitted or crocheted; of cotton, not elastic or rubberized	0.190617	LT1	122
Outerwear, knitted or crocheted, not elastic or rubberized; other, clothing accessories, nonelastic, knitted or crocheted	0.188632	LT1	374
Clothing accessories, knitted or crocheted, N.E.S.	0.183501	LT1	328
Outerwear knitted or crocheted, not elastic or rubberized; jerseys, pullovers, slipovers, cardigans, etc.	0.182652	LT1	1,166
Fabrics, woven, less than 85% of discontinuous synthetic fibers	0.181785	MT2	607

Source: Authors' calculations using UN Comtrade data. Technology classification is based on Lall (2000).
Note: See the note to table 4.2.

Table 4.16   Top 10 "Upscale" Commodities with the Highest Density in Indonesia, 2006

Short description	Density	Technology class	PRODY–EXPY
Outerwear, knitted or crocheted, not elastic or rubberized; jerseys, pullovers, slipovers, cardigans, etc.	0.37064	LT1	1,899
Fish, dried, salted or in brine; smoked fish	0.350937	RB1	5,558
Nickel ores and concentrates; nickel mattes, etc.	0.34071	RB2	3,758
Personal adornments and ornaments articles of plastic	0.338178	LT2	1,057
Peripheral units, including control and adapting units	0.336881	HT1	3,959

(continued on next page)

Table 4.16 *(continued)*

Short description	Density	Technology class	PRODY–EXPY
Crustaceans and mollusks, prepared or prepared, N.E.S.	0.336157	RB1	9,638
Petroleum gases and other gaseous hydrocarbons, N.E.S., liquefied	0.33395	PP	530
Fish fillets, frozen	0.330533	PP	7,188
Yarn, 85% synthetic fibers, not for retail; monofil, strip, etc.	0.330421	LT1	1,873
Pearls, not mounted, set ,or strung	0.328312	RB2	8,849

Source: Authors' calculations using UN Comtrade data. Technology classification is based on Lall (2000).
Note: See the note to table 4.2.

Figure 4.23 Product Space of Malaysia, 1987

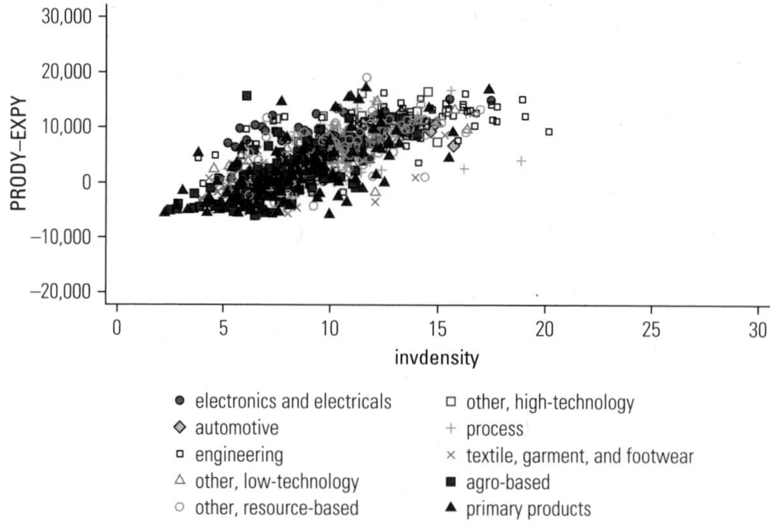
30,000
20,000
10,000
0
–10,000
–20,000
PRODY–EXPY
0
5
10
15
20
25
30
invdensity
electronics and electricals
automotive
engineering
other, low-technology
other, resource-based
other, high-technology
process
textile, garment, and footwear
agro-based
primary products

Source: Authors' calculations based on UN Comtrade data.

Relative to Indonesia and Malaysia, the Philippines' export performance was stronger in the early stages of industrialization; this is reflected in the tighter distribution of commodities in the product space for 1987 (see figure 4.25). However, compared with Indonesia and Malaysia, the Philippines did not capitalize as much on its initial advantages. Industrialization and export diversification in the Philippines has made headway, and although some medium- and high-tech products surfaced in the product space for 2006, they are fewer than for Malaysia and Indonesia (see figure 4.26 and tables 4.19 and 4.20).

Figure 4.24   Product Space of Malaysia, 2006

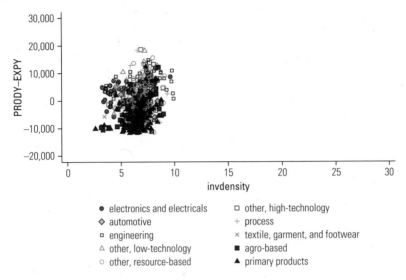

Source: Authors' calculations based on UN Comtrade data.

Table 4.17   Top 10 "Upscale" Commodities with the Highest Density in Malaysia, 1987

Short description	Density	Technology class	PRODY–EXPY
Radio receivers for motor vehicles	0.26207	MT3	4,424
Petroleum gases and other gaseous hydrocarbons, N.E.S., liquefied	0.261955	PP	5,272
Undergarments of textile fabrics, not knitted or crocheted; men's, boys' undergarments, other than shirts	0.232194	LT1	762
Umbrellas, canes, and similar articles and parts thereof	0.219664	LT2	2,429
Portable radio receivers	0.217257	MT3	4,871
Fabrics, woven, less than 85% of discontinuous synthetic fibers	0.214142	MT2	580
Undergarments, knitted or crocheted; of cotton, not elastic or rubberized	0.214104	LT1	95
Crude petroleum and oils obtained from bituminous materials	0.212354	PP	107
Other radio receivers	0.211516	MT3	961
Outerwear knitted or crocheted, not elastic or rubberized; women's, girls', infants' suits, dresses, etc., knitted, crocheted	0.209722	LT1	68

Source: Authors' calculations using UN Comtrade data. Technology classification is based on Lall (2000).
Note: See the note to table 4.2.

Table 4.18   Top 10 "Upscale" Commodities with the Highest Density in Malaysia, 2006

Short description	Density	Technology class	PRODY–EXPY
Crystals, and parts, N.E.S., of electronic components of heading 776	0.309486	HT1	4,860
Peripheral units, including control and adapting units	0.287641	HT1	353
Printed circuits, and parts thereof, N.E.S.	0.286852	MT3	3,420
Other radio receivers	0.280185	MT3	3,316
Electronic microcircuits	0.279775	HT1	4,568
Portable radio receivers	0.276732	MT3	5,459
Other sound recording and reproduction, N.E.S.; video recorders	0.275605	MT3	4,344
Other electrical machinery and equipment, N.E.S.	0.264674	HT1	2,889
Parts, N.E.S., of and accessories for apparatus falling in heading 76	0.252825	HT1	2,538
Parts, N.E.S., of and accessories for machines of headings 7512 and 752	0.250685	HT1	5,556

Source: Authors' calculations using UN Comtrade data. Technology classification is based on Lall (2000).
Note: See the note to table 4.2.

Figure 4.25   Product Space of the Philippines, 1987

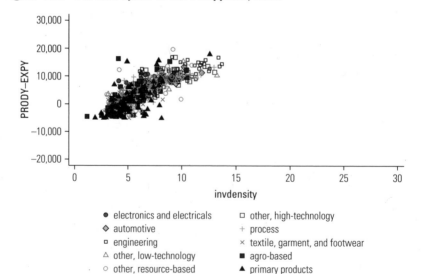

● electronics and electricals
◆ automotive
▫ engineering
△ other, low-technology
○ other, resource-based

□ other, high-technology
+ process
× textile, garment, and footwear
■ agro-based
▲ primary products

Source: Authors' calculations based on UN Comtrade data.

Figure 4.26   Product Space of the Philippines, 2006

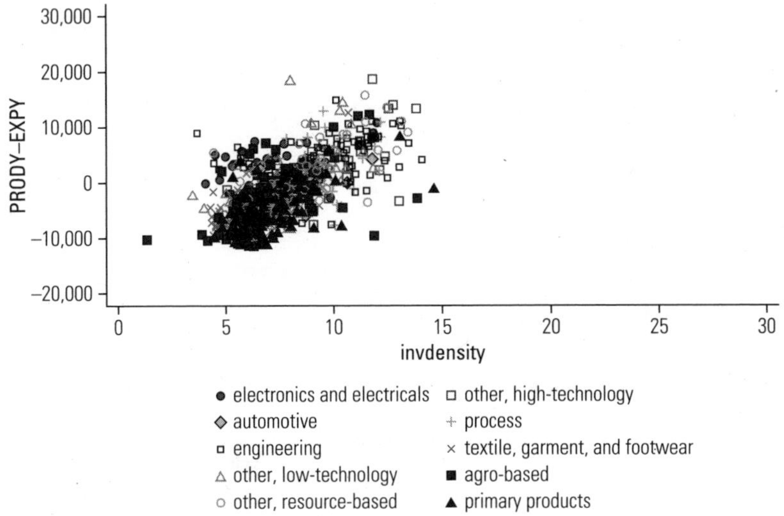

- ● electronics and electricals
- ◇ automotive
- ▫ engineering
- △ other, low-technology
- ○ other, resource-based
- ▫ other, high-technology
- + process
- × textile, garment, and footwear
- ■ agro-based
- ▲ primary products

Source: Authors' calculations based on UN Comtrade data.

Table 4.19   Top 10 "Upscale" Commodities with the Highest Density in the Philippines, 1987

Short description	Density	Technology class	PRODY–EXPY
Nickel ores and concentrates; nickel mattes, etc.	0.329816	RB2	3,270
Undergarments of textile fabrics, not knitted or crocheted; men's, boys' undergarments, other than shirts	0.319229	LT1	1,385
Manufactured goods, N.E.S.	0.317147	LT2	3,486
Clothing accessories, knitted or crocheted, N.E.S.	0.309774	LT1	924
Outerwear, knitted or crocheted, not elastic or rubberized; jerseys, pullovers, slipovers, cardigans, etc.	0.305111	LT1	1,762
Undergarments, knitted or crocheted; of cotton, not elastic or rubberized	0.298848	LT1	718
Women's, girls', infants' outerwear, textile, not knitted or crocheted; dresses	0.298766	LT1	438

(continued on next page)

Table 4.19 *(continued)*

Short description	Density	Technology class	PRODY–EXPY
Outerwear, knitted or crocheted, not elastic or rubberized; other, clothing accessories, nonelastic, knitted or crocheted	0.298534	LT1	971
Outerwear knitted or crocheted, not elastic or rubberized; women's, girls', infants' suits, dresses, etc., knitted, crocheted	0.297937	LT1	691
Tobacco refuse	0.290068	PP	1,310

Source: Authors' calculations using UN Comtrade data. Technology classification is based on Lall (2000).
Note: See the note to table 4.2.

Table 4.20 Top 10 "Upscale" Commodities with the Highest Density in the Philippines, 2006

Short description	Density	Technology class	PRODY–EXPY
Watches, watch movements, and cases	0.274277	MT3	8,885
Pearls, not mounted, set, or strung	0.22628	RB2	5,327
Printed circuits, and parts thereof, N.E.S.	0.225104	MT3	3,504
Crystals and parts, N.E.S., of electronic components of heading 776	0.221333	HT1	4,943
Clocks, clock movements, and parts	0.21449	MT3	2,448
Peripheral units, including control and adapting units	0.212142	HT1	437
Fish, dried, salted or in brine; smoked fish	0.20813	RB1	2,036
Electronic microcircuits	0.200308	HT1	4,651
Other electrical machinery and equipment, N.E.S.	0.188276	HT1	2,972
Flours and meals of meat, fish, etc., unfit for humans; greaves	0.187836	PP	846

Source: Authors' calculations using UN Comtrade data. Technology classification is based on Lall (2000).
Note: See the note to table 4.2.

Thailand's commodity distribution in the product space tightened between 1987 and 2006, and opportunities for diversification have increased (see figures 4.27 and 4.28). These include medium- and high-tech products—again, mostly electronic components displacing low-tech (e.g., garments and personal items) and resource-based commodities (e.g., food products) (see tables 4.21 and 4.22).

From the product space analysis, it appears that these four economies enhanced their industrial (and export) potential between 1987 and 2006. The promising areas of diversification and upgrading in 1987 were mostly within primary,

Figure 4.27   Product Space of Thailand, 1987

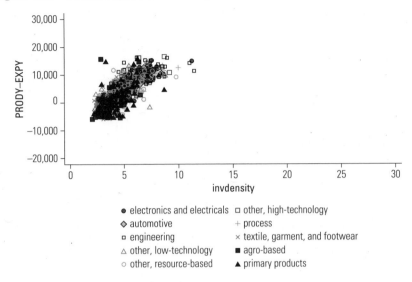

● electronics and electricals   □ other, high-technology
◇ automotive   + process
▫ engineering   × textile, garment, and footwear
△ other, low-technology   ■ agro-based
○ other, resource-based   ▲ primary products

Source: Authors' calculations based on UN Comtrade data.

Figure 4.28   Product Space of Thailand, 2006

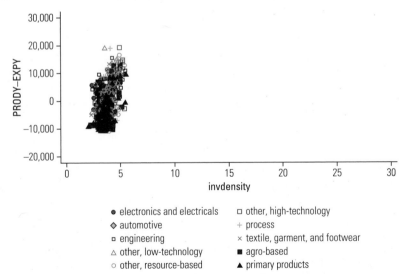

● electronics and electricals   □ other, high-technology
◇ automotive   + process
▫ engineering   × textile, garment, and footwear
△ other, low-technology   ■ agro-based
○ other, resource-based   ▲ primary products

Source: Authors' calculations based on UN Comtrade data.

Table 4.21 Top 10 "Upscale" Commodities with the Highest Density in Thailand, 1987

Short description	Density	Technology class	PRODY–EXPY
Undergarments of textile fabrics, not knitted or crocheted; men's, boys' undergarments, other than shirts	0.450218	LT1	778
Manufactured goods, N.E.S.	0.420227	LT2	2,879
Clothing accessories, knitted or crocheted, N.E.S.	0.410723	LT1	317
Outerwear, knitted or crocheted, not elastic or rubberized; jerseys, pullovers, slipovers, cardigans, etc.	0.409869	LT1	1,155
Undergarments, knitted or crocheted; of cotton, not elastic or rubberized	0.39557	LT1	111
Outerwear knitted or crocheted, not elastic or rubberized; other clothing accessories, nonelastic, knitted or crocheted	0.393131	LT1	363
Macaroni, spaghetti, and similar products	0.381835	RB1	1,357
Outerwear, knitted or crocheted, not elastic or rubberized; women's, girls', infants' suits, dresses, etc., knitted, crocheted	0.380661	LT1	84
Umbrellas, canes, and similar articles and parts thereof	0.374083	LT2	2,445
Travel goods, handbags, etc., of leather, plastics, textile, others	0.363848	LT1	365

Source: Authors' calculations using UN Comtrade data. Technology classification is based on Lall (2000).
Note: See the note to table 4.2.

resource-based, and low-tech products, because the Southeast Asian countries were more resource abundant on balance than the Northeast Asian ones (see table 4.23). By 2006, the steady development of electronic, automotive, and machinery industries via FDI had widened the options, primarily for Malaysia and Thailand. But the industrial deepening and backward linkages foreshadowed by the product space analysis have yet to be realized, and MNCs are not taking the lead in moving industrialization in these countries to the next level. For this to happen, diversification and upgrading[14] must be spearheaded by domestic firms with the requisite strategy and resources.[15] Without such firms, it is questionable whether the industrialization

---

[14]Upgrading is also dependent on the supply and quality of scientific and technical skills. Quality, in particular, remains poor throughout Southeast Asia, constraining technological capabilities and undermining the efforts to stimulate innovation.

[15]Kim (2007) maintains that the current trading arrangements are inhibiting the accumulation of social experience capital needed to enter more technology-intensive areas.

Table 4.22   Top 10 "Upscale" Commodities with the Highest Density in Thailand, 2006

Short description	Density	Technology class	PRODY–EXPY
Crystals and parts, N.E.S., of electronic components of heading 776	0.423955	HT1	5,657
Printed circuits and parts thereof, N.E.S.	0.417283	MT3	4,218
Peripheral units, including control and adapting units	0.395574	HT1	1,150
Electronic microcircuits	0.393997	HT1	5,365
Other sound recording and reproduction, N.E.S.; video recorders	0.377896	MT3	5,141
Clocks, clock movements, and parts	0.376103	MT3	3,162
Pearls, not mounted, set, or strung	0.373857	RB2	6,041
Other electrical machinery and equipment, N.E.S.	0.369362	HT1	3,686
Fabrics, woven, of continuous synthetic textile materials	0.368156	MT2	3,484
Parts, N.E.S., of and accessories for machines of headings 7512 and 752	0.353374	HT1	6,354

Source: Authors' calculations using UN Comtrade data. Technology classification is based on Lall (2000).
Note: See the note to table 4.2.

Table 4.23   Subsoil Assets, 2000
US$ per capita

Country	Subsoil assets
Malaysia	6,922
Indonesia	1,549
China	511
Thailand	469
Pakistan	265
India	201
Bangladesh	83
Korea, Rep.	33
Philippines	30
Japan	28
Singapore	0
Sri Lanka	0

Source: World Development Indicators Database.

of the Southeast Asian countries can proceed in the directions suggested by product space analysis.[16]

Trade Competition: China, India, and the Rest

So much for industrialization—now what of trade? The United States and the European Union absorbed the majority of Southeast Asia's exports through the mid-1980s. In 1983, 53 percent of the manufactured exports from Southeast Asian countries were to the United States and the European Union. The trend for direct exports to these regions has been downward, since more of the exports are being absorbed by final assemblers in China, who sell the bulk of their output in OECD (Organisation for Economic Co-operation and Development) markets (see figure 4.29).

Figure 4.29 Share of Manufactured Exports of Southeast Asian Countries Destined for the United States, EU15, and China

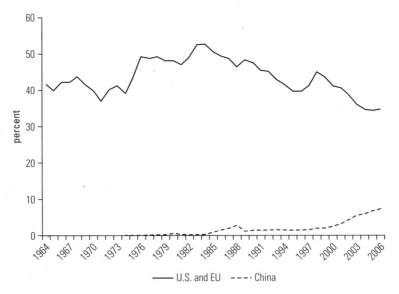

Source: Authors' calculations based on UN Comtrade data.
Note: Southeast Asian countries include Indonesia, Malaysia, the Philippines, and Thailand.

---

[16]Southeast Asian firms have demonstrated limited initiatives aimed at moving up the manufacturing value chain; in recent years, private investment has flowed more into finance, real estate, and retail services than into manufacturing.

Export Overlap with Southeast Asia

As recently as 1987, 70 percent of Southeast Asia's trade with India was in primary and resource-based products (see figure 4.30). Although these countries still export a significant amount of primary and resource-based products to India (for instance, Malaysia and Indonesia both export palm oil and petroleum, Thailand is an exporter of rice, and Indonesia also exports wood products), in recent years the composition of exports from Southeast Asian countries has altered to feature electronics and electrical components. In fact, the share of primary and resource-based products is now only half of what it was in 1987.

Imports by Southeast Asian countries from India consist of items such as cotton, oil seeds, meat, precious stones, and iron and steel. Although the exports of medium- and high-tech products from India to Southeast Asian countries increased between 1987 and 2006, primary and resource-based products still account for more than 60 percent, only a slight change from 1987 (see figure 4.31).

The overlap in exports between India and Southeast Asian middle-income economies has increased in the past 10 years, especially for the Philippines, although the degree of overlap is low compared to the overlap with China's exports (see figures 4.32 and 4.33).

The exports from middle-income Southeast Asian economies currently facing competition from India are low-tech products such as garments, textiles, and footwear, and medium-tech manufactures (see figure 4.34 and table 4.24). Looking

Figure 4.30   Composition of Exports from Southeast Asia to India, 1987 and 2006

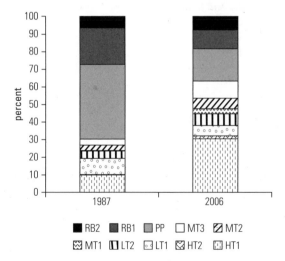

Legend: RB2 RB1 PP MT3 MT2 MT1 LT2 LT1 HT2 HT1

Source: Authors' calculations based on UN Comtrade data. Technology classification is based on Lall (2000).
Note: See the note to table 4.2.

Figure 4.31   Composition of India's Exports to Southeast Asian Countries, 1987 and 2006

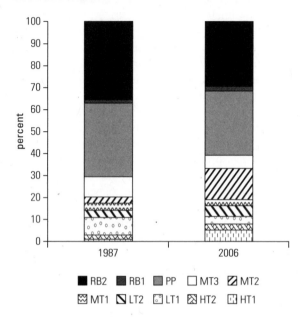

Legend: ■ RB2 ■ RB1 ■ PP □ MT3 ▨ MT2 ☒ MT1 ◹ LT2 ⊡ LT1 ▧ HT2 ⊞ HT1

Source: Authors' calculations based on UN Comtrade data. Technology classification is based on Lall (2000).
Note: See the note to table 4.2.

Figure 4.32   Share of Overlapping Trade Values between Southeast Asian Countries and India

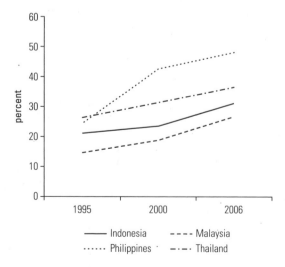

Legend: —— Indonesia - - - - Malaysia ······ Philippines — ·— · Thailand

Source: Authors' calculations based on UN Comtrade data.

Figure 4.33   Share of Overlapping Trade Values between Southeast Asian Countries and China

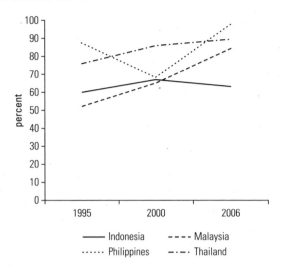

Source: Authors' calculations based on UN Comtrade data.

Figure 4.34   Share of Overlapping Trade Values between Southeast Asian Countries and India by Technology Class

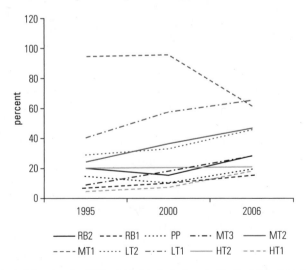

Source: Authors' calculations based on UN Comtrade data. Technology classification is based on Lall (2000).
Note: See the note to table 4.2.

Table 4.24 **Share of Overlapping Trade Values between Southeast Asian Countries and India by Technology Class**
percent

	1995	2000	2006
HT1	4.6	7.2	18.0
HT2	20.0	20.5	21.0
LT1	40.3	57.4	65.3
LT2	28.8	32.9	45.4
MT1	94.2	95.7	61.2
MT2	24.5	36.0	46.4
MT3	8.9	18.0	28.0
PP	14.7	10.2	19.3
RB1	6.7	10.1	15.1
RB2	19.9	15.3	28.2

Source: Authors' calculations using UN Comtrade data. Technology classification is based on Lall (2000).
Note: See the note to table 4.2.

ahead, the data suggest that competition could extend to other products as well; with the exception of automotive products, the overlap between the exports of middle-income Southeast Asian economies and those of India is increasing.

Compared with the case of India, exports from the middle-income countries in East Asia are facing much stiffer competition from China (see figure 4.35 and table 4.25). Exports of Southeast Asian countries are quite similar to those of China, except for primary products, automotive products, and resource-based products. This is partly a reflection of the nature of the production networks and intra-industry trade. However, it would be naïve to assume that such symbiotic arrangements can persist in the future. Given the current crisis and possible changes in external conditions, it is more likely that these countries will be competing head to head with China. We will explore this in more detail in chapter 6.

Industrialization and Trade of the Low-Income Asian Countries

With the exception of Vietnam, the low-income countries of South and Southeast Asia have been unable to progress beyond industrial adolescence. Inward-looking, protectionist policies and bouts of political disorder, arguably exacerbated by neighborhood effects, have hamstrung countries such as Pakistan, Bangladesh, Nepal, Sri Lanka, and Cambodia. The promise of the 1950s and 1960s, when economies such as Pakistan appeared to be on the threshold of rapid industrialization, was never realized. The growth performance of Pakistan, Bangladesh, and

Figure 4.35   Share of Overlapping Trade Values between Southeast Asian Countries and China by Technology Class

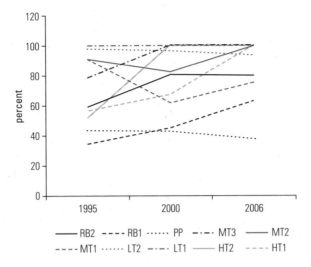

Source: Authors' calculations based on UN Comtrade data. Technology classification is based on Lall (2000).
Note: See the note to table 4.2.

Table 4.25   Share of Overlapping Trade Values between Southeast Asian Countries and China by Technology Class
percent

	1995	2000	2006
HT1	56.4	67.5	100.0
HT2	51.8	100.0	99.6
LT1	100.0	100.0	100.0
LT2	97.6	96.2	93.2
MT1	91.4	61.5	74.8
MT2	90.8	82.2	99.8
MT3	78.2	99.9	100.0
PP	43.4	42.8	37.3
RB1	34.6	45.4	63.0
RB2	59.3	80.6	80.0

Source: Authors' calculations using UN Comtrade data. Technology classification is based on Lall (2000).
Note: See the note to table 4.2.

Sri Lanka between 1975 and 2007 has been above the average for developing countries (see figure 4.36 and table 4.26), but it has not been reinforced as it was in East Asia by a local or FDI-led virtuous spiral of industrialization and exports.

Because the development of manufacturing industries did not extend much beyond textiles, garments, and other low-tech activities, the share of manufacturing (and industry) in GDP remains relatively low. An arrested industrial transition has impeded the transfer of workers from agriculture to industry, and the

Figure 4.36   GDP Growth

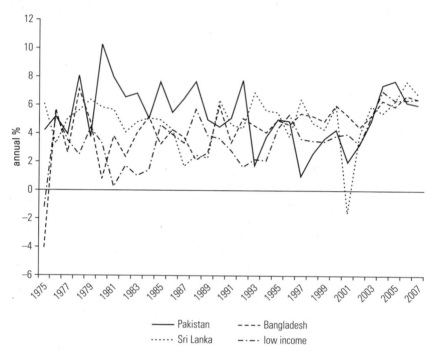

Source: World Development Indicators Database.

Table 4.26   Average Annual GDP Growth, 1975–2007

Country	Average annual GDP growth (%)
Bangladesh	4.32
Pakistan	5.31
Sri Lanka	4.88
Low-income countries	3.59

Source: World Development Indicators Database.

share of the primary sector remains close to 20 percent of GDP. Moreover, growth in these countries continues to fluctuate with reference to the fickle, weather-related fortunes of agriculture.

Partial industrialization is closely associated with two other characteristics of these economies. On average, they are less open and trade dependent than East Asian countries, and manufactures constitute a lesser share of exports. The stock of human capital is smaller and poorer in quality,[17] and percentagewise, the annual additions also tend to be modest. Furthermore, because industrialization has been marking time, the potential for growth- and productivity-enhancing technological change is also circumscribed.

Figures 4.37, 4.38, 4.39, 4.40, and 4.41 expose the factors underlying the performance of the low-income countries. Industry does not command a large enough share (Vietnam is a possible exception). The composition of manufactured exports leans toward textiles and light consumer items, and the fastest-growing exports are mainly low-tech, labor-intensive products with limited growth prospects.

Figure 4.37   Manufacturing, Value Added

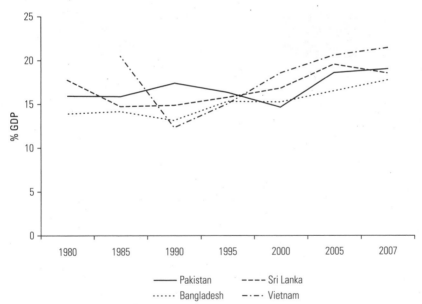

Source: World Development Indicators Database.

---

[17]Schooling quality and English language skills have stagnated or declined in each of these countries.

Figure 4.38   Industrial Composition by Type of Manufactures of Pakistan: 1981, 1990, and 1996

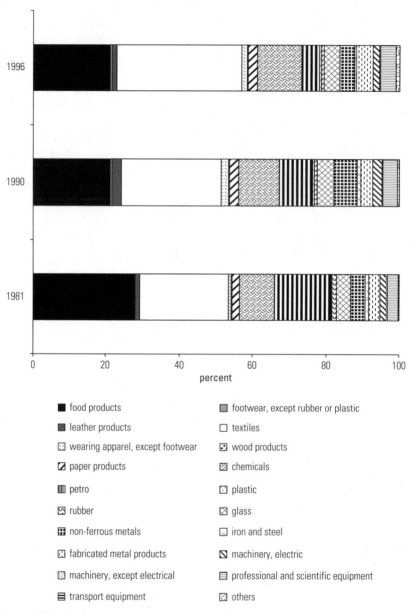

Source: UNIDO INDSTAT3.

Figure 4.39   Industrial Composition by Type of Manufactures of Bangladesh: 1981, 1990, and 1998

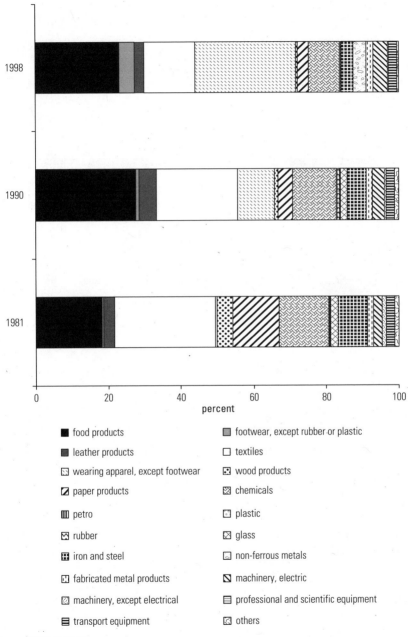

percent

■ food products	▨ footwear, except rubber or plastic
▦ leather products	□ textiles
▨ wearing apparel, except footwear	▣ wood products
▨ paper products	▨ chemicals
▥ petro	▣ plastic
▨ rubber	▨ glass
⊞ iron and steel	▨ non-ferrous metals
▣ fabricated metal products	◹ machinery, electric
▨ machinery, except electrical	▤ professional and scientific equipment
▤ transport equipment	▨ others

Source: UNIDO INDSTAT3.

Figure 4.40   Industrial Composition by Type of Manufactures of Sri Lanka: 1981, 1990, and 2001

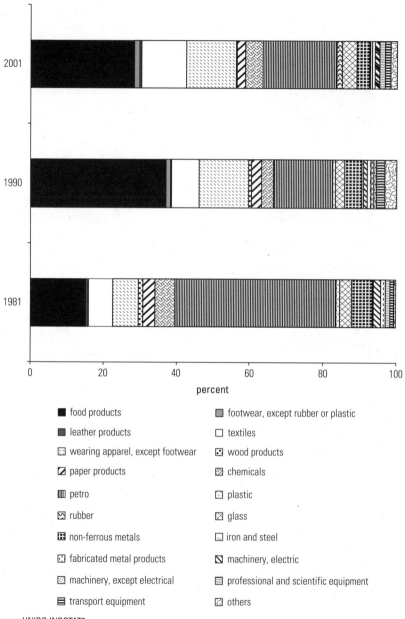

■ food products	▨ footwear, except rubber or plastic
▨ leather products	☐ textiles
▨ wearing apparel, except footwear	▨ wood products
▨ paper products	▨ chemicals
▥ petro	▨ plastic
▨ rubber	▨ glass
⊞ non-ferrous metals	▨ iron and steel
▨ fabricated metal products	▨ machinery, electric
▨ machinery, except electrical	▤ professional and scientific equipment
▤ transport equipment	▨ others

Source: UNIDO INDSTAT3.

Figure 4.41   Industrial Composition by Type of Manufactures of Vietnam: 2000, 2003

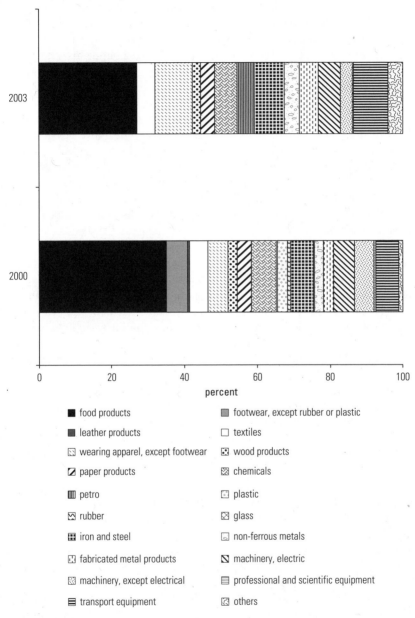

percent

■ food products	▨ footwear, except rubber or plastic
■ leather products	☐ textiles
▧ wearing apparel, except footwear	⦂ wood products
▨ paper products	▨ chemicals
▥ petro	▨ plastic
▨ rubber	▨ glass
▦ iron and steel	▨ non-ferrous metals
▨ fabricated metal products	◩ machinery, electric
▨ machinery, except electrical	▤ professional and scientific equipment
▤ transport equipment	▨ others

Source: UNIDO INDSTAT3.

The RCA calculations underscore the limited manufacturing capabilities of South Asian economies. More important, they point to the slow rate of change between 1985 and 2006. In Bangladesh, for example, jute products, garments, and textiles were among the products with the highest RCA in 1985. Twenty years later, jute products and garments retained the top spots, the difference being that garments had increased their dominance and had edged out primary commodities such as leather, tea, and shellfish (see table 4.27).

The evolution of Pakistan's comparative advantage is similar. In 1985, primary products such as rice, molasses, oil seeds, and raw cotton and simple manufactures such as carpets, cotton yarn, and fabric were among the most competitive products. By 2006, much like that of Bangladesh, Pakistan's comparative advantage had climbed a few notches to encompass a broader range of fabrics, garments, and other textile articles, all representative of an industrial beginner and not what one might expect of a country that had entered the race to industrialize at the same time as Korea and Taiwan, China (see table 4.28). In the 1960s, Pakistan looked like a winner; but its economic stride faltered in the following decades because of unfocused policies and protectionism.

Sri Lanka and Vietnam have much in common. Production and export of primary products such as fibers, oil seeds, tea, and rubber were Sri Lanka's strengths in 1985. By 2005, these exports were supplemented by garments (see table 4.29). Much the same description fits Vietnam (see table 4.30). The products differ, but the RCA story is the same—although by all accounts, Vietnam is industrializing faster through FDI, including investment by Chinese producers of light manufactures seeking lower-wage production platforms.

The United States and the European Union are the principal trading partners of Asia's low-income countries (see figure 4.42). Nearly 80 percent of exports from Bangladesh and Sri Lanka are absorbed by these two markets (and more than half of the exports of Pakistan and Vietnam). Exports to China and India are growing but are still fairly small, although China is becoming an important export destination for Vietnam, Bangladesh, and Pakistan (see figure 4.43). India has remained an insignificant market for these countries, except for Sri Lanka (see figure 4.44).

Imports are a different story, because China, in particular, is a highly competitive producer of the low- and medium-tech manufactures that these countries require. In fact, one-quarter of Bangladesh's imports now come from China, whose market share is expanding throughout South Asia (see figure 4.45). India is also enlarging its market share, but its penetration is most visible in Bangladesh and Sri Lanka (see figure 4.46). From tables 4.31 and 4.32 we can see the composition of the largest and fastest-rising imports into the low-income South Asian countries, as well as the origins of these imports. For the leading imports in terms of value, China is the major supplier of textiles and (with India) of lower-quality iron and steel products. India is a significant source of chemical products.

Product space analysis offers some clues as to the prospects for industrial diversification in South Asia and Vietnam. Compared with Southeast Asian economies,

Table 4.27   Top 10 Four-Digit-Level Commodities with the Highest RCA in Bangladesh: 1985, 2006

Short Description	RCA	PRODY	Technology class
1985			
Jute, other textile bast fibers, N.E.S., raw, processed but not spun	1392.27	255	RB1
Fabrics, woven, of jute or other textile bast fibers of heading 2640	817.86	278	LT1
Bags, sacks of textile materials, for the packing of goods	409.76	603	LT1
Live animals of a kind mainly used for human food, N.E.S.	98.07	6,188	PP
Under garments of textile fabrics, not knitted or crocheted; men's and boys' shirts	71.79	3,160	LT1
Leather of other hides or skins	68.47	852	LT1
Other fresh, chilled, or frozen meat or edible meat offal	52.92	8,045	PP
Yarn of textile fibers, N.E.S.	47.53	4,887	LT1
Crustaceans and mollusks, fresh, chilled, frozen, salted, etc.	36.86	5,548	PP
Tea	31.15	536	PP
2006			
Jute, other textile bast fibers, N.E.S., raw, processed but not spun	872.05	448	RB1
Fabrics, woven of jute or other textile bast fibers of heading 2640	370.46	842	LT1
Undergarments, knitted or crocheted; of other fibers, not elastic or rubberized	118.94	2,404	LT1
Undergarments of textile fabrics, not knitted or crocheted; men's and boys' shirts	72.04	3,979	LT1
Men's and boys' outerwear, textile fabrics not knitted or crocheted; trousers, breeches, and the like	64.01	4,528	LT1
Undergarments, knitted or crocheted; of cotton, not elastic or rubberized	61.63	5,645	LT1
Men's and boys' outerwear, textile fabrics not knitted or crocheted; jackets, blazers, and the like	51.06	4,466	LT1
Yarn of textile fibers, N.E.S.	46.36	6,319	LT1
Bags, sacks of textile materials, for the packing of goods	31.83	2,620	LT1
Outerwear, knitted or crocheted, not elastic or rubberized; jerseys, pullovers, slipovers, cardigans, etc.	30.96	10,190	LT1

Source: Authors' calculations using UN Comtrade data. Technology classification is based on Lall (2000).
Note: See the note to table 4.2.

Table 4.28   Top 10 Four-Digit-Level Commodities with the Highest RCA in Pakistan: 1985, 2006

Short description	RCA	PRODY	Technology class
1985			
Animal or vegetable fertilizer, crude	129.29	2,304	PP
Carpets, carpeting, and rugs, knotted	103.92	1,256	LT1
Castor oil seeds	96.86	1,134	PP
Tarpaulins, sails, tents, camping goods, etc., of textile fabrics	82.04	3,457	LT1
Molasses	74.45	2,490	RB1
Rice, semimilled or wholly milled	61.64	1,693	PP
Raw cotton, excluding linters, not carded or combed	57.63	1,690	PP
Cotton yarn	55.39	3,087	LT1
Cotton fabrics, woven, unbleached, not mercerized	52.70	2,484	LT1
Leather or other hides or skins	52.58	852	LT1
2006			
Articles of leather used in machinery or mechanical appliances, etc.	281.61	2,134	LT1
Cotton fabrics, woven, unbleached, not mercerized	120.97	2,527	LT1
Carpets, carpeting, and rugs, knotted	105.93	2,088	LT1
Linens and furnishing articles of textile, not knitted or crocheted	95.00	3,203	LT1
Undergarments, knitted or crocheted; of other fibers, not elastic or rubberized	92.18	2,404	LT1
Cotton yarn	90.10	3,830	LT1
Cotton waste, not carded or combed	89.76	2,954	PP
Rice, semimilled or wholly milled	82.28	2,678	PP
Molasses	52.38	1,680	RB1
Articles of apparel, clothing accessories of leather	49.40	5,318	LT1

Source: Authors' calculations using UN Comtrade data. Technology classification is based on Lall (2000).
Note: See the note to table 4.2.

the product space of Bangladesh hardly changed between 1987 and 2006 (figures 4.47 and 4.48). The densities of upgrading and diversification opportunities barely increased between 1987 and 2006, suggesting that the potential for diversifying did not improve after 1987, nor did the composition of the industrial opportunities (see tables 4.33 and 4.34). In both years, apparel is the favored product group, and few other manufactures enter the picture.

Pakistan's situation is a little brighter. The distribution of the product space moved closer to the origin and became tighter, suggesting a modest gain in industrial capabilities between 1987 and 2006 (see figures 4.49 and 4.50). However, closer inspection of the most promising products reveals that the majority are

Table 4.29   Top 10 Four-Digit-Level Commodities with the Highest RCA in Sri Lanka: 1985, 2005

Short description	RCA	PRODY	Technology class
1985			
Vegetable textile fibers, N.E.S., and waste	542.99	813	RB1
Tea	239.94	536	PP
Sesame seeds	115.90	1,662	PP
Fuel wood and wood charcoal	95.43	2,288	PP
Coconut (copra) oil	60.22	1,312	RB1
Castor oil seeds	53.63	1,134	PP
Spices, except pepper and pimento	38.35	1,272	PP
Natural rubber latex; natural rubber and gums	34.59	2,114	PP
Nuts edible, fresh or dried	34.02	2,294	PP
Men's and boys' outerwear, textile fabrics not knitted or crocheted; other outer garments	32.11	5,714	LT1
2005			
Vegetable textile fibers, N.E.S., and waste	809.67	1,186	RB1
Tea	350.52	604	PP
Copra	326.45	552	PP
Undergarments, knitted or crocheted; of other fibers, not elastic or rubberized	204.04	1,988	LT1
Spices, except pepper and pimento	74.72	1,387	PP
Precious and semiprecious stones, not mounted, set, or strung	70.31	3,167	RB2
Hydrogenated animal or vegetable oils and fats	68.80	2,966	RB1
Other tires, tire cases, tire flaps and inner tubes, etc.	60.96	7,593	RB1
Undergarments of textile fabrics, not knitted or crocheted; women's, girls', infants' undergarments, textile, not knitted, etc.	54.74	2,889	LT1
Undergarments, knitted or crocheted; of wool or fine animal hair, not elastic or rubberized	44.11	4,836	LT1

Source: Authors' calculations using UN Comtrade data. Technology classification is based on Lall (2000).
Note: See the note to table 4.2.

unchanged (see table 4.35 and 4.36). As in Bangladesh, the path to upgrading and diversification for Pakistan has not extended beyond apparel and some resource-based products.

Although a lack of data for Vietnam precludes us from commenting on its future industrialization, episodic information suggests that Vietnam is in a better position to diversify and upgrade its export basket relative to Bangladesh and Pakistan. In 2006, at least, the distribution of product space resembles that of the Southeast Asian rather than the South Asian economies, and the distribution

Table 4.30 Top 10 Four-Digit-Level Commodities with the Highest RCA in Vietnam: 2000, 2006

Short description	RCA	PRODY	Technology class
2000			
Roasted iron pyrites	273.64	7,484	RB2
Vegetable textile fibers, N.E.S., and waste	119.17	3,317	RB1
Rice, semimilled or wholly milled	50.90	2,459	PP
Pepper; pimento	48.90	2,739	PP
Men's and boys' outerwear, textile fabrics not knitted or crocheted; overcoats and other coats	42.84	2,745	LT1
Crustaceans and mollusks, fresh, chilled, frozen, salted, etc.	31.55	3,339	PP
Fuel wood and wood charcoal	26.24	2,363	PP
Tin and tin alloys, worked	24.23	6,731	PP
Coffee, green, roasted; coffee substitutes containing coffee	22.82	858	PP
Silk yarn and spun from noil or waste; silkworm gut	21.85	4,060	LT1
2006			
Anthracite, not agglomerated	113.24	1,809	PP
Copra	109.45	1,151	PP
Vegetable textile fibers, N.E.S., and waste	100.48	2,518	RB1
Pepper; pimento	38.27	2,205	PP
Rice, semimilled or wholly milled	37.42	2,678	PP
Men's and boys' outerwear, textile fabrics not knitted or crocheted; overcoats and other coats	28.87	4,230	LT1
Fish fillets, frozen	25.89	15,479	PP
Crustaceans and mollusks, fresh, chilled, frozen, salted, etc.	24.49	5,097	PP
Vegetable products, roots and tubers, N.E.S., fresh, dried	23.87	2,039	PP
Coffee, green, roasted; coffee substitutes containing coffee	23.42	1,120	PP

Source: Authors' calculations using UN Comtrade data. Technology classification is based on Lall (2000).
Note: See the note to table 4.2.

relative to South Asian economies is closer to the origin (see figure 4.51). However, Vietnam's short-term opportunities for diversification and upgrading also lie in primary, resource-based, and low-tech products, similar to the situation for the Southeast Asian countries in 1987 (table 4.37). Whether or not Vietnam can follow the Southeast Asian path to industrial development remains to be seen. As in Southeast Asia and China, the speed of transformation is likely to depend on Vietnam's ability to attract FDI in medium- and high-tech products, the level of domestic investment, and the emergence of domestic industrial and technological capabilities.

Figure 4.42   Dependence on U.S. and EU Markets

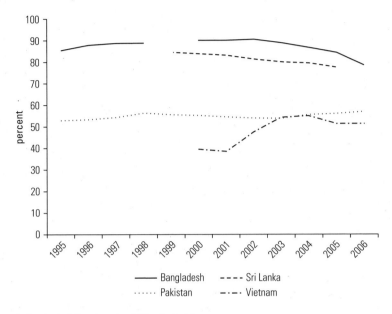

Source: Authors' calculations based on UN Comtrade data.

Given the slow pace of industrial progress in South Asian countries (excluding India), the prospect of catching up with the industrializing frontrunners is not improving. The production of textiles, food products, and processed commodities is the low and circuitous (and perhaps never-ending) path to industrial deepening. Pakistan, Bangladesh, Nepal, and Sri Lanka are specializing in low-value commodities, which occupy parts of the product space with fewer links to other commodity groups. Vietnam is a little different, but its industrial potential remains to be fully exploited.

The challenge facing South Asian countries is how to accelerate industrial change after decades of stagnation (although Pakistan, Sri Lanka and Bangladesh have all sustained GDP growth rates that are above the average for developing countries), and how to supplement consumption-driven growth with net exports by diversifying the export mix into medium-tech commodities promising better returns. There are some signs that such shifts may be implemented with the help of domestic entrepreneurship backed by domestic capital mobilized through the financial system. Foreign investment in manufacturing seems unlikely to mushroom in the near future; in fact, foreign investors have largely avoided industrial ventures in the low-income South Asian countries (except for India), because the business climate has been distinctly unfavorable there. Efforts at industrial and

Figure 4.43 Exports to China from Bangladesh, Sri Lanka, Pakistan, and Vietnam

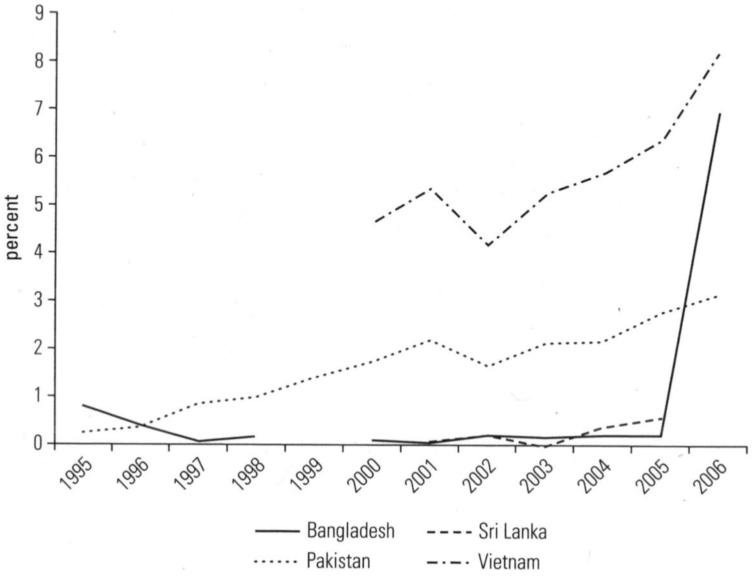

Source: Authors' calculations based on UN Comtrade data.

export diversification, should they intensify, would also confront intense competition from established producers in East Asia and the excess capacity in many industries. These problems will be compounded by less robust growth in import demand from some Western markets, most notably the United States. Marking time in industrial terms is economically and politically unpalatable for low-income countries, with growing and youthful populations, and facing mounting problems associated with unemployment, poverty, the looming challenge from climate change, and, in some cases, smoldering social unrest.

Chances are that the global economy will not regain the tempo it briefly achieved during 2005–07. With GDP growth and trade expanding more slowly, the countries of East and South Asia will need to strike a new equilibrium among themselves and with other countries. The most significant challenge will be the growing, reorienting, or downsizing of their industries in response to development strategies pursued by India and China and adjustment in the United States.

Technological Capabilities and Competitiveness

The external conditions may be not as favorable as in the past for the developing countries to diversify and deepen their industries by exploiting export opportunities.

Figure 4.44 Exports to India from Bangladesh, Sri Lanka, Pakistan, and Vietnam

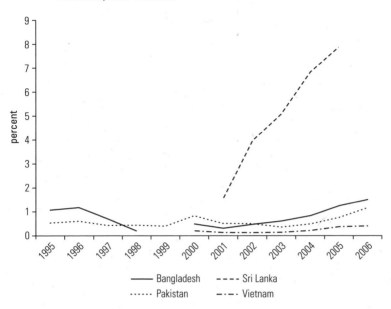

Source: Authors' calculations based on UN Comtrade data.

Consequently, Asian—mainly East Asian—countries are attempting to develop indigenous technological capabilities to cater to the wants of lower- and middle-income consumers in Asia, as well as buyers in industrialized countries.[18] In the face of stiffening competition within Asia, technology is coming to be viewed as a more important driver of growth than capital (Prahalad and Krishnan 2008). Following the example of Japan and Korea, countries are intensifying technology efforts and recognizing that FDI is only a partial answer, although such flow can facilitate technology transfer. There are several metrics that are used to assess the technological capabilities of a country. Some are input based, such as tertiary education enrollment and spending on R&D, and some are based on outputs, such as patents and published papers.

Tertiary Education

Except for Korea, Japan, and Thailand, Asian countries are lagging behind in terms of tertiary education enrollment (see table 4.38). While the gross enrollment rate in

---

[18]Some of this is through cost innovation that helps reduce the prices of manufactures and expands their markets.

Figure 4.45 China's Share of Imports in Bangladesh, Sri Lanka, Pakistan, and Vietnam

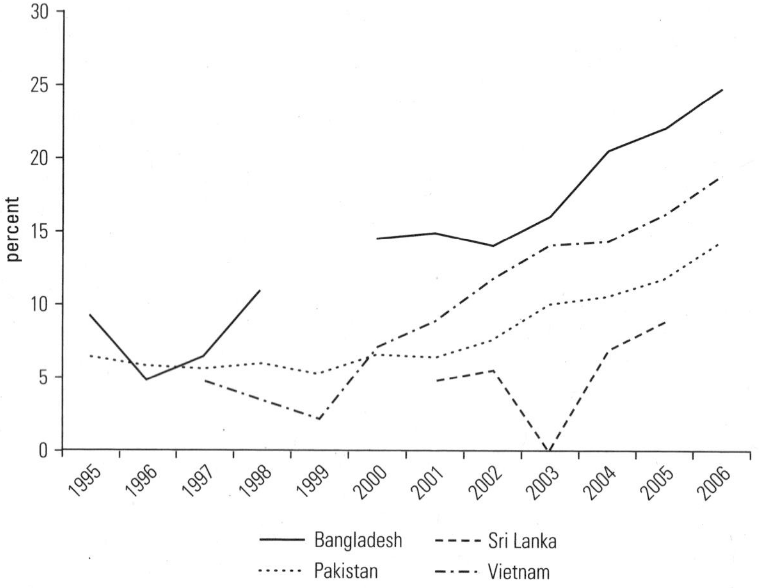

Source: Authors' calculations based on UN Comtrade data.

Korea is 93 percent (much higher than that of the United States), the enrollment rates in Japan and Thailand are 57 percent and 46 percent, respectively. Gross enrollment rates in other East Asian economies range from 17 percent in Indonesia to 29 percent in the Philippines. The gross enrollment rate in South Asia is low. India leads the pack with 12 percent, followed by Bangladesh (7 percent) and Pakistan (5 percent).

Enrollment in science and engineering fields is another indicator of the capacity to absorb and develop technology. More than half of all students in China, Japan, Singapore, and Thailand earn science and engineering degrees (see table 4.39). A significant percentage of students in Bangladesh; Hong Kong, China; Korea; and Taiwan, China; also earn their degrees in science and engineering fields, while relatively few students are graduating with science and engineering degrees in India, Pakistan, and the Philippines. The experience of East Asia suggests that to build indigenous technological capabilities, countries need to produce a sufficient supply of scientists and engineers, with these fields accounting for more than half of the total enrollment or graduation at the current stage of development. Quality of education must buttress quantity, and by all indications, the quality of education is wanting in Southeast and South Asian countries.[19] South and Southeast Asian

---

[19]On the quality of tertiary education in Southeast Asia, see Yusuf and Nabeshima (2010).

Figure 4.46   India's Share of Imports in Bangladesh, Sri Lanka, Pakistan, and Vietnam

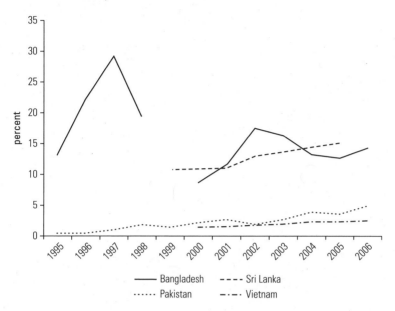

Source: Authors' calculations based on UN Comtrade data.

Table 4.31   Largest Imports of South Asian Countries
percent

Product	Product share	Share of U.S.	Share of EU15	Share of Japan	Share of China	Share of India
Gold, nonmonetary unwrought, semimanufactured	5.3	0.2	0.8	0.4	0.0	0.0
Polyethylene in primary forms	2.1	3.0	2.7	2.6	0.7	3.5
Polypropylene in primary forms	1.9	7.3	1.3	2.9	0.3	17.6
Iron/steel coils of other than high carbon steel	1.6	0.5	2.8	27.9	16.6	1.4
Fabrics mixed with fibers other than cotton, wool, etc.	1.6	0.8	4.7	9.6	31.8	0.8
Fabrics mixed mainly or solely with cotton	1.6	0.1	1.0	1.4	84.5	0.3
Blooms, etc., of other than high carbon steel	1.5	0.3	0.8	2.8	68.1	6.4
Refined copper, unwrought	1.4	0.0	0.5	2.9	0.1	5.6
Waste of other iron or steel	1.4	10.3	16.2	6.9	0.1	0.1
Sheets and plates of other than high carbon steel	1.4	0.6	5.1	19.2	31.1	3.2

Source: Authors' calculations based on UN Comtrade data.

Table 4.32   Fastest-growing Imports of South Asian Countries
percent

Product	Annual growth rate	Share of U.S.	Share of EU15	Share of Japan	Share of China	Share of India
Blooms, etc., of high-carbon steel	488.0	0.1	1.2	5.3	54.0	1.2
Vinyl chloride (chloroethylene)	463.3	0.0	0.0	32.7	0.1	1.1
Liquefied propane and butane	397.6	0.1	0.0	0.1	0.0	0.0
Diamonds, cut, otherwise worked, not mounted or set	390.1	0.7	5.5	5.5	0.1	0.5
Diamonds, sorted, rough, simply sawn	382.1	0.0	91.5	0.0	0.0	0.0
Unrefined copper	371.6	0.0	0.1	2.1	0.4	0.1
Skins and other parts of birds with feather	365.0	15.2	10.3	0.2	2.9	0.0
Slag, dross, etc., and waste from manufacture	357.3	0.0	0.0	35.3	0.0	63.9
Skins and other parts of birds	350.3	3.5	1.1	1.3	0.6	0.0
Ingots of iron or steel	334.4	0.0	0.1	0.0	36.3	51.0

Source: Authors' calculations based on UN Comtrade data.

Figure 4.47   Product Space of Bangladesh, 1987

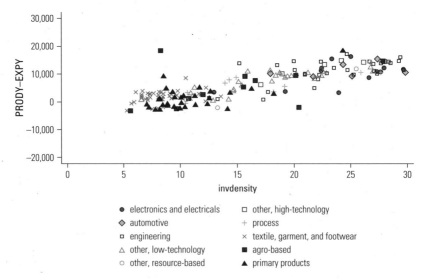

- ● electronics and electricals
- ◆ automotive
- ◘ engineering
- △ other, low-technology
- ○ other, resource-based
- □ other, high-technology
- + process
- × textile, garment, and footwear
- ■ agro-based
- ▲ primary products

Source: Authors' calculations based on UN Comtrade data.

Figure 4.48   Product Space of Bangladesh, 2006

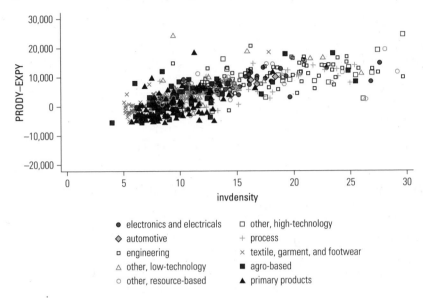

● electronics and electricals   □ other, high-technology
◆ automotive   + process
▫ engineering   × textile, garment, and footwear
△ other, low-technology   ■ agro-based
○ other, resource-based   ▲ primary products

Source: Authors' calculations based on UN Comtrade data.

Table 4.33   Top 10 "Upscale" Commodities with the Highest Density in Bangladesh, 1987

Short description	Density	Technology class	PRODY–EXPY
Undergarments of textile fabrics, not knitted or crocheted; men's, boys' undergarments, other than shirts	0.164584	LT1	3,512
Basketwork, wickerwork; brooms, paint rollers, etc.	0.15237	LT2	656
Women's, girls', infants' outerwear, textile, not knitted or crocheted; dresses	0.152142	LT1	2,564
Men's and boys' outerwear, textile fabrics not knitted or crocheted; jackets, blazers, and the like	0.152046	LT1	2,011
Men's and boys' outerwear, textile fabrics not knitted or crocheted; other outerwear	0.151764	LT1	1,615
Women's, girls', infants' outerwear, textile, not knitted or crocheted; other outer garments of textile fabrics, not knitted or crocheted	0.150978	LT1	1,437
Outerwear, knitted or crocheted, not elastic or rubberized; jerseys, pullovers, slipovers, cardigans, etc.	0.149653	LT1	3,888

(continued on next page)

Table 4.33 *(continued)*

Short description	Density	Technology class	PRODY–EXPY
Men's and boys' outerwear, textile fabrics not knitted or crocheted; trousers, breeches, and the like	0.144188	LT1	977
Undergarments of textile fabrics, not knitted or crocheted; women's, girls', infants' under garments, textile, not knitted, etc.	0.140466	LT1	1,357
Clothing accessories, of textile fabrics, not knitted or crocheted	0.14026	LT1	707

Source: Authors' calculations using UN Comtrade data. Technology classification is based on Lall (2000).
Note: See the note to table 4.2.

Table 4.34 Top 10 "Upscale" Commodities with the Highest Density in Bangladesh, 2006

Short description	Density	Technology class	PRODY–EXPY
Outerwear knitted or crocheted, not elastic or rubberized; other clothing accessories, nonelastic, knitted or crocheted	0.198168	LT1	1,397
Outerwear, knitted or crocheted, not elastic or rubberized; women's, girls', infants' suits, dresses, etc., knitted, crocheted	0.192436	LT1	293
Outerwear, knitted or crocheted, not elastic or rubberized; jerseys, pullovers, slipovers, cardigans, etc.	0.188801	LT1	4,263
Women's, girls', infants outerwear, textile, not knitted or crocheted; other outer garments of textile fabrics, not knitted or crocheted	0.182024	LT1	785
Undergarments, knitted or crocheted; of synthetic fibers, not elastic or rubberized	0.175899	LT1	230
Men's and boys' outerwear, textile fabrics not knitted or crocheted; other outer garments	0.171985	LT1	363
Fish, dried, salted or in brine; smoked fish	0.165889	RB1	7,922
Footwear	0.158627	LT1	12
Fish, frozen, excluding fillets	0.154622	PP	135
Corsets, garters, etc., not knitted or crocheted, elastic and nonelastic	0.153908	LT1	1,419

Source: Authors' calculations using UN Comtrade data. Technology classification is based on Lall (2000).
Note: See the note to table 4.2.

countries have a lot of catching up to do before they can expect to derive significant productivity gains from the technology push.

R&D Spending

Expenditure on R&D is another metric often used to judge the technological capabilities of a country. Japan is by far the largest spender on R&D as a share of

Figure 4.49   Product Space of Pakistan, 1987

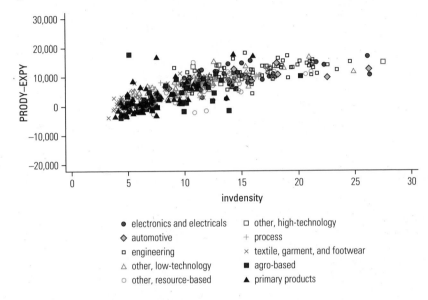

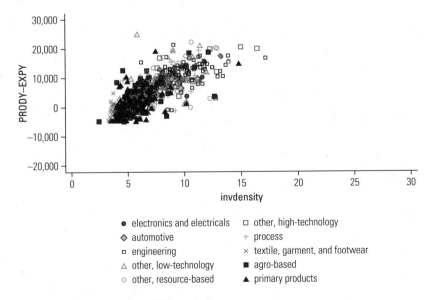

Source: Authors' calculations based on UN Comtrade data.

Figure 4.50   Product Space of Pakistan, 2006

Source: Authors' calculations based on UN Comtrade data.

Table 4.35 Top 10 "Upscale" Commodities with the Highest Density in Pakistan, 1987

Short description	Density	Technology class	PRODY–EXPY
Undergarments of textile fabrics, not knitted or crocheted; men's, boys' undergarments, other than shirts	0.268009	LT1	2,820
Men's and boys' outerwear, textile fabrics not knitted or crocheted; other outer garments	0.251025	LT1	923
Men's and boys' outerwear, textile fabrics not knitted or crocheted; jackets, blazers, and the like	0.241909	LT1	1,319
Women's, girls', infants' outerwear, textile, not knitted or crocheted; dresses	0.239259	LT1	1,872
Clothing accessories, of textile fabrics, not knitted or crocheted	0.23549	LT1	15
Women's, girls', infants' outerwear, textile, not knitted or crocheted; other outer garments of textile fabrics, not knitted or crocheted	0.234831	LT1	745
Outerwear, knitted or crocheted, not elastic or rubberized; other clothing accessories, nonelastic, knitted or crocheted	0.231841	LT1	2,405
Undergarments, knitted or crocheted; of cotton, not elastic or rubberized	0.230236	LT1	2,152
Silkworm cocoons and silk waste	0.228981	PP	1,116
Outerwear, knitted or crocheted, not elastic or rubberized; jerseys, pullovers, slipovers, cardigans, etc.	0.226621	LT1	3,196

Source: Authors' calculations using UN Comtrade data. Technology classification is based on Lall (2000).
Note: See the note to table 4.2.

Table 4.36 Top 10 "Upscale" Commodities with the Highest Density in Pakistan, 2006

Short description	Density	Technology class	PRODY–EXPY
Outerwear, knitted or crocheted, not elastic or rubberized; other clothing accessories, nonelastic, knitted or crocheted	0.289847	LT1	2,002
Undergarments, knitted or crocheted; of cotton, not elastic or rubberized	0.283071	LT1	322
Outerwear, knitted or crocheted, not elastic or rubberized; women's, girls', infants' suits, dresses, etc., knitted, crocheted	0.277122	LT1	897
Outerwear, knitted or crocheted, not elastic or rubberized; jerseys, pullovers, slipovers, cardigans, etc.	0.271571	LT1	4,867
Women's, girls', infants' outerwear, textile, not knitted or crocheted; other outer garments of textile fabrics, not knitted or crocheted	0.266353	LT1	1,389

(continued on next page)

Table 4.36 *(continued)*

Short description	Density	Technology class	PRODY–EXPY
Undergarments, knitted or crocheted; of synthetic fibers, not elastic or rubberized	0.262442	LT1	835
Men's and boys' outerwear, textile fabrics not knitted or crocheted; other outer garments	0.251116	LT1	968
Fish, dried, salted or in brine; smoked fish	0.249676	RB1	8,526
Fish, frozen, excluding fillets	0.244581	PP	740
Fabrics, woven, less than 85% of discontinuous synthetic fibers	0.240432	MT2	393

Source: Authors' calculations using UN Comtrade data. Technology classification is based on Lall (2000).
Note: See the note to table 4.2.

Figure 4.51   Product Space of Vietnam, 2006

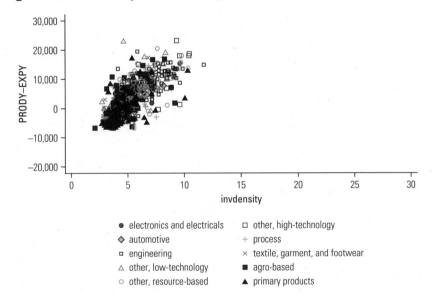

● electronics and electricals   □ other, high-technology
◆ automotive   + process
▫ engineering   × textile, garment, and footwear
△ other, low-technology   ■ agro-based
○ other, resource-based   ▲ primary products

Source: Authors' calculations based on UN Comtrade data.

GDP, with 3.4 percent of GDP so devoted in 2006 (see table 4.40). Korea has quickly ramped up its spending on R&D since 2000, and now it rivals Japan, with 3.2 percent of GDP channeled into R&D. Singapore also has been increasing its spending on R&D, which in 2006 accounted for 2.4 percent of GDP. The most impressive increase is in China, with the R&D outlay rising from 0.6 percent of GDP in 1999 to 1.4 percent in 2008. Given the rapid economic growth during this

Table 4.37   Top 10 "Upscale" Commodities with the Highest Density in Vietnam, 2006

Short description	Density	Technology class	PRODY–EXPY
Personal adornments and ornament articles of plastic	0.370375	LT2	2,158
Outerwear, knitted or crocheted, not elastic or rubberized; other clothing accessories, nonelastic, knitted or crocheted	0.351969	LT1	134
Outerwear, knitted or crocheted, not elastic or rubberized; jerseys, pullovers, slipovers, cardigans, etc.	0.341022	LT1	3,000
Fish, dried, salted or in brine; smoked fish	0.32256	RB1	6,659
Corsets, garters, etc., not knitted or crocheted, elastic or nonelastic	0.310899	LT1	156
Flours and meals of meat, fish, etc., unfit for human; greaves	0.306868	PP	5,469
Fish fillets, frozen	0.291687	PP	8,289
Base metal domestic articles, N.E.S., and parts thereof, N.E.S.	0.291541	LT2	960
Candles, matches, combustible products, etc.	0.289748	LT2	811
Crustaceans and mollusks, prepared or unprepared, N.E.S.	0.279235	RB1	10,739

Source: Authors' calculations using UN Comtrade data. Technology classification is based on Lall (2000).
Note: See the note to table 4.2.

Table 4.38   Gross Enrollment in Tertiary Education

Country/economy	1998	2000	2002	2006
Korea, Rep.	66.0	78.4	86.8	92.6
Japan	43.7	47.4	50.5	57.3
Thailand	—	35.2	41.0	45.9
Malaysia	22.1	25.9	28.0	30.2
Philippines	27.3	—	30.4	28.5
China	—	7.7	12.7	21.6
Indonesia	—	—	15.0	17.0
India	—	9.6	10.4	11.9
Vietnam	—	9.5	—	—
Bangladesh	—	5.4	6.0	6.8
Pakistan	—	—	2.5	4.5
Sri Lanka	—	—	—	—
Singapore	—	—	—	—
Taiwan, China	—	—	—	—

Source: World Development Indicators Database.
Note: — = not available.

Table 4.39   Percentage of First University Degrees in Science and Engineering

Country/economy	Year	Percentage
Bangladesh	2003	41.5
China	2004	56.2
Hong Kong, China	2004	37.7
India	2006	20.3
Japan	2005	63.3
Korea, Rep.	2004	45.6
Pakistan	2006	24.0
Philippines	2004	25.5
Philippines	2006	27.4
Singapore	2004	58.5
Taiwan, China	2005	40.8
Thailand	2001	68.9

Source: National Science Board (2008). Data for India, Pakistan, and the Philippines are from the World Bank Knowledge Assessment Methodology data set (http://www.worldbank.org/kam).

Table 4.40   R&D Spending by Country

Country	1996	2000	2002	2004	2005	2006
China	0.6	0.9	1.1	1.2	1.3	1.4
India	0.7	0.8	0.7	0.7	—	—
Indonesia	—	0.1	—	—	—	—
Japan	2.8	3.0	3.2	3.2	3.3	3.4
Korea, Rep.	2.4	2.4	2.5	2.9	3.0	3.2
Malaysia	0.2	0.5	0.7	0.6	—	—
Pakistan	—	0.1	0.2	—	0.4	—
Philippines	—	—	0.2	—	—	—
Singapore	1.4	1.9	2.2	2.2	2.4	2.4
Sri Lanka	0.2	0.1	—	0.2	—	—
Thailand	0.1	0.3	0.2	0.3	—	—
Vietnam	—	—	0.2	—	—	—

Source: World Development Indicators Database.
Note: — = not available.

period, the increase in the volume of resources committed to R&D is phenome-nal. The literature on R&D spending suggests that doubling such spending over a decade (along with a buildup of human capital and institutions supportive of inno-vation) can help lead to a technological takeoff for a country (Hu and Jefferson 2008). If China can sustain its research, it may emerge as a technology powerhouse in East Asia alongside Japan and Korea. But there is plenty of evidence to suggest that the efficient utilization of funds is probably the key to superior growth outcomes, and such efficiency is predicated on the accumulation of experience (managerial, research related, and marketing) in firms and research entities, which is a slow process.

Another indicator of technology potential is how R&D spending is distributed among the principal actors: private businesses, government, and higher education. In general, private firms are responsible for around two-thirds of R&D spending in OECD countries. In East Asia, firms account for a significant portion of R&D spending except in Indonesia and Vietnam (see table 4.41). In both Indonesia and Vietnam, government is the major source of R&D spending. This is also the case in South Asia. The share of government in R&D spending is more than 60 percent in India, Pakistan, and Sri Lanka. While the public sector is usually responsible for the bulk of basic and early-stage applied research, the task of technology development and the commercializing of innovation falls on firms. R&D spending during the development process can be viewed as a part of the effort to assimilate and internalize foreign technology while building the foundations of a national innovation system. During the rapid-growth phase of Japan, more than 30 percent of R&D was devoted to learning. Firms are in a much better position to identify the technologies that have the greatest commercial payoff, and they need to expend some effort in understanding these technologies. They must

Table 4.41   Composition of R&D Spending
percent

Country/economy	Business enterprise	Government	Higher education	Private nonprofit
China	71.1	19.7	9.2	—
Hong Kong, China	48.3	2.2	49.5	—
India	19.8	75.3	4.9	—
Indonesia	14.3	81.1	4.6	—
Japan	77.2	8.3	12.7	1.9
Korea, Rep.	77.3	11.6	10.0	1.2
Malaysia	71.5	10.4	18.1	—
Pakistan	—	67.6	32.4	—
Philippines	68.0	19.1	11.1	1.8
Singapore	65.7	10.4	23.9	—
Sri Lanka	5.5	61.0	33.6	—
Thailand	43.9	22.5	31.0	2.6
Vietnam	14.5	66.4	17.9	1.1

Source: UNESCO Institute for Statistics Data Centre.
Note: Hong Kong, China; India; Malaysia; Sri Lanka (2004). Philippines. Thailand (2003). Vietnam (2002). Indonesia (2001). — = not available.

also acquire the absorptive capacity through tailored organizational mechanisms and in-house research (Cohen and Levinthal 1990). Knowledge does not flow freely; it must be acquired.[20] The striking characteristic of research in the low-income economies of South Asia is the small share of the business sector, which explains, in part, the limited progress toward diversification in the past and threatens to hobble future efforts in this direction.

Patents

Tertiary education and R&D feed knowledge-generating activities, but they must be complemented by measures of output. A more sensitive—though far from adequate—measure of budding technological capabilities is the number of patents applied for and registered by the residents of a country (see Scotchmer 2004). This has tended to be based on the patents granted by the U.S. Patent and Trademark Office (USPTO) for several reasons. First, because the criteria for submission, the examination of patents, and the decision to award patents differ across countries, the number of patents granted by any one country is not directly comparable with that of another; in addition, the quality of patents differs. Using data from a specific patent office eliminates this incompatibility. Because the United States has been the major market for Asian economies, using data from the USPTO is appropriate. Second, applying to a foreign patenting office is more expensive. Therefore, only high-quality patents are submitted for approval, which serves to filter the data.

Table 4.42 lists the number of patents granted to Asian economies in 1992, 2000, and 2008. Japan is the leader by a wide margin, with more than 36,000 patents awarded in 2008.[21] Korea is a distant second, followed by Taiwan, China. The number of patents granted to these economies grew quite rapidly between 1992 and 2008. China now ranks fourth among Asian economies. In 2000, China received 163 patents—fewer than Singapore, with 242 patents, and comparable to India, with 131 patents. However, by 2008 Chinese residents were receiving triple the number of patents granted to Indian residents, and four times the number granted to residents of Singapore. Malaysia also saw the number of patents granted to its residents increase dramatically during this period, albeit from a base of just 11.

Patent grants are a good measure of technological capability, but they lag actual development by two to three years because of the time it takes to evaluate patent applications. Patent applications are a good indicator of how seriously countries are

---

[20]See, for instance, Kodama and Suzuki (2007) on the importance of proactive learning by firms.

[21]In fact, among the foreign countries, Japan receives the greatest proportion of awarded patents (60 percent), followed by Germany. In any given year, about half of all patents granted by the USPTO are to foreign residents.

Table 4.42 Number of Patents Granted by the USPTO

Country/economy	1992	2000	2008
Japan	23,151	32,922	36,679
Korea, Rep.	586	3,472	8,731
Taiwan, China	1,252	5,806	7,779
China	41	163	1,874
India	24	131	672
Singapore	35	242	450
Malaysia	11	47	168
Thailand	2	30	40
Philippines	7	12	22
Indonesia	9	14	19
Pakistan	1	5	7
Sri Lanka	2	5	2
Bangladesh	0	0	0
Vietnam	0	0	0

Source: U.S. Patent and Trademark Office (USPTO).

engaging in innovation activities, although the true informational content of this indicator can be overstated. Table 4.43 lists the number of patent applications by residents of different Asian economies. The relative rankings do not differ from those in table 4.42. What is notable is that lower-income countries such as Pakistan, Sri Lanka, Vietnam, and Bangladesh are now starting to apply for more patents.

Overall, Japan, Korea, and Taiwan, China, are currently the technological leaders in Asia, with the greatest capacity to exploit the opportunities for upgrading and diversifying manufacturing activities. They are in the best position to groom new industries as existing ones become unprofitable and begin to migrate. These economies may not avoid a further hollowing of their manufacturing sectors, but any such shrinkage will not be the result of inadequate attention to research. The true test will be the way this shift translates into innovations that are commercially profitable and that enable these economies to maintain their lead over competitors from China and India. China is rapidly building up its technological capacity, as is apparent from the growth in R&D spending and the increase in patents granted. India and Singapore, to a lesser extent, are also adding to this capacity. This is demonstrated in the speed with which they are catching up, but the innovation capabilities of these countries have yet to mature (see, for example, Dahlman 2007; Sigurdson and others 2006; Simon and Cao 2009; Thomson and Sigurdson 2008). Among Southeast Asian countries, Malaysia and Thailand are starting to give more attention to technological development in order to

Table 4.43   Number of Patent Applications Submitted to the USPTO

Country/economy	1992	2000	2008
Japan	38,633	52,891	82,396
Korea, Rep.	1,471	5,705	23,584
Taiwan, China	2,667	9,046	18,001
China	129	469	4,455
India	64	438	2,879
Singapore	89	632	1,226
Malaysia	16	104	297
Thailand	11	92	96
Philippines	10	32	69
Indonesia	11	9	13
Pakistan	2	7	13
Sri Lanka	0	6	12
Vietnam	0	0	10
Bangladesh	0	1	0

Source: U.S. Patent and Trademark Office (USPTO).

improve their indigenous technological capacity. Other economies in Asia are lagging far behind. They have yet to assign sufficient priority to urgently needed technology development, which will be a key determinant of how their manufacturing sectors evolve. Given the lead time in building R&D infrastructure and skills, their priority should be technology absorption. Once they accomplish that, they can move on to more ambitious goals.

Future Prospects

The external conditions that will face Asian countries in the years ahead are uncertain. A United States that is forced to rebalance its economy and a European Union that must accommodate similar rebalancing by several members, removes a vast amount of demand and injects a high degree of uncertainty for Asian exporters, because no one country or group of countries can substitute for U.S. and EU import demand. Asian exporters from the smaller economies must also contend with the likely partial dismantling of production networks. The emergence of production networking was the result of a decrease in transportation and communication costs, along with the willingness of firms in advanced countries to relocate and disperse their production around the globe. East Asian countries were able to catch the wave at the right moment, while others, including those in South Asia, allowed the opportunity to pass. Many hope that there will be another wave to catch; however, it is not clear that there will be any successors to the exports of garments and electronics, which facilitated the explosive growth of production networks. The rising energy costs, stemming from lower availability of fossil fuels and from environmental concerns, will temper the growth of trade in general and favor production in large markets (such as China and India). Given these likely external conditions, countries in Asia need to critically examine where their comparative advantage lies, whether they can sustain desired growth rates with the current suite of activities and if not, in which directions they can profitably diversify. For several East Asian economies, their comparative advantage and diversification opportunities may continue to reside in electronics. There is no new industry on the horizon that is likely to dislodge electronics. In addition to electronics, Southeast Asian countries have comparative advantage in resource-based products, reflecting their endowments. For South Asian countries, diversification opportunities are meager and are concentrated in labor-intensive, low-tech products, although the lack of significant change in their export composition and comparative advantage suggest that even such minimal diversification may be difficult to achieve. Without a significant strengthening of technological capacity, South Asian manufacturers other than India face a crisis.

Leading economies in Asia such as Japan, Korea, and Taiwan, China, are emphasizing domestic technological capabilities to stave off deindustrialization. Other Southeast Asian countries are just now realizing the importance of developing such capabilities. Their domestic technological capabilities are still low, although they are investing more in R&D and there are some (albeit few) signs of technological deepening. The problem countries are all in South Asia. They are poor in resources and human capital, and they lag the rest of industrial Asia by as much as three decades. Whether these countries can develop or attract firms that can compete with those in China and India will determine their industrial futures.

References

ADB (Asian Development Bank). 2009. *Asian Development Outlook 2009: Rebalancing Asia's Growth*. Mandaluyong City, Philippines: ADB.

Blanchard, Olivier J. 2009. "Sustaining a Global Recovery." *Finance and Development* 46(3): 8–12.

Cerra, Valerie, Ugo Panizza, and Sweta Chaman Saxena. 2009. "International Evidence on Recovery from Recessions." Working Paper WP/09/183, International Monetary Fund, Washington, DC.

Cerra, Valerie, and Sweta Chaman Saxena. 2008. "Growth Dynamics: The Myth of Economic Recovery." *American Economic Review* 98(1): 439–57.

Cohen, Wesley M., and Daniel A. Levinthal. 1990. "Absorptive Capacity: A New Perspective on Learning and Innovation." *Administrative Science Quarterly* 35(March): 128–52.

Cohen-Setton, Jeremie and Jean Pisani-Ferry. 2008. "Asia-Europe: The Third Link." Bruegel Working Paper 2008/04, Bruegel, Brussels.

Dahlman, Carl J. 2007. "China and India: Emerging Technological Powers." *Issues in Science and Technology* (Spring). http://www.issues.org/23.3/dahlman.html

Dooley, Michael P., and Michael M. Hutchison. 2009. "Transmission of the U.S. Subprime Crisis to Emerging Markets: Evidence on the Decoupling-Recoupling Hypothesis." Working Paper 15120, National Bureau of Economic Research, Cambridge, MA.

Economist Intelligence Unit (EIU). 2010. *India Country Forecast July 2010.* London: EIU.

Eichengreen, Barry, Ashoka Mody, Milan Nedeljkovic, and Lucio Sarno. 2009. "How the Subprime Crisis Went Global: Evidence from Bank Credit Default Swap Spreads." Working Paper 14904, National Bureau of Economic Research, Cambridge, MA.

Eichengreen, Barry, Yeongseop Rhee, and Hui Tong. 2004. "The Impact of China on the Exports of Other Asian Countries." NBER Working Paper Series 10768, National Bureau of Economic Research, Cambirdge, MA.

Fung, Victor K., William K. Fung, and Yoram Wind. 2008. *Competing in a Flat World: Building Enterprises for a Borderless World.* Upper Saddle River, NJ: Pearson Education Inc.

Gaulier, Guillaume, Francoise Lemoine, and Deniz Unal-Kesenci. 2004. "China's Integration in Asian Production Networks and Its Implications." Discussion Paper 04033, Research Institute of Economy, Trade and Industry, Tokyo.

Hu, Albert Guangzhou, and Gary H. Jefferson. 2008. "Science and Technology in China." In *China's Great Economic Transformation,* ed. Loren Brandt and Thomas G. Rawski. New York: Cambridge University Press.

Kim, Yong Jin. 2007. "A Model of Industrial Hollowing-out of Neighboring Countries by the Economic Growth in China." *China Economic Review* 18(2): 122–38.

Kodama, Fumio, and Jun Suzuki. 2007. "How Japanese Companies Have Used Scientific Advances to Restructure Their Business: The Receiver-Active National System of Innovation." *World Development* 35(6): 976–90.

Korinek, Anton and Luis Serven. 2010. "Real Exchange Rate Undervaluation: Static Losses, Dynamic Gains." World Bank Policy Research Working Paper 5250, World Bank, Washington, D.C.

Kose, Ayhan M., Christopher Otrok, and Eswar S. Prasad. 2008. "Global Business Cycles: Convergence or Decoupling?" Working Paper 14292, National Bureau of Economic Research, Cambridge, MA.

Kuijs, Louis. 2010. "China Through 2020: A Macroeconomic Scenario." World Bank China Research Working Paper 9, World Bank, Beijing.

Lall, Sanjaya. 2000. "The Technological Structure and Performance of Developing Country Manufactured Exports, 1985–98." *Oxford Development Studies* 28(3): 337–69.

Levy-Yeyati, Eduardo. 2009. "On Emerging Markets Decoupling and Growth Convergence." VoxEU.org.

Mathews, John. 2006. "China and the Developing World. Harnessing the Latecomer Effect for Industrial Catch-up—and the Case of Renewable Energy Sources in the 21st Century." Beijing Forum, Beijing.

National Science Board. 2008. "Science and Engineering Indicators." Arlington, VA: National Science Foundation. http://www.nsf.gov/statistics/seind08/.

Prahalad, C. K., and M. S. Krishnan. 2008. *The New Age of Innovation: Driving Cocreated Value through Global Networks.* New York; McGraw-Hill.

Prasad, Eswar. 2009. "Rebalancing Growth in Asia." Working Paper 15169, National Bureau of Economic Research, Cambridge, MA.

Reinhart, Carmen M., and Kenneth Rogoff. 2009. "The Aftermath of Financial Crises." *American Economic Review* 99(2): 466–72.

Republic of China (Taiwan). 2009. *National Statistics.* http://eng.stat.gov.tw/ct.asp?xItem= 25763&CtNode=5347&mp=5.

Scotchmer, Suzanne. 2004. *Innovation and Incentives.* Cambridge, MA: MIT Press.

Sigurdson, Jon, Jiang Jiang, Xinxin Kong, Wang Yongzhong, and Tang Yuli. 2006. *Technological Superpower China.* Northampton, MA: Edward Elgar Publishing.

Simon, Denis Fred, and Cong Cao. 2009. "China's Future: Have Talent, Will Thrive." *Issues in Science and Technology* (Fall). http://www.issues.org/26.1/simon.html

Steinfeld, Edward S. 2004. "China's Shallow Integration: Networked Production and the New Challenges for Late Industrialization." *World Development* 32(11): 1971–87.

Thomson, Elspeth, and Jon Sigurdson. 2008. *China's Science and Technology Sector and the Forces of Globalization.* Singapore: World Scientific Publishing.

World Bank. 2009. *Global Economic Prospects 2009.* Washington, DC: World Bank.

Yang, Yongzheng. 2006. "China's Integration into the World Economy: Implications for Developing Countries." *Asia-Pacific Economic Literature* 20(1): 40–56.

Yusuf, Shahid, and Kaoru Nabeshima. 2009. *Tiger Economies under Threat: Comparative Analysis of Malaysia's Industrial Prospects and Policy Options.* Washington, DC: World Bank.

———. 2010. "From Technological Mastery to Innovation." Washington, DC: World Bank.

5

The Drivers of Asia's Industrial Geography

The preceding chapters examined the evolving composition of industry in Asia and how countries are competing with China and India in global markets. In this chapter, we look at some of the factors that will affect industrial change and trade flows over the medium term. We highlight the following five factors:

- The adjustment and growth of the U.S. economy
- Savings and investment in China, India, and other major Asian economies
- Technological shifts
- Industrial networking, clustering, corporate competitiveness, and the pattern of trade
- The evolution of industrial capabilities in other Asian countries

These are by no means the only relevant ones—there are other economic and geopolitical factors that will play a mediating role; however, the above five deserve primacy for reasons we will explain.

Rebalancing the United States

For close to a quarter-century, the U.S. economy has served as the principal global locomotive—and a main contributor to the success of export-led growth in Asia. The willingness of the United States to open its market to exports from East Asia and Western Europe,[1]—as well as the strength of U.S. consumer demand for

---

[1]To build the economies of its Cold War allies, the U.S. pursued trade and exchange-rate policies that, over time, downsized a number of major domestic industries such as steel and autos.

imports—stimulated industrial development[2] in the exporting countries, while U.S. foreign direct investment (FDI) helped finance export-oriented industrialization and cemented trading relationships. A U.S. trade deficit of approximately 1.5 percent of GDP in the 1990s, which widened to a high point of 6 percent of GDP in 2006–07, enlarged the role of the U.S. market in the global trading system. This seemingly insatiable demand for imported manufactures, along with the associated hollowing of U.S. industry,[3] strongly bolstered manufacturing activities in China, India, and other Asian countries. Undoubtedly, the formation of the European Union and intraregional trade in Asia also fueled demand, but the United States was the most important mover and importer. A narrowing and gradual elimination of the U.S. current account deficit has massive implications for Asian countries that have depended upon exports to fuel their industrialization. The need to lower external debt and mobilize domestic resources to meet domestic priorities means that household savings (as a percentage of disposable income) must return to earlier U.S. trend rates of 8–10 percent, from the level under 5 percent witnessed in 2009, and government overspending must be curtailed.[4] Foreign borrowing to maintain current expenditure for the indefinite future is not a viable option for any country, not even one whose currency is an international unit of account and a store of value.[5]

Thus, the medium- and longer-term prognosis calls for higher U.S. domestic savings to finance investment priorities, to close domestic and external financing gaps, and to diminish the indebtedness of households—and of the government. This could mean lower potential growth as more of it derives from activities that produce smaller gains in productivity and are, on balance, less innovative. The potential growth rate of the U.S. economy over the long term is expected to fall by almost 1 percent per year—from about 3 percent to close to 2 percent. There are several reasons for this. First, household deleveraging and rebuilding of assets will most probably result in weaker demand from consumers. This is unlikely to be offset by increased investment, because spending on real estate may not climb

---

[2]Technology transfer from the United States through a number of channels also facilitated industrial development.

[3]Some of it happened through the transfer overseas of production facilities by U.S. multinational corporations (MNCs).

[4]The revival of consumption demand in the first quarter of 2010 pushed down household savings and foreshadows at least a temporary widening of the current account deficit.

[5]The "exorbitant privilege" enjoyed by the United States because of the dollar being the premier reserve currency is discussed by Reinhart and Reinhart (2010). This has been reinforced by the flight to safety precipitated by the financial crisis, causing the dollar to strengthen against the Euro. The degree to which this privilege is retained will depend upon regulatory measures to safeguard the attractiveness of U.S. financial markets and policy actions to rebalance the U.S. economy in the medium term (see Blanchard and Cottarelli 2010 on the 10 fiscal commandments for the Organisation for Economic Co-operation and Development (OECD) countries).

back to precrisis levels (Blanchard 2009). Both could adversely affect the change in total factor productivity. This rose by 0.9 percent annually between 1995 and 2000, but by 1.4 percent annually from 2001 through 2008. Unless export-led investment in manufacturing significantly contributes to productivity, a lower rate is in the cards. Compounding these is the anticipated decline in the growth of the labor force from 12.1 percent during 1998–2008 to 8.2 percent between 2008 and 2018 (Feldstein 2010; Lee, Rabanal, and Sandri 2010). Measures to limit global warming, if they are actively pursued, are also likely to raise the capital coefficient of development. With the U.S. economy generating less demand for Asian manufactures and U.S. firms competing more aggressively in foreign markets, industrialization and growth could be slowed in the smaller countries dependent on exports, as well as in countries at an early stage of industrial development with a narrow range of low-tech, raw material–based, and processed exports—countries such as Pakistan, Bangladesh, Cambodia, and Vietnam. The larger countries, such as China and India, have the resources, domestic markets, and growth momentum, while advanced economies such as Japan and the Republic of Korea have the technological capabilities and the corporate strength to compete in export markets, realize some of the opportunities associated with global warming, and take steps that will partially neutralize the long-run costs.

Savings and Investment

In the months immediately following the financial crisis of 2008–09 and its aftermath,[6] some believed that a savings glut[7] was resulting in underconsumption and trade surpluses in some Asian countries. Proponents of this view have argued that East Asian countries reacted to the pain inflicted by the crisis of 1997–98 by adopting domestic expenditure reduction and export-promoting exchange-rate and financial policies in order to accumulate foreign exchange reserves. This was in order to reduce their vulnerability to speculative attacks, sudden stops of capital, and capital flight.[8] The success of this effort at insuring against shocks is reflected in the vast foreign reserves held mainly by East Asian countries. In conjunction with the expansionary monetary and weak regulatory policies of some Western countries, along with their high public-sector indebtedness, the global

---

[6]For a succinet account of the causes of the financial crisis in the United States see Levine (2010). On factors contributing to increased subprime lending, see Mian, Sufi, and Trebbi (2010).

[7]Globally, the savings rate as a percentage of GDP has remained more or less static since 1995. It was 22.3 percent in the mid-1990s, declined to 20.6 percent in 2002, and rose to 22.8 percent in 2005. Mollerstrom (2010) maintains that for the U.S. current account deficits to be caused by capital inflows triggered by rising savings, U.S. investment—not just consumption—ought also to have risen by up to 4 percent.

[8]The crisis of 1997–98 also induced Asian borrowers to cut down short-term debts and to avoid mismatches in the maturity of their debt obligations.

economy is facing severe imbalances. One group of countries is consuming too much and borrowing to finance this spending, and another group may not be consuming enough. A solution advocated to promote the adjustment of Asian countries with current account surpluses—and to reduce the deficits of the United States, the United Kingdom, and some of the EU economies—is for East Asian households to increase their consumption so that domestic demand, rather than exports, becomes the engine of growth and raises the international demand for the exports of countries running deficits. A reduction in the so-called savings glut, it is argued, could (relatively) painlessly solve the adjustment issues for a handful of the most seriously affected countries and could restore growth.

A closer examination of savings in the Asian region indicates that they rose in only China, India, and Vietnam. This was mainly because of rapid growth and, in China's case, also because greater productivity and profitability of Chinese corporations[9] significantly increased corporate savings. The high savings of Chinese households and the rising savings of Indian households are also ascribed to precautionary motives: both countries lack adequate pension and health safety nets. In both countries, the limited access to finance compels families to save for children's education, down payments for the purchase of homes, the acquisition of major durables (cars particularly), and the accumulation of dowries for daughters—or the equivalent of bride prices for young women rendered scarce by sex imbalances (Chamon and Prasad 2007; Wei and Zhang 2009). Habit persistence and inertia in the face of rising incomes might be another factor explaining the rise in savings (Horioka and Wan 2006).[10] In the other Asian countries, savings remained constant or even declined, but in some cases, investment declined even more. This slowdown in investment is not entirely explicable, but it is linked to excessive, often speculative investment in the 1990s, prior to the crisis of 1997–98; to the overhang of capacity it created in the real estate sector and in manufacturing; and to the uncertain investment climate in some Southeast Asian countries. A number of industrializing East and Southeast Asian countries, which tended to run current account deficits prior to 1997–98—countries such as Thailand and Malaysia—welcomed trade surpluses and enlarged their foreign exchange holdings. Viewed as excessive by some, these reserves have nonetheless underwritten fiscal

---

[9]The bulk of the increased profits have accrued to only a subset of the state-owned enterprises, the largest beneficiaries being the producers of resource-based commodities, tobacco products, and suppliers of information technology (IT) services. Low dividend payout rates have contributed to the high levels of corporate saving and investment. Profitability has also been buttressed by low borrowing costs and other fiscal incentives provided to the corporate sector.

[10]Neither Prasad (2009) nor Horioka and Wan (2006) find that the age structure of the population explains Chinese savings. Household savings tend to follow a U-shaped rather than an inverted-U-shaped pattern, with young households and older households being the higher savers.

stimulus packages and assisted these countries in coping with the global economic contraction during 2009.

Are higher consumption propensities the recipe for faster growth in Asia and the world and the way to repair global resource imbalances? Although popular, this view needs to be treated with caution for two reasons. First, because the world could be heading toward a shortage of savings: savings in the advanced countries, in some instances already low, are projected to fall as the rising number of aging households begin to eat into their assets. This tendency will be exacerbated by higher dependency ratios (as the elderly population increases in number) and slowing growth of incomes. In several countries, expansionary fiscal policies have led to public dissaving and have generated large public-sector deficits that are likely to persist far into the future. These deficits and their servicing also need to be factored in as the adequacy of global savings is assessed.

Take, for example, the Indian case. India's national accounts for 2008 indicate that consumption as a percentage of GDP was 65 percent, while household savings were 24 percent. Meanwhile, investment was close to 39 percent of GDP, and the current account deficit was 1.4 percent of GDP. The large public sector deficits argue against increased public consumption. In theory, household consumption could grow faster—reversing recent trend rates—and this could offset a further deterioration of net exports or weakening of investment growth. In purely arithmetic terms, such rebalancing could sustain GDP growth rates of 7–8 percent per year for a few years, if foreign financing at affordable terms is available to accommodate continuing external deficits. However, given the likely shortage of savings globally, such affordability will be in question, and such widening of the current account deficit would raise the probability of foreign exchange becoming a constraint on growth.

Second, a premature focus on domestic consumption as a driver of growth in developing countries has future ramifications for industrial development. Demand from households, the majority of which are lower-middle- and middle-income households, will be weighted toward food, housing, transportation, light consumer goods, household goods, and services, whereas the faster-growing exports comprise higher-value manufactures and processed commodities. Quite likely, such a shift would significantly dampen investment in manufacturing activities that are more sophisticated, capital intensive, scale sensitive, and value adding. A reorientation of manufacturing and services to serve domestic consumers would also affect the investment in human capital: Tertiary-level professional and technical skills needed for an expanding higher-income overseas market would be less in demand, leading to slower increase in the stock of tertiary level science and technology (S&T) skills; there could possibly be more brain drain, especially of the most talented. The faster-growing segments of manufactured exports are also the ones that are more sophisticated, of higher quality, and with greater value added. By focusing on the domestic market, these countries may well forego exports that are more profitable and technology intensive; that can deepen domestic manufacturing capabilities; that can stimulate process and product innovation; and that can be the springboard for the emergence of corporate champions, the ones spearheading technology acquisition and investment in research and development (R&D). In addition, the imports of advanced machinery and components underpinning many of the exports serve as a vital conduit for R&D and technology transfer from more advanced trading partners. If they decline, most likely there would be a parallel decline in FDI in the more high-tech manufacturing and services activities in these countries.

Among the middle-income East and Southeast Asian economies, savings have very likely peaked in China and could decline as financial deepening and reforms of the health and social security systems lessen the need for precautionary savings and as the middle class's increasing wants for positional goods raises consumption. Barring an acceleration of growth in Southeast Asia, it is uncertain as to whether a dip in dependency ratios could push savings above existing levels. Indian savings could rise further if the economy expands at Chinese rates, or they could flatten out. In the rest of South Asia, savings will go higher if incomes begin rising more steeply, which is not likely. On balance, the outlook calls for a declining ratio of savings even if governments do not aggressively push consumption propensities.

Will there be a demand for these savings, or will a sizable fraction end up financing consumption and investment in the deficit-ridden postindustrial societies? There are four reasons for maintaining that the demand for investment will be greater in the future and that Asia may need to save more and not less.

First, most of Asia is still developing. Even in countries such as China and Malaysia, which have acquired significant industrial capabilities, the industrial base is not deep. For incomes to continue rising at a rapid (single-digit) pace, these countries must engage in further rounds of industrialization. More capital-, technology-, and skill-intensive activities—industry and services—need to be introduced, which will require costly investment. Healthcare and multimedia services are as capital intensive as, if not more than, manufacturing. South Asia— including India—lags far behind, and here much of the needed industrial base and infrastructure have yet to be built. In all, these countries' capital-to-labor ratios are a fraction of those in the United States.

Second, Asia's population is still mostly rural. Half of China's population, more than two-thirds of India's, and half of Indonesia's still are classified as non-urban. This has profound implications for the development of adequate urban housing and infrastructure to accommodate the almost inevitable transfer of the majority of these people to the cities. Affordable housing of decent quality, transport, communications, water, energy, sanitation, and sanitary waste disposal, to name the most essential, will consume immense amounts of capital. Aside from new investment to accommodate the urban population of the future, there is the vast backlog of investment to raise the living standards of existing urban inhabitants, many of whom live in slums[11] with the bare minimum of services—and often not even that. Asia's capital requirements for urban and infrastructure development have been frequently computed—and they are enormous—and as we indicate below, these projections might gravely understate the actual needs (see Asian Development Bank 2009).

Third, global warming will greatly increase the outlay on infrastructure of all kinds and, over time, require a replacement of production equipment, industrial boilers, coal-based power plants, and transport equipment. It will complicate the development process and enlarge investment needs. Inevitably, countries will be slow to face the new imperatives and delay will add to the costs, but eventually the bill will come due. For all Asian countries, global warming requires investments to conserve energy and water; to protect coastal and deltaic areas from rising sea levels; and to safeguard cities, in particular, from extreme weather events, be they heat waves or hurricanes. Cities and transport systems in Asia have evolved with the barest nod to design features that would mitigate carbon emissions and enhance livability. For too long, most municipalities in even the arid regions have avoided planning for the long haul and have preferred to assume that somehow the needed energy and water supplies will be forthcoming. Motorized vehicles are the preferred means of transport in even the poorest countries; it is this preference, reinforced by auto producers and affiliated industries and abetted by governments desperately seeking growth engines, that is determining the layout of cities. An extraordinarily small number of Asian cities are systematically developing comprehensive public transport systems and evincing a serious commitment to reducing greenhouse gas (GHG) emissions. It is unclear when a real change in thinking and lifestyles will occur. What is increasingly obvious is that with every passing day, decisions are being taken and investments being made that will be costly to reverse or modify in the future, when reversing mistakes may become unavoidable—barring, of course, the miraculous discovery of one or more technological fixes. Poorly designed and insulated buildings; energy inefficient appliances, equipment, and processes; urban spatial designs that further embed automobility into living and travel arrangements; and water extraction, sanitation, delivery, and industrial use practices that reduce the availability of clean water—together these are hastening the onset of warming and leading to water scarcity and storing problems for the future. The day will come when cities will need to be incrementally or hastily deconstructed and rebuilt to conform with lifestyles that consume much less fossil fuel–based energy. The longer the delay in making the switch to such a lifestyle, the greater will be the eventual burden of adjustment.

Fourth, social expenditures will add to the claims on investible resources. One is the needed investment in skills to narrow the technological gap between

---

[11]About 1.2 billion urban dwellers worldwide live under slum conditions.

developing Asia and the advanced countries, as well as to build the knowledge capital that will stimulate innovation. More education, training, and research will absorb higher-level skills; in addition, upgrading education will call for large expenditures on capital-intensive facilities—not just classrooms, but also laboratories, computers, and state-of-the-art communications technology. Raising both the level and quality of education in much of Asia and bringing technological capabilities of all countries up to the level that Korea is at today will be a huge and costly undertaking.

For several of the Asian societies that can anticipate a sharp increase in the proportion of the elderly in the next two decades, facilities must be created and resources put aside to accommodate the medical and other expenses of the non-working old—making cities elder friendly, for example. If the thinking and research on elder care in Japan is an indication of what is to come, a variety of medical, robotic, and information and communication technology (ICT)–based devices could contribute to the quality of life of the elderly through heightened mobility, monitoring and care, entertainment, access to services, and routine medical assistance. A substitution of relatively scarce labor by capital is in the cards.[12] Societies where a fifth or more of the population is over 65 years of age will require a different mix of urban furniture, services, equipment, and life support systems. In a word, the elderly will enjoy decent living standards only if societies are willing to make the investments in the R&D, capital assets, and facilities necessary to cope with steeply rising dependency ratios.

The potential demand for investment is there, enough to absorb the current level of savings and more. That this demand is not manifesting itself has to do with the divide between private and social returns, distorted tax and other incentives, and risk perceptions that are diverting resources into the financial sector[13] and real estate—distortions that are accentuated by increasing income disparities and greater imbalances in power relationships. The transport, energy, and financial industries, for example, strongly and effectively oppose measures that would constrain their prospects. Both public and private entities are reluctant to boldly plan for the future and embark on risky schemes—some inciting strong political opposition from industries and vested interests. In several cases, governments lack the foresight, planning skills, and resources to engage in investment or underwrite the risks of the private sector.

---

[12]An increasing number of these will be single children who would need to take care of two sets of parents. Even if these children decide to rely on external services for the care, the number of available caregivers is insufficient.

[13]More than 25 years ago James Tobin (1987) expressed skepticism as to the real economy outcomes of financial activity (and the mushrooming of transactions resulting in paper gains and losses) although he staunchly believed in the advantages of financial market efficiency.

Although higher consumption spending in East Asia would provide a welcome boost to demand in the medium term and may help deficit countries to adjust,[14] those Asian households that are accumulating precautionary savings as incomes rise are doing the right thing from a purely private perspective, and they might also be contributing to the larger social good over the long term. It is now up to governments to compensate for the market's myopia and ensure, with the help of the price mechanism and other incentives and signals, that the resources are efficiently invested in the interests of long-term sustainability. It is increasingly apparent that unaided market forces subject to myriad distortions and manipulation will certainly lead to suboptimal outcomes.

Major Technological Shifts

We noted earlier that a succession of general-purpose technologies have been associated with periods of rapid growth. Most recently and spectacularly, semiconductors and other advances in the realm of electronics, computers, the Internet, and mobile telecommunications are jointly responsible for bringing an enormous spate of innovations across diverse segments of the economy, for inducing investment, and for nudging the global growth to unprecedented heights. There is plenty of impetus left in the electronics and IC technologies, and this could be used most fruitfully in conjunction with technological innovation in low-carbon energy generation, new materials, urban transport systems, robotics, and bioinformatics. Significant advances in these areas through basic and applied research could help to sustain rapid development in Asia. The importance of these technologies is widely recognized, and five Asian economies are committing large sums to research that could have a bright commercial future. Of the five—Japan; Korea; China; Taiwan, China; and India—Asia's two most populous economies have arguably the most at stake and the most to gain for several reasons.

First, by participating in technological breakthroughs, they could reap early-mover advantages and corner a sizable share of the global market, instead of having to acquire and assimilate the technology from abroad and then compete with other countries to secure a piece of the global export trade. Second, successful innovations would be a boost to industry, with many spillovers, and the basis for productivity growth. They would launch a flotilla of firms, both small and large, among which could emerge a few world-class suppliers able to establish global brands and provide the two Asian countries with much-needed corporate heft. For China to nurture an innovative firm such as Samsung or Canon in an expanding field would represent tangible progress.

---

[14]This, of course, assumes that these deficit countries can expand their exports substantially when much of their manufacturing capacity has already relocated outside of the country.

Third, both China and India are urbanizing and industrializing economies with much ground still to cover. These countries are currently building their research infrastructure, training large numbers of researchers, and attempting to define their areas of comparative advantage in R&D. By entering relatively new fields with many scientific and technological secrets yet to be unlocked, China and India can enhance the productivity of their spending on research. The fact that they are at an earlier stage of development means that there is more scope for incorporating new technologies into manufacturing equipment and urban infrastructure. This process is also incentivized and expedited by the ongoing, large-scale investment in fixed assets in both countries. Thus, by achieving a pole position in leading-edge technologies that are still relatively immature, China and India can gain an edge on industrialized—and especially postindustrial—economies where the share of manufacturing is shrinking.

In this race to take the lead in the signature technologies of a "green economy," China has a considerable advantage over India. The scale of its R&D effort is far greater—it is producing many more researchers every year—and Chinese companies are near the forefront in the production of photovoltaic cells (PVCs), wind turbines, and high density batteries.[15] Moreover, Chinese research in nanotechnology, which is likely to affect the development of advanced materials, is yielding promising results.

R&D in green technologies represents an important facet of a broader strategy to deepen industrial capabilities and competitiveness using technology as the lever. All of the industrialized and industrializing countries are engaged in this technological arms race, and the stakes are high, because competitiveness and return on capital are increasingly a function of quality, design, and innovation. For standardized and labor-intensive products, costs of labor certainly matter a good deal; however, even in these product categories, process innovation that reduces costs and product innovation that differentiates a product and enhances its value contribute to profitability. In more valuable products, sophisticated technologies can confer a decisive advantage. As noted above, the frontrunners are Japan and Korea, if the metric used is R&D expenditure relative to GDP. They also lead others in Asia in the number of patents registered with the U.S. Patent and Trademark Office (USPTO). Taiwan, China; Singapore; and China are in third, fourth, and fifth places, respectively. The larger Southeast Asian economies and India follow, with the other South Asian countries trailing far behind. The latter have not entered the technological race thus far, which

---

[15]China invested heavily in nonfossil sources of energy during the 11th Plan and intends to redouble its efforts in this regard during the 12th Plan. Solar power for instance, is being heavily subsidized, especially for projects in remote regions ("Hedging all bets" 2010). See Adams, King, and Ma (2009) on China's R&D effort. The Indian firm Suzlon is also one of the foremost manufacturers of wind turbines, while China's BYD is a leader in high-density batteries.

partly explains their industrial composition and export competitiveness, and the characteristics of their narrowly circumscribed product space.

Among the industrializing countries, China is clearly setting the pace. The most striking aspect of its performance are the rates of change of key indicators. These are quite startling and overshadow those of India. In purchasing power parity (PPP)–adjusted terms, China is now the second-largest spender on R&D and has the second-largest contingent of researchers in the world after the United States. On its current trajectory, China should pull ahead of Korea and Taiwan, China, with respect to patents and papers in the near future. Moreover, because China's research spans many more subsectors, it is also likely to prove more fruitful overall than that of these two economies. Japan currently enjoys a huge lead over all other Asian economies but is having difficulty translating this into manufacturing success across a broad front and into GDP growth. Japan is likely to retain innovation-based competitiveness in autos, consumer electronics, and manufacturing equipment, and Korea has a well-honed and seemingly durable advantage in electronics, mobile telecommunications, white goods, and transport equipment. However, firms in both countries face intensifying competition from up-and-coming rivals in China—and within a decade, most likely from India as well.

As the research on innovation has convincingly established, the bulk of the downstream applied R&D, the kind that leads to commercial outcomes, is conducted by firms. A number of larger firms, especially, collaborate with scientists in universities and research institutes and monitor the research published by the scientific press. They are ready to acquire intellectual property (IP) with commercial promise from such institutions, but the innovativeness of the manufacturing industry and how it fares in the hard school of international competition depends upon how effectively firms deploy their own generated and acquired technologies. The Japanese, Korean, and Taiwanese miracles may have been sparked and sustained by the guiding hand of the state, state-directed financial bodies, and specialized research institutes established by the state, but large Japanese firms and trading houses, large Korean conglomerates, and small- and medium-sized Taiwanese firms—networked with MNCs—built the manufacturing engines of these three economies and actually delivered the miracles. Starting with modest production facilities, low-tech products, and no research or international marketing expertise (and no brand names), firms in the "miracle economies" acquired the manufacturing, research, and marketing capabilities and the much-coveted brand recognition. Whether the three countries remain competitive in the areas they now dominate or enter and colonize new industries will be decided by the competencies and the inventiveness of manufacturing firms.

So it will be in the rest of Asia. Recognizing this, the Chinese government and Chinese firms are trying hard to become global players and to establish a secure foothold in major product categories through their price competitiveness, technological upgrading, homegrown innovation, acquisition of IP from other sources, takeover of foreign firms and their brands, and determined efforts to build their own brands.[16] Indian firms are beginning to engage in a similar effort. But throughout the rest of Asia, almost four decades of industrialization, while it has led to the birth of a number of industrial conglomerates and major firms (frequently through the midwifery of governments), have not given rise to manufacturing powerhouses with global ambitions that have contributed to the industrial achievements of the leading economies.

Clustering of Industrial Activities

Manufacturing activity is primarily an urban phenomenon. In East Asia, the most dynamic and fastest-growing manufacturing industries emerged in a relatively small number of cities. In key instances, groups of firms in an industrial subsector formed integrated clusters through the use of a common labor pool, buyer-supplier relationships, collaboration to refine and develop technologies, joint marketing efforts, information gathering and training systems, and, in order to present a united front when lobbying for government support. Where cluster networking took root, it helped internalize technological spillovers and, in the most successful cases, achieve the balance between competition and cooperation that can be the basis for a virtuous growth spiral. Realizing the benefits of industrial clustering, governments (national as well as subnational) throughout East Asia have sought to grow clusters—in particular, clusters of high-tech firms. They have pursued clustering by seeding selected urban locations with science parks, incubators, and extension services; by encouraging local universities to engage in research and establish industrial linkages; by inducing venture capitalists to invest in small and medium enterprises (SMEs) in the area; and by attracting a major anchor firm, local or foreign, that could trigger the in-migration of suppliers and imitators. Governments have supported these initiatives with investment in infrastructure and urban services and through a variety of tax and financial incentives (see Yusuf, Nabeshima, and Yamashita 2008).

Some clusters materialized autonomously; others congealed as a result of initiatives by national and local governments, frequently in close coordination with industrial associations. In many instances, attempts to create the cluster effect led

---

[16]The Chinese firms making headway in this regard are Haier, Lenovo, Huawei, and ZTE. Lenovo's experience with the acquisition of IBM's PC business and that of TCL with the takeover of Thomson's TV arm suggests that the acquisition of large foreign firms with brand names can bolster the fortunes of ambitious Chinese companies—if they can muster the managerial expertise to harness and grow the reputational capital of the acquired foreign assets and to cope with the challenges posed by transnational operations. (On Lenovo's circumstances, see "Short of Soft Skills" 2009.) The acquisition of Volvo, the Swedish carmaker, by Geely, the privately owned Hangzhou-based Chinese manufacturer, will be another important test case of whether Chinese firms can turn around an ailing foreign company and effectively sustain and capitalize on its reputation.

nowhere, even when a number of firms established production facilities at an urban location. Over the span of nearly four decades, East Asia notched up enough successes to become the global hub of manufacturing, from the beginnings in Japan followed by the growth of industrial clusters in Korea; Taiwan, China; Southeast Asia; and then China. Dense urban-industrial agglomerations, some with networked clusters of firms, have been vital to the growth of productivity, for technological change, and for promoting further industrialization by opening opportunities and stimulating supplies of capital and skills.

This is the past; what of the future? One striking aspect of recent industrialization and clustering in Asia is its slowing in many countries. In Japan, industrialization has been in retreat for two decades, with many lower-tech clusters withering and a hollowing even of higher-tech clusters. There are no new industrial hotspots in Japan, although manufacturing clusters flourish in cities like Nagoya and Kyoto. New clusters of "green manufacturing" could arise in Kyushu, for example, but they are more likely to displace existing activities than to expand the industrial base. Deindustrialization in Korea is at an earlier stage; here, as in Japan, it is possible that the investment in "green" technologies, in the life sciences, and ICT could trigger an upsurge of manufacturing activities in existing locations, with emergent clusters displacing or complementing the old. However, Korea, much like Japan, is a maturing industrial country increasingly unlikely to foster new industrial clusters or reclaim the industrial ground it has lost mainly to China and Southeast Asia.

The high-tech electronics, IT, and biotech industries of Taiwan, China, are in a healthy steady state, but most of the low- and even medium-tech industries, which are sensitive to labor costs, have migrated to the mainland. The principal manufacturing clusters in Taiwan, China, remain robust; however, the odds are against new clusters springing up on the island with the cost structure, market access, and supply of skills favoring the mainland.

That future industrialization is more likely in developing Asia is no surprise. What is surprising is the virtual absence of budding industrial agglomerations in Southeast Asia, with the exception of Vietnam. Industrial growth continues in all the leading Southeast Asian economies; however, it is largely through densification in existing industrial agglomerations and in already established industrial subsectors. From the perspective of industrial clustering in these countries, what is remarkable from the earlier assessment of production patterns, exports, and value added is the limited evidence of industrial deepening through backward linkages to the manufacturing of components, intermediates, and production equipment.

In Thailand, clusters of firms producing auto parts, electronics, foodstuffs, textiles, and engineering products are mainly in the Bangkok metro area and its vicinity. In spite of the government's efforts at dispersing industry, industrial agglomerations have not begun to coalesce elsewhere in the country. The existing Malaysian centers of manufacturing in KL/Klang Valley, Penang, Malacca, and

Johor Bahru are holding onto their electrical and engineering industries, but rising costs are eating into the competitiveness of labor-intensive assembly operations. Textiles and footwear are declining. Again, new urban agglomerations of manufacturing are not springing up in other parts of the country.

Widening of activity in established industrial centers and existing lines of production is also apparent in Indonesia and the Philippines, but there is scant evidence of diversification or of deepening, or signs of nascent industrial agglomerations that could breed tomorrow's manufacturing clusters.

During the past decade, new centers of manufacturing have blossomed, and a clustering of textiles and light consumer electronics manufacturing may be ongoing in a few Vietnamese cities—principally Haiphong, Hanoi, Ho Chi Minh City, and Da Nang.[17] Further west in South Asia, industrialization in Pakistan, Bangladesh, and Sri Lanka remains concentrated in a few of the main urban areas. The clusters that exist are mainly focused on textiles and garments. In Pakistan there is a well-known cluster producing surgical instruments and sports equipment, mainly soccer balls. According to trade and production statistics, production has risen in all three countries, but the mix is static and potential backward and forward linkages are not thickening the domestic value chain. The surgical instruments cluster in the Pakistani city of Sialkot, for instance, has not diversified into more sophisticated, derivative products. Nor, for that matter, have textile producers in Dhaka used R&D in new synthetic materials to serve other industries, using their expertise as a point of departure. Garment manufacturers in Sri Lanka, many in the vicinity of Colombo, have increased domestic value added through the domestic production of lace, ribbons, zippers, and buttons but have not diversified into other industries. A combination of factors, including adequate profits from existing production lines, risk aversion, the scarcity of skills, research bottlenecks, entrepreneurial shortsightedness, financing constraints, and market uncertainties, might explain why old clusters have not evolved and few new ones have emerged. But the fact remains that the manufacturing sector is stagnating in the three countries.

India is a different story, with more evidence of industrial acceleration and diversification, but by no means on the scale of China's from the 1980s through 2008. India's industrial capacity is deepening and diversifying in the Mumbai, Nasik, Pune urban region, and around Delhi and Agra, Chennai, and Kolkata. Textile clusters continue to flourish in Tirupur, as do farm machinery clusters in Punjab and Haryana. It is too early to know if the investment in the auto, petrochemicals, iron and steel, and engineering industries will create new clusters, increase domestic value added, spur innovation (in metallurgical and chemical fields, for example), and put India firmly on the path to higher-tech industrialization.

---

[17]Kuchiki (2007) notes the formation of an electronics cluster anchored by Canon in Hanoi and of a garments cluster in Haiphong.

That some Indian firms are scrambling to enlarge their global presence suggests that change is afoot. How dramatically this will affect India's industrial composition and geography will depend upon the country's supply of skills and market opportunities (domestic as well as foreign), entrepreneurial energies, and elasticity of financing.

This leaves China, where three major urban industrial agglomerations—the Pearl River Delta (PRD), Changjiang, and Bohai regions—have given rise to multiple clusters producing everything from toys, footwear, and garments to computers and autos. Industrial deepening in these three regions is continuing; in addition, industrial agglomerations are expanding in Chengdu, Chongqing, Xian, Wuhan, and Dalian, and in Henan, Jiangxi, Guangxi, and Guizhou provinces, as some industries are moving out of the crowded PRD in search of space, labor, and lower costs. Industry is also booming in Anhui, along the coast in Fujian, and is reviving in the northeastern provinces such as Liaoning and Jilin.

As a full-spectrum industrializer, with a commitment to deepening and upgrading of manufacturing capabilities and pursuit of high-tech opportunities, China is likely to enhance its capacity and competitiveness in virtually every manufacturing subsector. Given the strong gains in labor productivity throughout the manufacturing sector, there is little reason to anticipate a decline in China's competitiveness in light manufacturing. Ceglowski and Golub's (2007) computing of China's unit labor costs in manufacturing underscores its advantage over its competitors. It is an advantage deriving from productivity gains that have outpaced the increase in wages and, thus far, the appreciation of the exchange rate. A weakening of East Asian currencies and the Euro relative to the dollar in 2009–10 led to an appreciation of China's trade-weighted real effective exchange rate. China's decision to end the implicit pegging of the renminbi to the dollar and intensifying wage pressures are likely to result in further appreciation of the real effective exchange rate. This will be offset by the migration of labor and land intensive activities to lower cost inland cities and by falling transport costs. How this plays out is difficult to gauge, but it would be unwise to assume that China is ready to forsake labor intensive manufacturing with several hundred million underemployed workers in agriculture and significant productivity gains to be realized. Hence, other early-stage industrializing Asian countries will have to battle Chinese producers if they want to expand their global market share or export to China. For the South Asian economies, it is not enough to maintain a competitive advantage in garments, textiles, and light manufactures; they need to break out of these old industrial strongholds and compete in other areas with better growth prospects, which India is doing. At the other end of the spectrum, Chinese firms—some allied with MNCs—are already emerging as formidable competitors in electronics, pharmaceuticals, metallurgical products, transport equipment, and engineering equipment. Thus, they will be competing with manufacturers in Japan and Korea, many of which have set up production facilities in China.

The map of Asian manufacturing viewed from this angle shows a gradual withdrawal of manufacturing activities from the Eastern rim economies—Japan, Korea, and Taiwan, China—and a transfer of labor-intensive production to China and Southeast Asian countries, among others. Manufacturing is positioned to grow in China, with new centers joining the old, as infrastructure development and rising costs in coastal areas push some of the more footloose industries into the interior. Manufacturing capabilities will also deepen, and more Chinese firms will be operating near the technological frontiers in key industries.

The industrial prospects of Southeast Asia are uncertain. A country such as Vietnam has a future in light manufacturing and processing, because MNCs will want to maintain multiple sources of supply, and Chinese FDI is transferring some labor-intensive activities to Vietnam. Singapore will need to specialize in high-tech niche areas and depend on the competitiveness of services. For reasons we will elaborate later, Malaysia, the Philippines, Thailand, and Indonesia risk a manufacturing stasis or even a partial rollback unless they can make the leap in technological and manufacturing capabilities to compete with China, India, and the Northeast Asian countries at the higher end of the technological spectrum. Likewise, South Asian countries other than India could remain in a low-level manufacturing equilibrium barring political and policy breakthroughs—national and international—that focus the leadership on more ambitious development objectives, radically change the opportunity set, and begin to significantly ease the shortages of skills, infrastructure, and capital.

Shift in Global Production Networks

The manufacturing industry in East Asia is notable for its export orientation and the degree to which production of tradables throughout the region is integrated into international production networks. These buyer- and supplier-driven value chains have arisen out of investment and sourcing decisions of MNCs and buyers in the industrialized countries. They are the legacies of strategies, of incentives of technologies facilitating dispersed production, and of an era when energy was cheap and the United States displayed a seemingly limitless appetite for the manufactures of East Asia.

Production networks have supported and motivated a sprawling industrial archipelago extending from Singapore to Korea. In South Asia, India, Bangladesh, and Sri Lanka have a role in the manufacturing of garments, but it is a relatively minor role that has developed in the past decade. The core of the system lies in East Asia, China, and Southeast Asia. Dispersed manufacturing permits efficient specialization, redundancy in sources of supply, and great supply elasticity. Most of the risk resides with the myriad suppliers scattered over a half-dozen economies competing in a cutthroat market managed by buyers and integrators who serve as intermediaries for final buyers.

The heyday of production networking might be passing for several reasons, and its slow atrophy will affect the spatial distribution of manufacturing in Asia.

First, networking has resulted in hypercompetitive markets for standardized, modular products with codified technologies. This may have done wonders for intra-industry trade and greatly benefited consumers in the high-income importers of finished products, but with quasi-rents sharply reduced, producers of items feeding international value chains have difficulty accumulating the resources to grow out of low-end unskilled labor-intensive processing activities.[18] They stay relatively low-tech; they have difficulty, given the nature of products and the chains, to diversify or upgrade skills and products. This partly explains why Malaysia has been unable to climb out of assembly and processing of electronics into other products. This is not the only reason, but it is one of them. Networks have a locking-in effect for the many production cogs that feed the ocean-spanning value chains. Networking, apparently, is not a ladder out of low- or midlevel manufacturing activities.

Second, networking, for all its virtues and presumed efficiency, is a complex, energy-intensive activity entailing significant transaction costs for all the players. These add to the cost of products and will rise with energy prices.[19]

Third, dispersed production makes it harder for assemblers to plan and develop products, and the risks involved have implications for inventory holding and for the flexibility of production. In most instances, a clustering of assemblers and suppliers is the most cost-effective approach. It facilitates coordination, makes possible just-in-time delivery, and reduces insurance and warehousing costs. It also simplifies design and development of products—even in the Internet era (Moody 2001; Eberhardt and others 2004).[20] In fact, most final producers are consolidating their production chain and prefer to deal with as few suppliers as possible, and co-location is an advantage. Moreover, buyers are also finding that purchasing from fewer reputable producers is more efficient than buying from many suppliers scattered over several countries.[21] By focusing purchases, a number of costs are minimized, including the costs of monitoring compliance with labor,

---

[18]This may account for the continued specialization of countries such as Bangladesh, Sri Lanka, and Pakistan in garments and textiles (Almeida 2010).

[19]The likelihood of oil prices rising can be envisioned from some simple statistics. The per capita daily consumption of oil is 2.5 gallons in the United States. It is 1.9 gallons in Korea and 1.4 gallons in Japan. Were China to approach Korea's level by 2020, its consumption would reach 40 million barrels per day (bpd) as against approximately 8 million bpd in 2009. This would imply, for instance, a rising stock of light vehicles reaching 225 million from approximately 60 million in 2010, based on annual domestic production of 15 million cars as against 13 million in 2009 (Kopits 2010). On the rising cost of seaborne trade, see Rubin (2009).

[20]These matter less for standardized commodities produced using mature technologies.

[21]On such trends in the apparel industry, see Gereffi and Frederick (2010).

environmental, and phytosanitary rules, along with rules having to do with security regulations in importing countries. If this practice spreads, networks will be severely pruned.

Fourth, the sunk capital in MNC production facilities in a number of Asian countries and the long-standing relationships with local suppliers and governments have provided a certain inertial stability to networks. Furthermore, many MNCs, while recognizing the advantages of concentrating production in China, have been loath to put all their eggs in one basket. To a certain extent, the purpose of diffusion of production sites was to exploit trade agreements, to circumvent trade restrictions (such as highly restrictive garment trades), and to avoid trade disputes, especially between United States and other East Asian economies. If such restrictions and concerns over trade frictions remain, there will still be some dispersion of production activities. However, the crisis of 2008–09, a slowing of U.S. demand for imports, and the increasing relative prominence of the Chinese market over the medium and longer term could reinforce other tendencies, leading to a shakeout and concentration of industrial production in Asia, as well as a greater readiness to locate facilities in China and to buy from producers in China.[22] If this happens, more of the production currently scattered over East and South Asia will gravitate toward clusters in China's industrial cities, and intra-industry trade could decline. This will reduce costs all around; in addition, a concentration of suppliers and sources of supply will increase the bargaining power of suppliers and help widen profit margins.[23]

This signifies a substantial reduction of standardized commodity production in the middle- and lower-middle-income Asian countries and its relocation in China and possibly India. Low-income Southeast Asian and South Asian countries might continue to hold on to their markets for garments and textiles,[24] but the transition to other standardized commodities (e.g., electronics) traded via global networks could be far more difficult than it would have been 20 years ago, when Southeast Asian countries were entering the markets for manufactured commodities. In fact, the prospects for these countries to further their industrialization using the leverage provided by trade have dimmed. Unless regional trading opportunities can impart the needed stimulus, it is unlikely that the domestic markets in the smaller South Asian countries will boost industrialization—something they have failed to do thus far.

---

[22]Between the fourth quarter of 2008 and the third quarter of 2009, industrial production fell in all but these six countries: China, India, Kazakhstan, Norway, Singapore, Korea, and Vietnam (Bloomberg 2010).

[23]Sturgeon and Van Biesebroeck (2010) examine the concentration of auto manufacturing in large middle-income countries such as China.

[24]For example, there is scope for trade in textiles between India and China because of differences in areas of specialization. China's exports of finished textiles could lead to imports of intermediate yarn and cloth from India (Cerra, Rivera, and Saxena 2005).

Indian producers are, to a degree, integrated into the production network for textiles but not for other products; hence, a shrinking of these vehicles for trade would affect growth. It will also affect the scale of diversification into products imported by advanced countries via networks. Were India to become an alternative hub to China for a wide range of standardized products, then it is possible to foresee industrialization along traditional lines. Barring that, and assuming slow or moderate growth of world trade over the medium run, industrialization in India will be paced and directed more by domestic demand. India might yet surprise the world by matching China's past performance using services (not just IT services) as the principal driver of growth and exports, by relying less on FDI, and by deriving more of the industrializing impetus from domestic demand and not from network-mediated exports to the United States and the European Union. This would be a significant achievement. From the perspective of Asian industrial geography, it would lead to an even greater relative concentration of manufacturing activity in China and parts of Southeast Asia. The outcome would be an unusual state of affairs. China would become the undisputed leader in many subsectors of manufacturing, and other Asian countries would be more dependent on services for growth and the balancing of their trade. Instead of using a broad manufacturing base as the ladder to higher incomes, the rest of Asia would have to place their bets on a number of high-tech and capital-intensive manufacturing industries, on innovation, on productivity growth from services, and from intensively trading services. Although services is the dominant sector in most Asian countries, we know little about the potential of a services-led model to deliver high and sustainable growth rates for low- and middle-income countries.[25] Indian experience with the off-shoring of impersonal services holds out some hope, but the contribution of the sector to employment and the GDP is small and empirical evidence underlying its long-term potential as a driver of growth is slender indeed.

References

Adams, Jonathan, Christopher King, and Nan Ma. 2009. *China: Research and Collaboration in the New Geography of Science*. Philadelphia: Thomson Reuters.

ADB (Asian Development Bank). 2009. *Asian Development Outlook 2009: Rebalancing Asia's Growth*. Mandaluyong City, Philippines: ADB.

Almeida, Rita K. 2010. "Openness and Technological Innovation in East Asia: Have They Increased the Demand for Skills?" World Bank Policy Research Working Paper 5272, World Bank, Washington, DC.

---

[25]See Grabowski (2009), which sketches an Indian model of growth that partially skips a stage of manufacturing development and moves to higher tech industry and to tradable services.

Blanchard, Olivier. 2009. "Sustaining a Global Recovery." *Finance and Development* 46(3): 8–120.

Blanchard, Olivier and Carlo Cottarelli. 2010. "Ten Commandments for Fiscal Adjustment in Advanced Economies." VoxEU.org.

Bloomberg. 2010. http://www.bloomberg.com.

Ceglowski, Janet, and Stephen Golub. 2007. "Just How Low Are China's Labour Costs?" *World Economy* 30(4): 597–617.

Cerra, Valerie, Sandra A. Rivera, and Sweta Chaman Saxena. 2005. "Crouching Tiger, Hidden Dragon: What Are the Consequences of China's WTO Entry for India's Trade?" Working Paper WP/05/101. International Monetary Fund, Washington, DC.

Chamon, Marcos, and Eswar Prasad. 2007. "Why Are Savings Rates of Urban Households in China Rising?" IZA Discussion Paper 3191. Institute for the Study of Labor.

Eberhardt, Markus, Julie McLaren, Andrew Millington, and Barry Wilkinson. 2004. "Multiple Forces in Component Localisation in China." *European Management Journal* 22(3): 290–303.

Feldstein, Martin. 2010. "U.S. Growth in the Decade Ahead." Working Paper 15685. National Bureau of Economic Research, Cambridge, MA.

Gereffi, Gary, and Stacey Frederick. 2010. "The Global Apparel Value Chain, Trade and the Crisis: Challenges and Opportunities for Developing Countries." World Bank Policy Research Working Paper 5281, World Bank, Washington, DC.

Grabowski, Richard. 2009. "An Alternative Indian Model?" *Journal of Asian Economies* 20: 50–61.

"Hedging All Bets". 2010. The Economist Intelligence Unit, April 12.

Horioka, Charles, and Junmin Wan. 2006. "The Determinants of Household Saving in China: A Dynamic Panel Analysis of Provincial Data." Working Paper 12723. National Bureau of Economic Research, Cambridge, MA.

Kopits, Steven R. 2010. "EIA: The China Syndrome." Econbroswer.com.

Kuchiki, Akifumi. 2007. "Agglomeration of Exporting Firms in Industrial Zones in Northern Vietnam: Players and Institutions." In *Industrial Agglomeration and New Technologies*, ed. Matsatsugu Tsuji, Emanuele Giovannetti, and Mitsuhiro Kagami. Cheltenham, UK: Edward Elgar Publishing.

Lee, Jaewoo, Paul Rabanal, and Damiano Sandri. 2010. "U.S. Consumption after the 2008 Crisis." IMF Staff Position Note. International Monetary Fund, Washington, DC.

Levine, Ross. 2010. "An Autopsy of the U.S. Financial System." NBER Working Paper 15956. National Bureau of Economic Research, Cambridge, MA.

Mian, Atif, Amir Sufi, and Francesco Trebbi. "The Political Economy of the Subprime Mortgage Credit Expansion." NBER Working Paper 16107. National Bureau of Economic Research, Cambridge, MA.

Mollerstrom, Johanna. 2010. "The Source of the Global Trade Imbalances: Saving Glut or Asset Price Bubbles?" VoxEU.org.

Moody, Patricia E. 2001. "What's Next after Lean Manufacturing?" *MIT Sloan Management Review* 42(2): 12–13.

Prasad, Eswar. 2009. "Rebalancing Growth in Asia." Working Paper 15169. National Bureau of Economic Research, Cambridge, MA.

Reinhart, Carmen M., and Vincent Reinhart. 2010. "Is the US Too Big to Fail?" VoxEU.org.

Rubin, Jeff. 2009. *Why Your World Is about to Get a Lot Smaller.* New York: Random House.

"Short of Soft Skills: Lenovo's Bid to Become a Global Brand Is Coming Unstuck." 2009. *Business China,* June 8.

Sturgeon, Timothy J., and Johannes Van Biesebroeck. 2010. "Effects of the Crisis on the Automotive Industry in Developing Countries: A Global Value Chain Perspective." World Bank Policy Research Working Paper 5330, World Bank, Washington, DC.

Tobin, James. 1987. *Policies for Prosperity: Essays in a Keynesian Mode.* Cambridge, MA: The MIT Press.

Wei, Shang Jin, and Xiaobo Zhang. 2009. "The Competitive Saving Motive: Evidence from Rising Sex Ratios and Savings Rates in China." Working Paper 15093. National Bureau of Economics, Cambridge, MA.

Yusuf, Shahid, Kaoru Nabeshima, and Shoichi Yamashita, eds. 2008. *Growing Industrial Clusters in Asia: Serendipity and Science.* Washington, DC: World Bank.

6

Industrial Strategy at a Crossroads

For at least three decades most of the industrializing economies of East and South Asia have delivered rates of growth that are above average for developing economies. With a few exceptions, such as the Philippines, East (including Southeast) Asian economies grew much faster than the norm, and with the exception of Nepal, the South Asian economies stayed above the rates for the rest of the developing world. The outstanding performers among these economies all hewed to a model of growth whose drivers were investment—domestic and foreign—and exports. Other factors such as political stability, fundamentally sound macropolicies, trade liberalization, and human capital no doubt contributed, but these would have been insufficient in the absence of the virtuous spiral generated by the dynamic intertwining of exports and domestic investment in technology and productive assets. Export-led growth was the rallying cry throughout East Asia; it was what kept "animal spirits" high through good times and buoyed or revived economies when the economic climate soured because of a domestic shock or an international downturn. After the East Asian crisis of 1997–98, many commentators were quick to announce the demise of the East Asian model; however, the economies of the region defied the odds and recovered—although, because of weakening investment and a slowing of export growth, only China regained the precrisis momentum.

Rapidly increasing exports complemented by high rates of investment eluded most of the South Asian economies, with only India able to crank up domestic investment to over 30 percent of GDP—and that only after 2003; hence, growth in South Asia was slower, because countries in the region relied mainly on the export of garments, textiles, and resource-based products. When India's growth reached levels comparable to those of East Asia, it was a boom in the exports of services that served as the catalyst. This aroused entrepreneurial activity in India, stimulated domestic capital spending, and began attracting investment from abroad.

No such catalytic development occurred in the other South Asian countries; instead, several have had to cope with domestic sociopolitical issues that have darkened the investment climate.

The great global recession of 2008–09 is forcing a reappraisal of development strategies in Asia and in other regions as well. At the heart of this reappraisal are conjectures regarding the future sources of growth, the course of globalization, and the roles of the United States, the European Union (EU), China, and, in the distance, India, Brazil, and the Russian Federation. For the purposes of decision making, policy makers and business managers cannot avoid making such conjectures and must develop a coherent view to inform plans and guide investments. In the remainder of this chapter, we will sketch three different scenarios and, on the basis of certain assumptions, identify the one we believe is most likely to prevail, as well as the consequences for the industrial geography of the Asian region.

Scenario 1: Business as Usual

The most analytically convenient scenario is inevitably one with minimal changes. With minor modifications, perceived trends are extrapolated into the future.[1] This has its advantages, because extrapolation with only a small amount of tweaking is safer than the alternatives, as it involves the least amount of judgment. Under this scenario, the world economy gradually recovers during 2010–11 and resumes full-bore growth equivalent to the average for the period 2004–07, with trade growing in due course by 6–7 percent.[2] Growth of East Asian economies rebounds to 6 percent or more, with the Japanese economy expanding at close to 2 percent and China achieving high single-digit rates of GDP growth. South Asia, with India at the forefront, also begins to accelerate, with the performance of individual countries in the region influenced by political factors and the weather. As in the past, growth would be pulled by investment and trade, with domestic consumption playing a greater or lesser part depending on the stage of development, the maturity of the financial sector, the adequacy of social safety nets, and the openness of individual countries.[3] Manufacturing industry and exports of manufactures would again serve as the principal motors of the economies, complemented in China and India by infrastructure development and a deepening of business

---

[1]Serven and Nguyen (2010) maintain that the post 2008–09 crisis "configuration of current account deficits might not differ from the pre-crisis situation" (p. 14) because many of the determinants are unchanged.

[2]The World Trade Organization forecasts that global trade will grow by 9.5 percent in 2010.

[3]According to computable general equilibrium (CGE) model simulations, further trade liberalization would deliver gains amounting to not much more than 0.2 percent of global GDP by 2015, and these would favor the developed countries and industrializing countries such as China and Brazil, not the poorer countries (Anderson and Martin 2005; Polaski 2006; Ackerman 2006).

services.[4] Southeast Asian middle-income countries would continue to benefit from rising intra-industry trade in intermediate products, with China and Japan providing the twin axes of production networks, mainly serving retail markets in the United States and the EU. For the lagging South Asian economies to improve their game, capital spending on infrastructure and manufacturing would need to rise sharply, with more of the increased and diversifying production of industrial items being exported. In every case, the recipe for industrial development is virtually the same. Each country attempts to enlarge its shares of existing product markets, to upgrade existing product groups, and to diversify into products that leverage acquired comparative advantage. For the foreseeable future, assembled and processed commodities, which have served as the vanguard of export-led growth, would dominate manufactured exports. There is change, but it is of the incremental kind. There are no projections of disruptive technologies or new technological epochs, or of a radical reorientation of trade flows from the United States and the EU to China; there is only more of the same, perhaps with some of the low-income countries and India aggressively pushing industrialization.

This scenario—while it is surely plausible for the near term, in view of the recovery of most Asian economies—rests on the critical assumption that the demand for Asia's exports will return to the levels reached during 2001–07, with only moderate changes in the mix of products exported. The recovery of East Asia's trade that started in the second half of 2009 is a positive sign, but the buoyancy of trade in the medium run is likely to be tempered by four factors. First is the high likelihood that demand from the United States will remain low for years. Consumers in the United States sustained the East Asian export machine from the 1970s until at least 2007. Import demand from other nations certainly reinforced U.S. demand, but the centrality of the U.S. market for Asian suppliers went largely unchanged and was underscored by the speed at which trade flows began drying up after U.S. import demand plunged in 2008. With U.S. consumers eventually having to raise their savings (above 4–5 percent rates) and deleverage, and with the United States forced to narrow its current account deficit through a combination of slower growth, a depreciation of the dollar, and a variety of measures to enhance the competitiveness of its tradables (whether goods or services), its trading partners can expect weaker demand for imports and greater competition from U.S. exports. Some of the EU countries will also need to curb their demand for imports in order to erase their twin deficits. The expanding public sector debts and contingent liabilities of several Organisation for Economic Co-operation

---

[4]China's investment rate rose to 46 percent in 2009 as a result of increased spending on infrastructure, housing, and manufacturing capacity. This will have steepened the decline in the marginal product of capital that was already apparent (Brooks and Barnett 2006). Under the circumstances, further increasing investment to sustain growth would be counterproductive.

and Development (OECD) countries narrow the scope for reflationary policies.[5] So also does the level of external indebtedness, particularly of the United States. That the East Asian countries will continue to bankroll the United States' large current account deficits through the purchase of U.S. Treasuries is likely in the medium term[6] but questionable in the long run.

A second factor, related to the first, is the potential for growing the international trade of light consumer goods, electronics and electrical products, auto parts, and other manufactured commodities. These are standardized goods trading in relatively saturated markets. In several industries there is global excess capacity, fierce price competition, and narrow profit margins. China is now the ranking producer of steel, cement, aluminum, and glass. It is pulling ahead of the Republic of Korea in shipbuilding, and it produced more cars than the United States in 2009. As a result of continuing investment in capacity in these industries and others in the absence of an exit of smaller inefficient producers (of cement and steel, for example), capacity utilization rates in 2008 had fallen into the 75 percent range for steel, cement, and aluminum, and even lower for methanol, polycrystalline silicon, and wind power equipment. This partly explains the declining investment in manufacturing capacity in a number of Southeast Asian countries in recent years and the shift toward real estate and business services. If future growth is likely to be slower, a rebound in private investment in East Asia may not materialize and, under these conditions, it is not clear that India could enter the market for electronics and auto parts without increasing the pressure on all participants to levels that could force a major shakeout of industry across Asia, triggering a bout of protectionism. Investors are being cautious elsewhere as well. American companies are husbanding large cash assets, which they are unwilling to plough into productive assets because the outlook for manufacturing is uncertain with stock market movements providing little guidance as they are influenced much more by the ample supply of liquidity and low interest rates than by the prospects of the real sector.

A third factor, linked to the first two, is the maturing of the electronics and information and communication technologies, which underpinned the latest stage of industrialization in East Asia. Although bio- and nanotechnology and renewable energy–related technologies all have promise, none has developed in a manner conducive to a new wave of industrialization with significant consequences for GDP growth and employment. Biotech has been viewed as a promising industrial force for almost two decades; it has led to important advances in medicine and the agricultural sciences, for example. But the multiple subfields nourished by biotechnology have

---

[5]Concerns that monetary easing and fiscal stimuli administered during 2009–10 could lead to higher rates of inflation are adding to the worries of policy makers in some countries.

[6]Caballero, Farhi and Gourinchas (2008) and Caballero (2010) argue that the world is short of safe AAA-rated assets and that emerging economies have made little progress in generating these. Hence, countries will continue to accumulate U.S. Treasuries and finance U.S. external account imbalances.

neither individually nor collectively provided the foundations for a new base of industry with significant growth, employment, and export prospects. Nanotech, advanced materials, and energy technologies may begin to show traction, but it might be a decade or more before they become more than niche industries.[7] It is difficult to identify an industrial technology that could promise a sustained acceleration of growth rates.

The fourth factor is the cost of energy and raw materials. So long as they were low (stable or falling), they could be conveniently ignored and used to generate globe-spanning, energy-intensive production networks. In 2007–08, the increase in the prices of fossil fuels and critical metals served as a forewarning of pressure on suppliers (see figure 6.1). Prices eased when the global economy went into a tailspin, but if growth rates were to approach the levels attained in 2006–07, the supply elasticities for energy and raw materials are such that inflationary tendencies would very quickly resurface. Evidence of this possibility became apparent in 2010. Rising prices would curb demand[8] and begin undermining the viability of industries and trading systems built on cheap energy and mineral supplies. Growth would be caught between the pincers of rising costs and weakening demand.[9]

Asian economies were sustained during 2006–07 by asset bubbles generated by expansionary monetary policies and financial innovations in advanced economies that encouraged leveraging and consumption, side by side with high savings in the Middle East and East Asia that facilitated borrowing. A return to the state of affairs that precipitated the great recession of 2008–09 is scarcely desirable. Were it to happen, the global economy would experience, at the very best, another year or two of uneasy expansion that could not last.

Scenario 2: Concentration of Economic Activities in China and India

Business as usual will be difficult to restore for more than a handful of years. A possible scenario for the Asian economies starts with a return to near normalcy in 2010–11 but then veers in a different direction.

Consider the implications of prolonged sluggish growth in the United States and the continuation of its struggle to adjust the current account deficit to accommodate

---

[7]It is notable that the venture capital industry in the United States, which is flush with funds, has few outstanding successes to report since the end of the dot-com boom. Over the past five years, only Facebook and Twitter have yielded the high returns that venture capitalists seek.

[8]Oil priced at over $85 per barrel could depress economic activity in the United States.

[9]In the 1980s and the 1990s, global economic expansion was buoyed by low energy prices. With extraction costs rising and "peak oil" approaching, another energy dividend is not in the offing, and greenhouse gas (GHG) concerns argue for a tax on carbon.

Figure 6.1 Global Commodity Prices

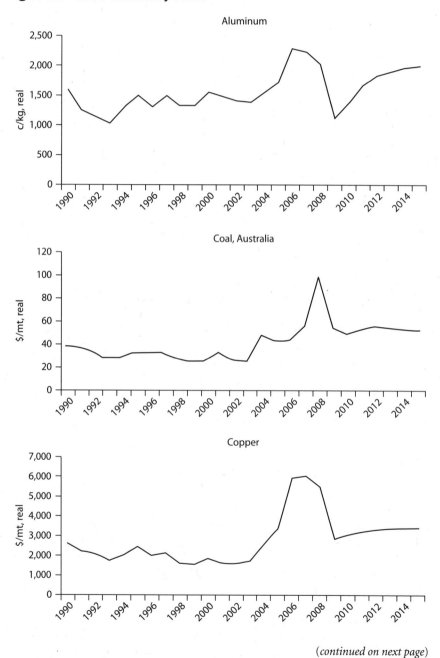

(*continued on next page*)

Figure 6.1   *(continued)*

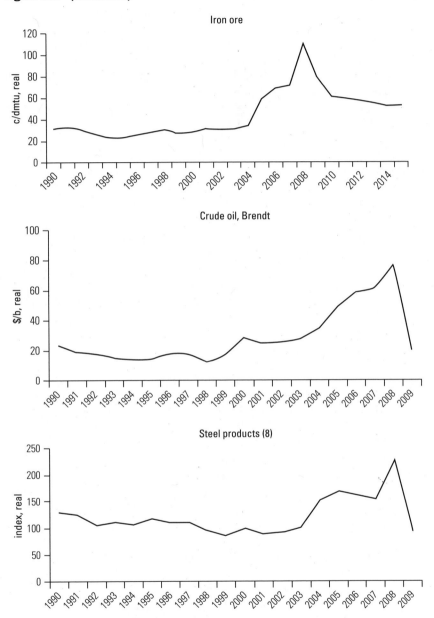

Source: Global Economic Monitor Database, World Bank.
Note: $ = U.S. dollar: c = U.S. cent; mt = metric ton; dmtu = dry metric ton unit; b = barrel. "Steel products (8)"
includes rebar (concrete reinforcing bars), merch bar (merchant bars), wire rod, section (H-shape), plate (medium),
hot rolled coil/sheet, cold rolled coil/sheet, and galvanized iron sheet.

a waning foreign appetite for U.S. Treasuries. This situation could be paralleled by a depreciation of the dollar relative to other major trading currencies (the dollar has depreciated significantly against the yen but strengthened vis-à-vis the euro),[10] which would further quench the U.S. appetite for imports from Asia while, arguably, diverting resources into tradables and discouraging the overseas transfer of production, including the outsourcing of services.[11] If the United States exports more and imports less, either other countries take up the slack by growing faster and importing more—in which case world trade expands—or past U.S. deficits, which contributed so lavishly to global demand, are transferred to other countries, which then run smaller surpluses or incur larger deficits. Either way, there is likely to be some decline in export growth from Asia to the United States, particularly of manufactures. Until a realignment of trade flow occurs, the growth impulse from trade surpluses enjoyed by several Asian countries will diminish.

Alternatively, the United States could face bigger deficits as the European countries forced to eliminate large current accounts that cannot be financed by capital inflows push adjustment onto other countries. Accommodating the adjustment of Spain, Italy, Greece, and other European countries running deficits would require a reduction in the surpluses of other members of the EU, in particular Germany, and of East Asian trading partners, especially China. A fiscally conservative stance by Germany, and other European countries with surpluses would redirect most of the pressure onto China and the United States, i.e., China would export less to the EU countries and derive less growth from trade and/or the United States would experience a widening of its deficit absent significant fiscal tightening. In any event, rebalancing would be painful and could affect the direction of globalization.

A narrowing of the U.S. external deficit by moderating demand for the imports of manufactures could accelerate a number of developments signaled by recent trends in trade and industrialization across Asia. As noted above, East Asian trade has flourished in part because of manufacturing activities that, as a result of national incentive regimes, foreign direct investment (FDI), and opportunities for trade, were integrated into international production networks. These delivered final goods to U.S., EU, and Japanese markets by mobilizing the region's production capabilities in a cost-effective way. An electronic gadget might be assembled in one country, but its parts might come from three others. These might take a circuitous route through yet another country, where some of the parts are assembled into a module and additional work is done on the module itself to prepare it for the recipient assembler. By distributing demand among a host of suppliers, the vertical disintegration of the production process led to much greater intra-industry

---

[10]Feldstein (2010) maintains that the dollar must also depreciate against the euro and that the euro area may need to run an overall current account deficit to balance surpluses elsewhere.

[11]Liu and Trefler (2008) estimate that the insourcing of services to the United States is outweighing outsourcing.

trade, which we documented in chapter 2. By combining productive assets and specialized skills from several countries, networking allowed sharing of the benefits from trade. To the degree that the network consolidated dispersed East Asian manufacturing activities into one reasonably well-articulated system, it facilitated a mutually advantageous coexistence. This is why several empirical studies do not find much evidence of China (or India, for that matter) intensifying pressures on neighboring countries. On the contrary, countries worried about competition from firms in China (and later in India) but welcomed the upsurge of demand from China, somewhat mediated by production networks. In spite of inevitable tensions, the Asian symbiosis sustained the export-led model, although barely.

Production networking as practiced in East Asia has its costs. Vertical specialization of production among firms in different countries gives rise to numerous problems noted earlier—communication, defining specifications and designs, monitoring work practices, and meeting delivery schedules. There are problems also of customs, insurance, shipping, invoicing, and fulfillment. These transaction costs are nontrivial and can add 10 percent or more to the cost of the product (Sirkin, Hemerling, and Bhattacharya 2008). There is also the cost of shipping intermediate products back and forth. The time factor for goods that have to be shipped from distant places means that users need to hold precautionary inventories and tie up working capital. Although networks have knit suppliers together, assemblers and parts producers can have difficulty working closely on design and jointly coordinating refinements in technologically fast-moving industries. As with just-in-time production and delivery, there is no substitute for proximity in contributing to the efficient conception, design, development, and manufacture of a product. The more sophisticated the product, the more customized the individual components; and the more complex the task of integration, the greater the efficiency gains and (vertical) technological spillovers[12] from a clustering of firms jointly engaged in the product's manufacture.

This leads to efforts among East Asian economies to increase domestic value added by localizing more segments of the value chain. In countries where a focus on assembly and processing activities means that domestic value added in most export-oriented manufacturing rarely exceeds 30 percent, raising GDP growth by increasing value added is the constant focus of policy makers. The creation of local manufacturing clusters that internalize multiple production activities is one of the uppermost objectives of governments in Asia. The agglomeration of suppliers and assemblers in clusters is more likely to occur where the potential local markets are largest, because this facilitates design and testing and lessens risk. The presence of large markets confers other benefits such as access to credit and to skilled workers, and the presence of many buyers makes it easier to realize economies of scale and of scope. Clustering is also more likely in economies hosting

---

[12]These are more common than horizontal spillovers and strengthen the case for clustering.

major firms with expertise in integration and a focus on research and development (R&D) to bolster international competitiveness (see Yusuf 2008).

In East and South Asia today, China and India are the two major economies with good growth prospects and emerging homegrown multinational corporations (MNCs) with the ambition to innovate. Japan's economy is as large as China's, but it is unlikely to expand by more than 1–2 percent per year. Although Indonesia is a populous country, it is at an earlier stage of industrialization. Hence, if production networks are to coalesce in the urban-industrial regions of individual countries, China and India are the most likely sites.

If trade grows more slowly, energy costs remain high or even climb higher, competition in product markets intensifies, and MNCs move to rationalize their production in the Asia region—all eminently plausible outcomes that could occur together—then a decline in vertical specialization and a transfer of intermediate and component production to China and (eventually) India is definitely possible. It will be a gradual process, and the rest of Asia would certainly not be denuded of manufacturing, but value chains could become concentrated in clusters, and more of these clusters could be located in Asia's giant economies. Furthermore, a larger share of their production would be aimed at the domestic market under the assumption that trade would not provide the opportunities it once did. The evidence presented on intra-industry trade in chapter 2 points to this trend, as does increasing competition between Chinese producers and others in East Asia and OECD markets.

The losers would be the smaller economies of Asia and those with unattractive business climates. Relative to East Asian economies, especially those in the northeast, business climates in Pakistan, Bangladesh, Nepal, and Sri Lanka are far more challenging, and these countries are ranked low according to various measures of competitiveness (see tables 6.1, 6.2, and 6.3). Some are also prominent in the failed state index (table 6.4). Because of the unfavorable business climate and high risks, South Asian countries (with the exception of India) also do not receive much FDI (see figures 6.2 and 6.3). With slower-growing trade and little FDI inflow, these countries are likely to be characterized by low growth.

Middle-income countries in East Asia also face difficult challenges. Countries such as Malaysia could lose most of their component manufacturing to China and India as MNCs restructure their operations, cut excess capacity, and prune the extra costs of shipping parts from one place to another. With both China and India having integrated into the global economy, maintaining several production units for insurance purposes will be less important. Lean operations that benefit from cluster-induced spillovers could dominate decision making in a world where more of the growth comes from two major Asian economies.[13] Hence, for the

---

[13]The lean approach to manufacturing and retailing has been reinforced by years of intensifying competition and, most recently, by the global recession. Companies have mobilized

(*continued on next page*)

Table 6.1   Doing Business Indicators (Rank)

Country/economy	2006	2007	2008	2009
Singapore	2	1	1	1
Japan	10	11	12	12
Thailand	20	18	15	13
Malaysia	21	25	24	20
Korea, Rep.	27	23	30	23
Taiwan, China	35	47	50	61
Pakistan	60	74	76	77
China	91	93	83	83
Vietnam	99	104	91	92
Sri Lanka	75	89	101	102
Bangladesh	65	88	107	110
India	116	134	120	122
Indonesia	115	135	123	129
Philippines	113	126	133	140

Source: World Bank 2005, 2006, 2007, 2008.

leading Southeast Asian industrializing countries to sustain their competitiveness, it is vital to secure medium-term performance in electronic and automotive products, and it is only through a rapid accumulation of domestic technological capacity that they can grasp fresh industrial and trade opportunities. Fortunately (or unfortunately), they have rich natural resources to lean on while they build up indigenous capabilities. The risk is that countries are distracted by other social and political issues and are unable to muster the consensus needed to press ahead with industrialization in difficult times with no obvious models to guide them. A loss of momentum could lead to a slow retreat of manufacturing in Southeast Asia, with countries becoming mainly resource-based commodity exporters with low and volatile growth rates.

Japan, Korea, and Taiwan, China, have developed their technological capabilities sufficiently to accommodate and benefit from this kind of scenario. Even so, Chinese

---

(*continued from previous page*)
a variety of techniques and software to reduce cycle times, warehousing, equipment downtime, energy costs, and material wastage. Producers, moreover, have redoubled their efforts to customize products for individual markets and to use the wealth of data now at their disposal to identify the preferences of customers and use marketing tools to target them more effectively (Womack and Jones 1994; Moody 2001).

Table 6.2   Global Competitiveness Index

Country/economy	1997	2003	2009–10
Singapore	1	8	3
Japan	14	13	8
Taiwan, China	8	16	12
Korea, Rep.	21	23	19
Malaysia	9	26	24
China	29	46	29
Thailand	18	31	36
India	45	37	49
Indonesia	15	60	54
Vietnam	49	50	75
Sri Lanka	—	57	79
Philippines	34	65	87
Pakistan	—	75	101
Bangladesh	—	91	106

Source: Lopez-Claros and others 2006; Porter, Schwab, and Sala-i-Martin 2007; World Economic Forum 2010.
Note: — = not available.

Table 6.3   Global Competitiveness Ranking

Country/economy	2004	2006	2008	2009
Singapore	2	3	2	3
Japan	21	16	22	17
Malaysia	16	22	19	18
China	22	18	17	20
Taiwan, China	12	17	13	23
Thailand	26	29	27	26
Korea, Rep.	31	32	31	27
India	—	27	29	30
Indonesia	49	52	51	42
Philippines	43	42	40	43

Source: IMD World Competitiveness Yearbook 2009.
Note: Ordered by rank in 2009. — = not available.

and Indian firms will begin exerting great pressure on the established firms from Japan, Korea, and Taiwan, China. Their ability to sustain their lead over competitors from China and India will depend upon the productivity of innovation systems and the agility of firms in developing and marketing new ideas.

Table 6.4   Failed-States Index (Rank)

Country	2006	2009
Pakistan	9	10
Bangladesh	19	19
Sri Lanka	25	22
Philippines	68	53
China	57	57
Indonesia	32	62
Thailand	79	79
India	93	87
Vietnam	70	94
Malaysia	98	115
Korea, Rep.	123	153
Singapore	133	160
Japan	135	164

Source: Failed States Index 2009.

Scenario 3: New Industrial Epoch, New Opportunities

A third scenario (and the one least likely to materialize in the near term, but whose likelihood will increase with time) revolves around the dawning of a new technological epoch that gives industrialization a major jolt, triggering another virtuous spiral. The technological epoch could arise, for example, from a global consensus that highly damaging climate change is a near certainty unless radical measures are taken to arrest GHG emissions, and, moreover, that shared rising prosperity will demand innovations to significantly conserve energy and other exhaustible materials. This is a fairly utopian scenario.

East Asian industrialization was the outcome of a serendipitous coming together of a number of factors. One deserving primacy is the revolution in electronics and communication technologies, which opened up a broad avenue for industrial development. Key decisions leading to the modularization of the technology and to standardization facilitated a dispersal of production and of innovation, both product- and process-related. Spearheaded by FDI, the off-shoring of electronics assembly inducted several East Asian economies into MNC production networks and launched the most important phase of export-led industrialization in East Asia. Its significance can be gauged from the gulf that separates industry in South Asia from that of East Asia. South Asia—India excepted, which never managed to attract FDI in electronics—remains wedded to the manufacturing of textiles and garments, whereas most East Asian economies transitioned rapidly from textiles and resource-based goods to the processing of electronics—moving as a result into the middle-income category.

Figure 6.2   Foreign Direct Investment, Net Inflows

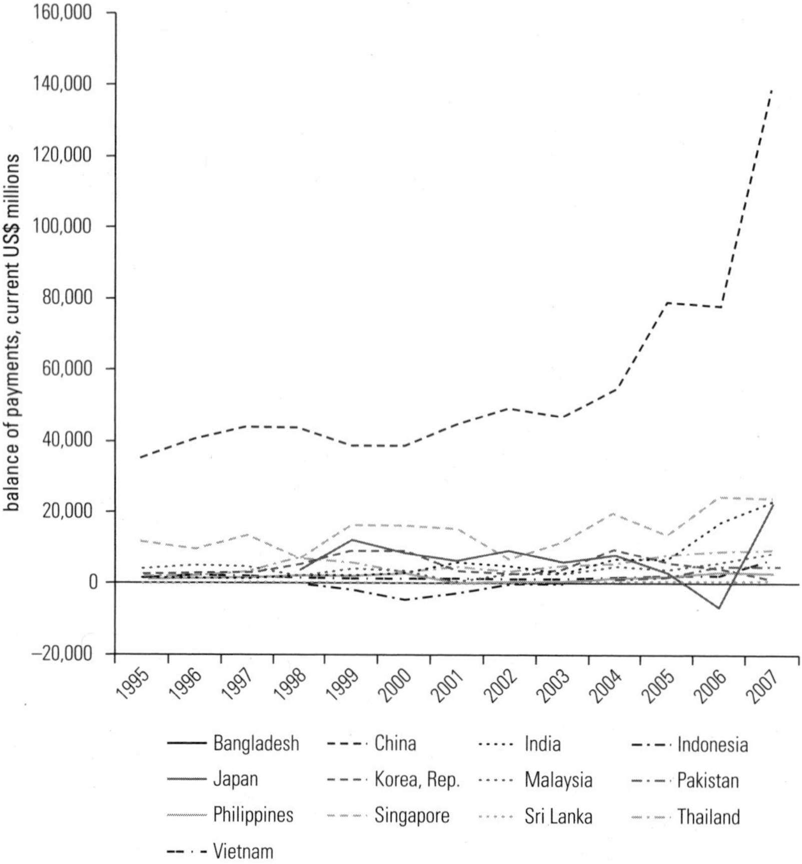

Source: World Development Indicators Database.

The electronics/ICT revolution is by no means a spent force.[14] However, unless innovation and demand continues spiraling (and not just from the United States), the East Asian countries graduate into the design and manufacturing of complex components and production equipment for the electronics industry, and the South Asian economies move into significant niches they vacate, electronics alone will not be the pathway to successively higher stages of industrialization. What, then, are the options on the horizon? The most likely is a cluster of activities under

---

[14]There is more innovation apparent in software than in hardware.

Figure 6.3 Foreign Direct Investment, Net Inflows, Excluding China

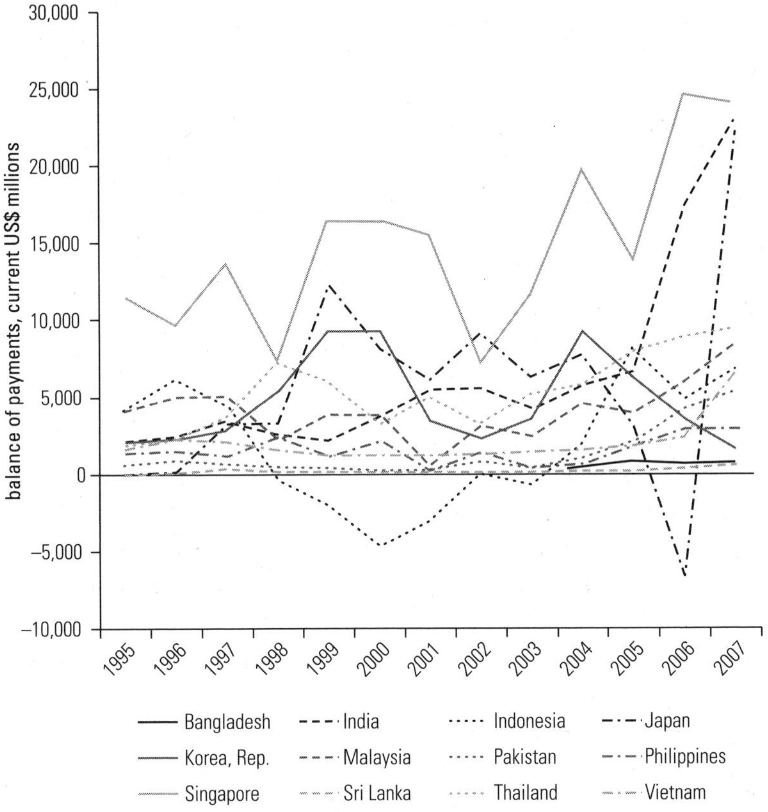

Source: World Development Indicators Database.

the rubric of "green technologies." This is still an ill-defined set of possibilities, but the avenues for technological advances and new manufacturing are becoming clearer.[15] What is not clear yet is how a focus on green technologies will affect total output, investment, production methods, employment, and industrial geography.[16]

[15]In the future, the emphasis of sustainability in the various dimensions of development will multiply the opportunities for innovation. Countries pursuing sustainability through policy, regulation, standard-setting, investment, and incentives will stimulate companies to innovate in particular ways (Prahalad and Krishnan 2008).
[16]A note of caution is warranted. High-tech sectors, in spite of being the focus of innovation and leading the field with respect to gains in productivity, often are too small to drive

(*continued on next page*)

Green technologies range from energy and water conservation to nanotechnology, advanced materials, and waste disposal. The core manufacturing activities that will translate green technologies into industrial change are likely to be those producing material and equipment for generating renewable energy and transmitting it over smart grids; new materials that are lightweight, biodegradable, or recyclable and can be manufactured with the smallest release of carbon; transport equipment and power supplies that meet green criteria; building materials; and household and industrial equipment that will promote conservation and the inputs for a low-carbon urban infrastructure. As currently perceived, most of these products are research-, skill-, and capital-intensive. Few are likely to employ armies of production line workers, although value added per worker would surely rise. Perhaps the industries that best fit the profile of a breakthrough technology with dense manufacturing linkage are new automotive and transport technologies. Assuming that the global stock of automobiles—more broadly, internal combustion engines—will need to be replaced by propulsion devices with a negligible direct carbon signature, and that future additions will be mainly green technology–based vehicles, we stand on the threshold of a new industrial revolution. The three biggest sources of GHGs (if we exclude humans, rice cultivation, deforestation, and cattle) are power plants, transport equipment, and buildings. Should the vast majority of these sources need to be replaced to minimize climate change, and should "green" become the order of the day, manufacturing industry will have to take on a challenge. And once green is "it," every other activity will be affected, requiring redesign, retooling, and change in the structure of industry.

Is Asia positioned to compete for this type of manufacturing activity with all that it entails in terms of technology and human capital? Some countries are, and those that can develop research capabilities and absorb the new production technologies will be the big winners and will participate in what could turn out to be a new industrial epoch (see Felipe, Kumar, and Abdon (2010) for a ranking of countries).

Concluding Observations

Economists and other social scientists are discovering that forecasts based on the models and empirical techniques we currently employ are subject to large margins

---

(*continued from previous page*)
GDP growth directly. The U.S. semiconductor industry at its peak in 2000 contributed just 0.6 percent of GDP. The information technology (IT) industry in India accounts for 0.7 percent of GDP. Technological spillovers raise the contribution of these sectors, but the fact remains that the bulk of GDP growth from manufacturing or services derives from traditional industries such as food processing and construction materials and mid-tech transport and engineering industries (McKinsey Global Institute 2010).

of error.[17] But there is no escape from forecasting—from making educated guesses as to what the future holds. Explaining the past can be satisfying, but if economics becomes an extension of history, its utility as a guide to decision making could be greatly reduced. The decision-making process would be substantially impoverished.

In this book we have looked back in time using data series and the literature on development to size up a process, to understand the unfolding pattern of changes in Asia affecting trade and industry, and to hypothesize about the future dimensions of one critical part of national economies: the manufacturing sector. Our understanding of the development process leads to the proposition that growth in Asian economies has thus far been inseparable from industrialization and from the expanding trade in manufactures. Furthermore, the economies that have successfully graduated into high-tech manufacturing activities have all first acquired a solid base of manufacturing capabilities in electronics and electrical engineering industries. Hence, when we look ahead, our working hypothesis is that the development and growth of low- and middle-income economies—and even high-income economies—will be a function both of industrialization and of the form it takes. A corollary of this proposition is that trade will strongly influence the pace and characteristics of industrialization. This is more applicable to the smaller economies, but even the larger ones are unlikely to thrive if the growth of trade slows—or worse, grinds to a halt.

Through a review of recent trends, we have tried to determine how manufacturing activities are evolving in Asia and to highlight the role of China and India, which are the fastest growing among the industrializing Asian economies and which have major roles in the world trading system.

Out of this analysis, reading the trends and reviewing the information on some of the significant corporate players brings us to a prognosis of a slowing of growth and trade in Asia, a greater concentration of manufacturing and associated research capabilities in China, a more gradual increase of such capabilities in India, and stagnation or decline in manufacturing in other Asian countries (Vietnam being a possible exception, because it is somewhat coextensive with the economy of Southern China). Services may partially compensate for the arrested development of manufacturing in some countries, but past experience suggests that they may prove to be less dependable vehicles for rapid and sustainable growth rooted in innovation and improving productivity. Nor do we see a continuing acceleration in the trade in services fueled (as was the case with manufacturing) by demand from the United States and, to a lesser degree, from other OECD countries. On the contrary, this demand will be

---

[17]Taleb (2007) has drawn attention to the now infamous and unpredictable "black swans." Others have pointed to the unexpected threats and opportunities that are hidden in "fat tails" of event distributions.

slower to materialize from the United States and some countries in the EU, which also will need to compete far harder to balance their books with the rest of the world.

If industrialization and growth languishes in the rest of Asia, China's gains—and India's—will be partially negated by weaker external demand, by the threat of trade frictions, and by an unwinding of globalization.

We think that this outcome is avoidable, although just barely. As the Doha Round of talks has shown, hammering out compromises that partially and fairly address the competing interests of nations is a difficult business.[18] Making and implementing long-term development policies in the current political circumstances of most Asian countries is also a formidable undertaking. Doctrinal differences in approaches to development, as well as varied readings of the evidence on the sources of growth, the gains from freer multilateral trade, factor flows, the contribution of urbanization, and how global warming can be arrested, make it hard to define clear objectives and to chart a course for a diverse assortment of countries.

Rather than attempt the impossible, which is to set forth a detailed roadmap for all of Asia, we offer a parsimonious set of proposals that could enable Asian countries—and others—to achieve higher rates of sustainable growth.

It appears that the world needs to enter a new technology-induced spiral that entails a large amount of spending on fixed assets, generating massive employment and the promise of substantial returns over the longer term. Neither biotechnology, advanced materials, nor nanotechnology—all of which hold promise—have yielded these. However, the new industrial green revolution could conceivably deliver the goods. With the threat of global warming providing irresistible motivation, a rapid and systematic development of technologies in the following five areas can stimulate the development of new industries:

- Low-carbon urban infrastructure and services delivery
- Low-carbon transport solutions and energy-delivery infrastructure
- Low-carbon energy infrastructure
- Water delivery, purification, management, and conservation technologies for urban and rural uses
- Lean natural resource use technologies for industry

Exploiting currently available technologies in each of these areas and exploring fresh possibilities, if aggressively pursued, would generate the growth and the

---

[18]A multifaceted dissection of the global trading environment following the collapse of trade in 2008 and with reference to the issues arising from the Doha Round can be found in Baldwin (2009). See also Hufbauer and Stephenson (2009).

employment that Asian countries are seeking. It would harness electronics technologies and give a focus to research on new materials and nanotechnologies.[19] Moreover, it would yield the much-needed bonus of cutting GHG emissions, containing water use, and lessening the depletion of nonrenewable resources and environmental damage. Another benefit of more compact cities designed for walking would be the improvement in public health.

A new technological epoch will require a strong push and incentives from government—both negative and positive. Public spending on infrastructure, support for research, and underwriting of some risk capital would need to be combined with a multitude of other reinforcements and sanctions, including standards for equipment and infrastructure, pricing regimes, and regulatory arrangements. A neoliberal state that trusts in the market and adopts a fundamentalist low profile is less likely to achieve results.

The successful launch of a new technological epoch would give rise to a round of cross-sectoral investment incentives that would fuel growth directly and from gains in productivity arising from innovation and improved efficiency. Middle- and high-income countries would have new industries to expand into, and technological change would rejuvenate existing industries. Ideally, this would lead to a regionwide reshuffling of industrial shares, with the technologically more advanced countries going down new industrial pathways, and the low-income countries moving up the industrial ladder and occupying the spaces vacated by middle-income countries, as well as finding new niches of their own creation.

A new technological epoch that makes possible sustainable growth and curbs global warming will absorb an enormous volume of resources. The winners will be countries that can mobilize resources and maintain high levels of investment.

References

Ackerman, Frank. 2006. "Assessing the Effects of Trade Liberalisation: A Critical Examination." *QA—Rivista dell' Associazione Rossi-Doria* no. 3.

Anderson, Kym, and Will Martin. 2005. "Agricultural Trade Reform and the Doha Development Agenda." Policy Research Working Paper 3607. World Bank, Washington, DC.

Bai, Chunli. 2005. "Ascent of Nanoscience in China." *Science* (309): 61–63.

Baldwin, Richard. 2009. *The Great Trade Collapse: Causes, Consequences and Prospects.* London: Centre for Economic Policy Research.

Brooks, Ray, and Steven A. Barnett. 2006. "What's Driving Investment in China?" IMF Working Paper 06/265. International Monetary Fund, Washington, D.C.

Caballero, Richard. 2010. "Understanding the Global Turmoil: It's the General Equilibrium, Stupid." VoxEU.org.

---

[19]China's efforts to become a leader in nanotechnologies are described by Bai (2005), and the opportunities for middle income countries are discussed by Niosi and Reid (2007).

Caballero, R., E. Farhi and P. Gourinchas. 2008. "Financial Crash, Commodity Prices, and Global Imbalances." NBER Working Paper 14521. National Bureau of Economic Research, Cambridge, MA.

"Failed States Index 2009." *Foreign Policy.*

Feldstein, Martin. 2010. "Is the Euro Overvalued?" http://www.project-syndicate.org.

Felipe, Jesus, Utsav Kumar, and Arnelyn Abdon. 2010. "As You Sow So Shall You Reap." Asian Development Bank, Manila.

Hufbauer, Gary, and Sherry Stephenson. 2009. "Trade Policy in a Time of Crisis: Suggestions for Developing Countries." Policy Insight 33. Centre for Economic Policy Research, London.

IMD (International Institute for Management Development). 2009. *World Competitiveness Yearbook.* Laussane, Switzerland: IMD.

Liu, Runjuan, and Daniel Trefler. 2008. "Much Ado About Nothing: American Jobs and the Rise of Service Outsourcing to China and India." Working Paper 14061. National Bureau of Economic Research, Cambridge, MA.

Lopez-Claros, Augusto, Michael E. Porter, Klaus Shwab, and Xavier Sala-i-Martin. 2006. *The Global Competitiveness Report 2006–2007.* New York: Palgrave Macmillan.

McKinsey Global Institute. 2010. *How to Compete and Grow: A Sector Guide to Policy.* Washington, DC: McKinsey & Company.

Moody, Patricia E. 2001. "What's Next after Lean Manufacturing?" *MIT Sloan Management Review* (Winter): 12–13.

Niosi, Jorge, and Susan E. Reid. 2007. "Biotechnology and Nanotechnology: Science-based Enabling Technologies as Windows of Opportunity for LDCs?" *World Development* 35(3): 426–38.

Polaski, Sandra. 2006. *Winners and Losers: Impact of the Doha Round on Developing Countries.* Washington, DC: Carnegie Endowment for International Peace.

Porter, Michael, Klaus Schwab, and Xavier Sala-i-Martin. 2007. *The Global Competitiveness Report 2007–2008.* New York: Palgrave Macmillan.

Prahalad, C. K., and M. S. Krishnan. 2008. *The New Age of Innovation: Driving Cocreated Value through Global Networks.* New York: McGraw-Hill.

Serven, Luis, and Ha Nguyen. 2010. "Global Imbalances Before and After the Global Crisis." World Bank Policy Research Working Paper 5354. World Bank, Washington, DC.

Sirkin, Harold L., James W. Hemerling, and Arindam K. Bhattacharya. 2008. *Globality: Competing with Everyone from Everywhere for Everything.* New York: Business Plus.

Taleb, Nassim Nicholas. 2007. *The Black Swan: The Impact of the Highly Improbable.* New York: Random House.

Womack, James P., and D. T. Jones. 1994. "From Lean Production to Lean Enterprise." *Harvard Business Review* (March–April): 93–103.

World Bank. 2005. *Doing Business in 2006.* Washington, DC: World Bank.

———. 2006. *Doing Business in 2007.* Washington, DC: World Bank.

———. 2007. *Doing Business in 2008.* Washington, DC: World Bank.

———. 2008. *Doing Business in 2009.* Washington, DC: World Bank.

World Economic Forum. 2010. *The Global Competitiveness Report 2009–2010*. New York: World Economic Forum.

Yusuf, Shahid. 2008. "Can Clusters Be Made to Order?" In *Growing Industrial Clusters in Asia: Serendipity and Science*, ed. Shahid Yusuf, Kaoru Nabeshima, and Shoichi Yamashita. Washington, DC: World Bank.

Index

Figures, notes, and tables are indicated by *f*, *n*, and *t*, respectively.

A
agriculture
  biotechnology and, 228
  in China, 32, 33*f*, 33*t*, 35–36, 41, 47–48*f*, 217
  Doha Round negotiations, 70*n*4
  in India, 56*f*, 59*f*, 62
  in low-income economies, 172–73
apparel industry. *See* textiles industry
Association of Southeast Asian Nations
  (ASEAN), 80
automotive industry
  in China, 44
  future prospects, 228
  in India, 78
  intraregional and intra-industrial trade in
    Asia, 74, 76–78, 78*f*, 82*f*

B
balance of payment (BOP) crisis (1991), India, 4
Bangladesh
  clustering in, 216
  competitive advantage, 99–101, 101*t*, 102*t*
  EXPY, 108, 109*t*
  future industrial prospects in, 234
  intraregional and intra-industrial trade, 79
  manufacturing and GDP growth in, 170, 172*t*,
    173*f*, 175*f*, 183
  patents, 198
  product space analysis, 180, 181, 188–89*f*
  RCA in, 178, 179*t*
  tertiary education in, 186
  textiles industry in, 219*n*18
  top 10 commodities, 178, 179*t*, 180, 188–90*t*
  trading partners, 179, 183–85*f*
  U.S. economy, rebalancing of, 205
  wage rates and productivity in, 88*t*, 90
  WTO, effects of China's accession to, 125
biotechnology, 228–29

BOP (balance of payment) crisis (1991), India, 4
BPO (business process outsourcing) activities in
  India, 4–5, 54–55
Brazil, 44*n*11, 226
business process outsourcing (BPO) activities in
  India, 4–5, 54–55

C
Cambodia, 130, 170, 205
capital investment and savings. *See* savings and
  investment
"cellular" economic model in China, 51–52, 52*t*
CGE (computable general equilibrium) models,
  226*n*3
China, 1–4, 31–54
  agriculture in, 32, 33*f*, 33*t*, 35–36, 41,
    47–48*f*, 217
  automotive industry in, 44
  branding and product category dominance,
    213–14
  "cellular" economic model in, 51–52, 52*t*
  change in type of manufacturing, 32–34,
    34*f*, 35*t*
  clustering in, 217
  competitive advantage in. *See* competitive
    advantage
  Cultural Revolution, recovery from, 4
  decentralized approach to, 31–32
  electronics industry in, 39, 41, 42, 43*f*,
    125–26
  energy costs in, 200
  export composition and growth, 30*f*, 40–48,
    41–44*f*, 45–47*t*
  fastest-growing manufacturing industries and
    exports, 94*t*
  FDI, role of, 4, 18*f*, 65, 98–99, 112–16
  forecasts regarding, 69–70
  Foreign Trade Corporations, 4